What the pros are saying
MAKING VIDEOS FOR MONEY

"From making the initial contact through pre- and postproduction, this book is a practical guide for anyone interested in video production. Here are the upsides and downsides and in-between sides. And best of all, it is dated for the here and now. It's complete with fresh examples. You're gonna like it."

> —Paul Tharp, Administrative Director, Marketing
> and Planning, Sonora Community Hospital

"Barry Hampe has written the definitive beginner's text on producing videos: logically organized, clearly written, easy to learn from. A 'must read' for every student or professional looking to make money in this lucrative field."

> —Tim Hawthorne, Chairman, Hawthorne Direct, Inc.,
> and author of *The Complete Guide to Infomercial
> Marketing*

"Like [Hampe's] other works, this well-organized, easy-to-understand resource is packed with useful, detailed information, real-life examples, time-saving techniques, and advice for anyone using video to make money. Barry's experiences and guidance will save the reader precious time and money by eliminating the guesswork and potential mistakes in producing a video. The detailed production budget checklist has saved me countless hours by eliminating the need for me to develop this material from scratch."

> —Michael Ruiz, Aerospace Engineer,
> NASA—Johnson Space Center

"This book is a valuable addition to the resources available to anyone wanting to make videos for money. The section on infomercials is an excellent starting point for anyone diving into the world of direct response television."

> —Jennifer Harding, Manager, Public Relations,
> NIMA International, the association representing the
> electronic retailing industry worldwide

Experts on documentary offer high praise for Barry Hampe's
MAKING DOCUMENTARY FILMS AND REALITY VIDEOS:
*A Practical Guide to Planning, Filming, and Editing
Documentaries of Real Events*

"A highly valuable book that covers the many aspects of producing a documentary. I recommend it to anyone embarking on such a project."   —Gordon Quinn, Kartemquin Films,
Executive Producer, *Hoop Dreams*

"This important new entry in the literature of documentary filmmaking . . . [explains] why there is so much more to making an effective documentary than just being in the right place to photograph the events of the day. Barry Hampe, a longtime pro in the field, has amassed a highly informative and readable volume. . . . He goes beyond the basics to describe avoidable pitfalls just as carefully as he explains what is entailed in devising a documentary that transcends mere reportage."   —*American Cinematographer*

"This is a very useful book for everyone who cares about the subject. Clear, informative, and a valuable resource that combines professional expertise with personal experience."
—Betsy McLane, Ph.D., Executive Director,
International Documentary Association

"This well-written book covers all aspects of documentary film and video, from the ethics of the documentary to postproduction techniques, and everything in between. Especially helpful are the chapters on recording natural human behavior—in other words, how to record people as though there were no camcorder present."   —*Videomaker*

"I found [Hampe's] book *Making Documentary Films and Reality Videos* informative, insightful, and useful—the same qualities that are lacking in many documentaries today. [The] text helps newcomers to the field learn the basics and can help good documentary producers become even more creative in their approach."
—Michael Cascio, Vice President, Documentary Programming,
Arts & Entertainment Network (A&E)

An Owl Book, available at your bookseller

MAKING
VIDEOS
FOR
MONEY

BARRY HAMPE

Making VIDEOS FOR MONEY

: PLANNING
: AND
: PRODUCING
: INFORMATION
: VIDEOS,
: COMMERCIALS,
: AND
: INFOMERCIALS

AN OWL BOOK

Henry Holt and Company

New York

Henry Holt and Company, LLC
Publishers since 1866
115 West 18th Street
New York, New York 10011

Henry Holt® is a registered trademark
of Henry Holt and Company, LLC.

Library of Congress Cataloging-in-Publication Data
Hampe, Barry.
Making videos for money : planning and producing information
videos, commercials, and infomercials / Barry Hampe.
— 1st Owl Book ed.
p.   cm.
"An Owl book."
Includes bibliographical references and index.
ISBN 0-8050-5441-3 (pb)
1. Video recordings—Production and direction.
2. Television advertising.   3. Infomercials.   I. Title.
PN1992.94.H36   1998
791.45'0232—dc21   97-33173

First Owl Books Edition 1998
Designed by Victoria Hartman

Printed in the United States of America

10 9 8 7 6 5

This book is dedicated to my sons,
Jeffrey, Scott, Gregory, and Christopher,
who as children brought me great joy
and as adults—immense pride.

CONTENTS

. . . .

FOREWORD

Making *Videos for Money* is a wonderfully relevant book for anyone interested in media production work. While many media production students dream of becoming the next Steven Spielberg, the hard cold reality of the modern media industry is that there are very few opportunities to break into large-scale entertainment production roles. There are, however, burgeoning opportunities for media production entrepreneurs in independent and corporate video production.

In the pages that follow, Barry Hampe tells you everything you need to know to get into and thrive in the corporate video production business. The book demystifies the complexities of this market and describes clearly in very practical terms how to establish a client base and how to produce marketable media products.

The book is replete with juicy war stories that provide the reader with personal knowledge gained from the "school of hard knocks" about the world of working with clients. Reading the chapters that follow will give the reader an opportunity to master these hard-earned lessons vicariously, rather than unnecessarily suffering the many bumps and bruises it may otherwise take to learn how to make videos for money.

—Gary L. Kreps, Ph.D.
Dean and Professor
School of Communication
Hofstra University
Hempstead, New York

PREFACE

Making *Videos for Money* is the third in a series of books on the theory, concepts, and day-to-day reality of video production. While most video books and almost all video instruction concentrate on the technology of the medium, my interest has always been in how one thinks about production in terms of achieving the content that will be shown to an audience. Everyone knows that you need to have the picture in sharp focus. But I am astounded by the number of people who set out to make a video without recognizing that it's equally important to be well-focused on the concept.

I get a certain amount of e-mail from people who have read my previous books. And I'm still astonished to receive a message that says, essentially:

> Thank you for your book on making documentaries. I'm going off to some remote part of the world to make a documentary. I haven't decided what the topic will be. What kind of camera do you recommend?

And I wonder what part of the book the person read. Because I always say—as I've said in this book—I'm not a technical person. Cameras don't make videos, people do. A good video, whether it's a documentary made on location in Africa or a commercial shot in your hometown, depends far more on good ideas, well executed, than on the latest technical marvel from the equipment makers. I'm not opposed to technology. It's just that I've learned over a couple of decades of doing this work that the way we record the pictures changes all the time, but the need to be clear about what we are doing—especially the need to shoot for editing—doesn't.

This is a book about the bread and butter of video production—making videos for clients who pay you to do it. You'll find almost as much about the care and feeding of clients in this book as you will about thinking your way through the production of a video. That's because clients are the overshadowing presence at any time that one is making a video for money. You have to satisfy yourself for the video to be any good. And you have to satisfy your clients in order to get paid.

A NOTE ON THE EXAMPLES

The examples of commercials, information videos, and infomercials are taken from the period in which the manuscript was researched and written. Therefore if you pick up this book some time later, the specific videos may be gone, but the principles of videomaking that they exemplify remain.

Also, I've spent my professional life in Philadelphia, Honolulu, and Las Vegas. So it is only natural that a lot of the examples I give have taken place in one of these three areas. But not all. When one makes videos for money, one often gets an all-expense-paid trip to somewhere else.

I hope you enjoy my book. But more important, I hope it helps you to make money while making videos.

Feedback
On-line, you can reach Barry Hampe by e-mail at:
WriteHampe@aol.com
If you are not on-line, you can write to:
Barry Hampe
Making Videos for Money
Henry Holt and Company
115 West 18th Street
New York, New York 10011

ACKNOWLEDGMENTS

To my partner in life and work, Sylvie Hampe: There comes a time in the writing of a book—about two-thirds of the way through the manuscript—when I lose confidence in what has been written and become unsure how to finish. This is the point at which you read what is written, mark what needs to be changed, and even more important, point out something that you really like. That's usually all it takes to put the book back on track. As the editing half of The Writing & Editing Company, you get credit as the defensive back, who ferrets out misspellings, typographical errors, and mistakes in usage in the manuscript before it goes to the publisher. But your contribution is so much more than that. In every sense you are a partner and collaborator in my work.

To my clients: Without you, your needs, and your financing, my body of work might be limited to one student production and not much else. This is the most expensive medium in the world, and it has been your sponsorship that made it possible for me to practice my craft.

To my agents, Michael Larsen and Elizabeth Pomada: Thank you for your faith and encouragement and your hard work on my behalf.

To my editor, Cynthia Vartan: I am delighted that my work goes to you. I relish your phone calls, faxes, and pointed, accurate commentary on my manuscripts.

To my fellow ITVA Blue Ribbon Panel Judges, Larry Eder, Rose

Kimball, Mary Lynn Nichols, John Prin, Denise Taylor, and G. Warren: You are one of the nicest groups of people with whom I have ever had to spend long hours in close quarters. My thanks for your friendship and your insights.

To Chris Jones, Susan Steger Welsh, and Tyson Greer: Thank you for letting me tell the story of our experiment in scriptwriting and for allowing me to reproduce portions of the scripts.

To the infomercial experts I interviewed: Your thoughts and stories about infomercial production have been invaluable. I am grateful to Sam Catanese of Infomercial Monitoring Service, Carter Clews of Infomation, Vince Clews of Vince Clews & Associates, Susan Delaney of National Media, Bob Leubber and Steve Smith of Paradigm Communication Group, Jennifer Harding of NIMA International, Tim Hawthorne of Hawthorne Communications, Jack Kirby of Quantum Television, John Kogler of Jordan Whitney, David Savage of American Telecast Corporation, and Mark Williams of Mark Williams Entertainment Organization.

To Gina Schlichenmayer at the Aladdin Hotel and Casino: Thanks for permission to reprint the script in figure 8.1.

To all the videomakers who sent me copies of their videos for review as part of the preparation for this book: Thank you for sharing your work with my readers and me. A few of your videos have been described and mentioned by name in the text of the book. But whether mentioned or not, all of them have contributed to the work and deserve to be acknowledged. I am grateful to Randall Becker of Black & Becker Productions for "Hope House: Building Hope for the Future," Lorna Domke of the Missouri Department of Conservation for "Legacy of Life," Jay Heard of Multivision, Inc. for "Digital Hi-Note and HiNote Ultra," Melanie Hecht-Yonks of GTE Directories Corporation for "Safety," David Hoffman of Varied Directions International for "Hit the Road, Jack," Bob Johnson and Jim Gulian of Media Partners Corporation for "Bridging the Gap" and "The Guest," Mike Kanser of Consumers Power for "Direct Deposit," Kristofer Kindem of 3M Center for "Imagine," Rochelle Langford of JCPenney for "Marian Wright Edelman Biography," Sandra L. McCrimmon of Meyocks and Priebe Advertising for "Excursion II," Mark O'Brien of AARP for "Fr. Joe Carroll," David Poulshock of

David Poulshock Productions for "Jetnet," Steve Prather of Best Buy
Company for "The In Stock Zone," Bill Ronat of Brandt/Ronat & Co.
for "Are You Ready? Get Ready!," Ryan Rose of Walcoff & Associates
for "Don't Let It Slide" and "Say Yes," Dusty Rumsey of Park Production Group for "Service Squad—A Case of Trust," Dr. Jan Smith of
Hewlett-Packard for "Synergies," Ron Stone of Stonefilms of Texas for
"Amazing Grace," Mark Thornberry of Wachovia Creative Services
for "Main Street Jazz," Stephen Watkins of Flagstar Creative Services
for "Save the Children: A Partnership for a Purpose," Dean Wetherell
of Wetherell & Associates for "Personal Protective Equipment" and
"Seat Belt Safety," Dan White of USDA Forest Service for "Continu-
ally Correcting Course," Joan Thompson of Raychem for "Raychem
World Report 4Q94," and David Zdon of CME Video and Film for
"Welcome to CAP."

Finally, I owe an incredible debt of gratitude to all the people—
many of them anonymous—who in spite of their best intentions have
made videos that are flawed and even sometimes really bad. Without
knowing it, they have given us all a great gift, because there is so
much to be learned from a sincere, dedicated effort that didn't
make it.

Making

Videos

For

Money

PART I

SPONSORED VIDEOS

THE VIDEO MARKET EXPLODES

Making *Videos for Money* is probably the first book on video production that looks beyond how to operate television technology to the ways it actually is used to earn a living. Production people go to film school or to a school of communication to learn how to make feature films or television programs. But most of you will spend your careers making information videos, commercials, and infomercials. And the chances are that you may have had little or no preparation for this. University film departments teach making movies, not making money. The idea is that if you have the talent and promotional ability of a Spielberg or a Lucas, the money will come. If not, you'd better have the technical skills to get a job.

Some video departments, unfortunately, are run by academics who may have TV station experience somewhere in the past (often at a public broadcasting or university station where budget is always a consideration, but actually making money isn't) but have never lived the stressful life of a small video production company. Few of these teach how to deal with clients, prepare budgets, and sell products, ideas, or services.

Others, fortunately, do draw their faculties from working professionals and do give their students a real world perspective. If you've had that advantage, you're in luck, and you'll know how to use the information on these pages. But if you haven't, you need this book.

CLIENTS WANT TO MAKE VIDEOS

Making videos for money—which usually means making videos for clients—has exploded into the lucrative field we've always dreamed it could be. Business, government, and nonprofit organizations are as likely to think of making an information video when they have something they want to communicate as they are to consider putting out a brochure, a written report, or a newsletter.

There are a lot of reasons for this expanded demand for video production, not the least of which is that making a video is a lot sexier than making yet another written report. One thing that has made this shift from print to moving image possible is that today it can cost no more to produce and distribute an information video of a reasonable length than to put out a first-quality, four-color brochure. And for now, at least, the video is likely to command more attention from the audience than the brochure, which may be perceived as "just one more damn thing to read."

A New Generation of Viewers—and Clients

The headset generation has a very low experience level with reading for information and, indeed, will often go to great lengths to avoid reading to find out something they need to know and understand. In some cases, as we're now being made painfully aware, they've managed to go through school without ever learning *how* to read for information. They'll phone everyone they know to see if anyone has the answer, even when what they want to know about is sitting next to them in written form. They will, however, take information from a video.

Most of today's middle management is composed of people from the first generation that grew up with TV as a constant companion and baby-sitter, the first generation of modern Americans who felt no need to read for entertainment, let alone information. And these are the people who are now starting to fill top executive positions. So it's no surprise that they have no problem with the idea of communicating through video. It's their primary medium.

Corporate Communication and Sponsored Videos

The use of video in corporate communication has become a multibillion-dollar industry. The kid who used to run the copy machine is now a video technician. The former editor of the company newsletter now produces a monthly, weekly, or sometimes even daily company closed-circuit video newsmagazine. Corporate videos are used in human resources to present everything from new employee orientation to changes in the company benefits package. Corporations also have turned to videos as a public relations medium to carry specific messages to their investors, their customers, their neighbors, and even their critics.

Sponsored videos can include virtually any message the sponsoring organization wants to communicate to a target audience. Companies use them for sales, public relations, and training. Government agencies regularly make videos to explain—or brag about—what they are doing. And nonprofit organizations are turning to information videos as a way to carry their message—and often their fund-raising appeals—to a larger audience.

Commercials and Infomercials

Cable and satellite television are revolutionizing broadcast television. It's hard to believe—in these days of sixty- to one-hundred-channel cable systems—that not much more than a generation ago there were just three networks. PBS didn't exist. Independent stations were few to none, and where they did exist they showed old movies in black and white and reruns of less successful series. Today, cable television threatens to grow to five hundred channels as increasing numbers of cable networks dedicated to a single theme come on-line. And direct satellite broadcasting has established a beachhead on the multichannel monopoly currently held by cable. No one knows in what form it all will end, but it's a safe bet that for the foreseeable future Americans will have a lot of television channels available in their homes at a reasonable price.

For videomakers that means production of commercials will continue to be a growth area, because every cable company sells reasonably priced commercial spots in the local market. Retailers who once would have been happy to run an ad in the weekly community shopping publication now find they can afford to be on TV. Production of commercials, which was once the province of local TV stations on the low end of the budget scale and of advertising agencies and a few production companies on the high end, is wide open to independent videomakers throughout the country.

The expansion of available air time through this proliferation of channels has also made direct marketing by infomercial a growing market for videomakers. And infomercials are thirty-minute programs rather than 30-second spots.

Documentaries

Documentary production has increased incredibly, and the budgets for documentaries can be remarkably good. Once relegated to public broadcasting, they are now a staple on many cable channels. The answer to the question, "If PBS doesn't do it, who will?" is A&E, Bravo, Discovery, the History Channel, Home Box Office, the Learning Channel, the Travel Channel, Turner Broadcasting, and many others.

There has always been a small market for sponsored documentaries—what were once called "industrial films"—and that has grown tremendously with the ease, convenience, and economy of video production. Any time there's a unique event with the end in doubt, there's the potential for a documentary. You just have to find a sponsor to pay for it.

Retail Videos

Retail videos are usually just a special form of information video produced to be sold to consumers. Health and fitness videos and travel videos have been around for a long time. But almost any topic that will interest a paying audience can find shelf space in video stores, gift shops, and increasingly in bookstores and even drugstores. An acquaintance of mine produced and distributes a video guide to Nevada's legal brothels. Last year I wrote and directed a video for a client on child safety in the home.

And the market for retail videos continues to grow as the cost of production and duplication drops the price into the affordable range. Today, you can watch a program on television—especially on the cable channels—and as it is going off you'll be invited to call an 800 number to order the program you've just seen on video.

MAKING THE MOST OF THIS BOOK

In short, every area of video production is expanding rapidly. And with this has come a demand for informed professional production to meet this exploding need for programming.

If you are a videomaker with professional experience, you can come to this book to find specific information. If you've never planned, written, or produced an infomercial, you'll find a section dedicated to making infomercials. If you're aware that producing a commercial may be a little harder than it looks, you'll find a section on making commercials.

And so on.

If you're a beginner—and I have known several people who have decided to go into the video business even though they had no experience or training in the field—you may want to start at the beginning and read straight through to the end. This will give you an overview of the video production field and many of the ways to make money within it.

If you are a student, you may or may not find any emphasis in the video production courses you're taking on how to make money with the skills you're acquiring. Film schools teach the feature film with an occasional side trip to the documentary. Video courses tend to focus on broadcast journalism and making film-style documentaries. But most of the jobs you'll find available will be either in corporate video or with an independent production company, where you'll make your living doing information videos, commercials, and infomercials. Even if you go to work for a TV station, you're more likely to find yourself making commercials than doing news and documentaries.

Yes, you can learn a lot in a short time on the job. But this book can help you get off to a good start.

PRODUCTION STORY—JUST BECAUSE IT'S FUN
DOESN'T MEAN YOU SHOULDN'T MAKE MONEY

One of my early jobs in production was as a one-man media department in an education center. I'd load my car with thirteen cases of equipment—I counted them every time I loaded them in or out—drive to a school somewhere in New Jersey, and shoot all day on a production. Then I'd go back to the center and spend hours editing what I had shot into a coherent visual statement that would both make sense to an audience and achieve the sponsor's goals.

I remember sitting in the editing room, late one night, putting a program together. I'd just created a great cut and I said out loud, "God, I love doing this. If they only knew—I'd do it for nothing."

But, of course, I never told them.

And that's what this book is about. Someone—a sponsor or client—has to put up the money to pay for the tools and supplies and give us an income so that we can practice our craft. We owe these clients our best skills at making these kinds of projects. That's what they're paying for.

And they owe us a decent fee, paid in a timely fashion.

That's what *Making Videos for Money* is all about.

WHAT VIDEOS DO WELL—
AND WHAT THEY DON'T

Television attracts more viewers than any information or entertainment medium in history. But video's undeniable appeal to a large audience does not mean it is a panacea for all communication problems. As with any other medium, video has its weaknesses as well as its strengths. And trying to force all of your clients'—or your company's—information needs into this one medium is no more likely to be successful than trying to solve all of their transportation needs with a single vehicle.

For instance, in the early days of video there were a lot of grant-supported experiments in the use of TV in education. What many educators wanted to do was to videotape a master teacher conducting a class and then show the tape to other classes. Actually, that gave the students the worst of two worlds. They lost the interactivity of a live teacher working with a live class able to answer *their* questions and personalize the class for them. And they also lost video's ability to provide demonstrations and visual evidence and to condense and intensify information through editing. Videotaping a teacher conducting a class is no more creating an information video than is videotaping the pages of a book and asking the audience to read it from the screen. It's simply stuffing the content of one medium into another.

On the other hand, the videotape of the master teacher might have been a good demonstration piece to use for training other teachers. At that point the content of the video would become how a master teacher works with a class, rather than a lesson in history or geography or whatever subject the teacher was trying to get across to the students.

There's an old homily that has been around the audiovisual business for the past sixty years that says people remember only some small percentage—15, 20, 25 percent, depending on who's telling the story—of what they hear but can recall some much larger percentage—60, 70, 80 percent—of what they see. It was based on flawed research during World War I. But it sounded so good, especially to A-V people, that it has been repeated over and over again until it has taken on a life of its own. Forget it. The fact is, if you let people hear something they care about, they'll remember it. And if you show them something that has no relevance for them, they probably won't retain it.

Studies have shown that some people may prefer one medium over another or may give primacy to one sense over the others. In spite of the old adage that *seeing is believing,* some people will accept what they are *told* even when it contradicts something that they have *seen* for themselves. And others, to quote Eliza Doolittle, say, "Don't talk . . . show me!"

VIDEO'S STRONG POINTS

What video does very well is to show things that can be recorded and played back on a TV screen. It can provide a visual demonstration of the way a product or process actually works—or fails to work. It can dramatize ideas and events to make them come to life. It can sometimes make it possible to illustrate and visualize abstract ideas and events that cannot be photographed in reality. It can provide access to real events beyond the direct experience of most viewers—anything from explaining major surgery to riding in the space shuttle—by presenting visual evidence of that reality. And it can combine all of these strengths into a compelling presentation to make a strong emotional appeal to an audience.

Visual Demonstration

Video is great at showing how things work. From its earliest days, television has played upon the ability of the medium to demonstrate products effectively. One of the best series of commercials is the one for a laundry detergent in which a man who never speaks pours a stain-maker on a handkerchief, tears it in half, and washes half in a clear beaker of cold water with his detergent and half with another detergent. The half with his detergent always comes out cleanest.

When one of the casinos in Las Vegas decided to step into the twenty-first century with a new kind of slot machine that did away with coins, their ad agency asked me to do a video to show players how the new machine operates. The coin-free slot machine accepts paper money and racks up credits equal to the amount paid. It "pays out" by printing out a bar code strip which may either be inserted in another coin-free slot for credit or taken to the cashier's cage where it is scanned for payment in cash. In the video we demonstrated how to use the new machines and also hammered away at benefits, such as not having to carry around heavy trays or buckets of coins and not getting your fingers dirty from constantly handling coins.

Most infomercials about products are demonstrations. They show you the automobile finish that is so glassy that water drops roll right off rather than stopping to cause a dirty spot. They show the exercise equipment demonstrated by people who are in great shape. And they show people using all the cooking gadgets that promise a healthier, more economical, and easier way to prepare food.

Demonstration is an excellent way to gain acceptance for a new product. One of my clients sells a lubricant additive that helps car engines run smoother and cooler. He called me about doing a documentary-style infomercial in which we would treat a car's engine with the additive, drain all the oil out of the crankcase, replace it with water, and then drive the car for a thousand miles through the desert including a pass through Death Valley. The reason you haven't seen it on TV is that after I presented the budget for the video he didn't call me back. But it would have been one heck of a demonstration.

Dramatization

The top video when I judged a recent ITVA International Video Festival was a marketing piece made for Hewlett-Packard called "Synergies." It went just a step into the future and dramatized rescue efforts during a disastrous earthquake, showing the rescue workers using Hewlett-Packard products which either existed in prototype or were under development. Carefully planned and beautifully made, this video grabs the viewer's attention right from the opening scene and holds it unabated for fourteen enthralling minutes.

Taster's Choice has gotten us all interested in the lives of their two Manhattan apartment dwellers whose soap opera romance, played out in 30- and 60-second installments, revolves around instant coffee.

Other videos among the ITVA finalists were information and training tapes which used parodies of classic television series such as *The Twilight Zone* and *Dragnet* to help get their message across to their viewers.

Dramatization can be an effective way to arouse viewer interest and present information in an exciting way that viewers will remember. But a dramatization must stay on message. No matter how interesting its story may be, a mini-movie that wanders off the point is not doing the job the client paid for.

Illustration and Visualization

The marriage of computers and video has made it possible to create and animate charts and graphs, breathing life into what might otherwise seem to be dull, dry figures. For instance, in researching a video on the need for affordable housing in the Minneapolis–St. Paul area, I came across what I felt were significant statistics. In the treatment I listed among the key copy points for the video:

> Rental housing is scarce. While construction of single-family homes in the past five years has run at 115 percent of the average for the years 1970–1994, construction of rental housing of all types has slowed to just 54 percent of the rate for the past twenty-five year period. There has been a shortfall of 18,750 rental housing units over the past eight years.

As I reread that paragraph, I find it hard to follow, even though I know what I meant when I wrote it. But in the video I planned to use animated graphics which would show that the area was currently building single-family homes at a rate 15 percent higher than normal at the same time that it had cut construction of rental property to little more than half of what had been the normal rate for the past quarter century. It would go on to show that if rental construction had contin- ued at the normal rate, then the housing market would now contain an additional 18,750 rental units. Their mere existence would ease the inflationary pressure on the rental market, thereby dropping the rent on less desirable properties into the affordable range.

Animated video can also allow us to create a visual analog for events that occur outside the world of normal videography. We've all seen network animation of a space shuttle docking. This is an event that actually occurs in the real world, but where there may be no video camera outside the spacecraft to show us what happens.

By now we've all "seen" the double helix DNA molecule, even though it is actually no more than a concept which has been inferred through a powerful chain of logic from a preponderance of scientific evidence.

Presenting Visual Evidence

Video is also, obviously, the primary medium for documenting real events and bringing their substance to an audience. One or two peo- ple with a video camera and some sound gear can go where an audi- ence of hundreds or thousands not only wouldn't fit but might not be welcome. You can't take a crowd along to shoot the behavior of ani- mals in the wild. And most of us will never take a safari to Africa or spend several months in the Alaska bush to see it for ourselves.

But video can also make accessible to an audience experiences closer to home that they have simply never noticed. I made a docu- mentary about the way young children learn for a teacher training project in early childhood education. We recorded kids from a few weeks old up to the age of five to show the tremendous amount of learning that takes place long before a child ever sets foot in a class- room. We did it with a three person crew, shooting everywhere from a local park to a bathroom where a thirteen-month-old boy was taking a bath. And shot everything within twenty-five miles of our production office.

With this documentary we made accessible to teachers on four continents a view of young children that most had never seen before. A *Young Child Is* . . . was a breakthrough at the time, because it showed young children doing *whatever* they chose to do. Until then, most documentaries on early childhood were scripted by an academic expert and shot to illustrate whatever theories the expert propounded. This led to such travesties as labeling heroic two-year-olds as "the terrible twos." In my documentary two-year-olds were stars.

Similarly, the auto lubricant documentary infomercial that never got made would not only have been a demonstration but a piece of visual evidence taken from a real event.

Making an Emotional Appeal

Video works well as an emotional medium. It can use the elements of dramatization and demonstration along with music and powerful visual evidence to evoke strong feelings in an audience.

Those late night commercials to save the starving children, showing lots of images of children in distress, are an emotional appeal. But so are the beer commercials that show healthy young people having fun.

In politics, negative campaign commercials on television are effective because they are emotional appeals, whereas "campaigning on the issues" usually requires a longer, more fact-based and intellectual presentation—the sort of thing that often doesn't play well on TV.

VIDEO'S WEAKNESSES

As we've seen, video shines when it deals with the visual, the dramatic, and the emotional. And it becomes less effective when it gets away from those strong points. Video is not especially good at verbal presentations, at presenting abstract, nonvisual information, or at making an intellectual argument.

Verbal Presentations

There has been a tendency in recent years to create video programs which consist of nothing but people talking. Certainly, if the speaker is someone the audience would stand in line to hear anyway, this can be quite interesting. But in spite of the many talk shows on TV, video is not a great verbal medium. The network talk shows are, after all, a form of stylized entertainment dealing primarily in emotion. Issue-oriented talk shows, found mainly on public television stations and public affairs cable channels, are often examples of death by boredom. They take the kind of panel discussion that might draw a few dozen people if offered in a university lecture room and put it on television where it draws a limited audience.

The primary problem is simply the medium's limited ability to handle words. A TV half hour with wall-to-wall talk (not something I would ever recommend) would contain roughly thirty-five hundred to four thousand words, or about as many words as there are in the next chapter of this book. That's not a lot. A moderately good reader can take in about three times as many words in the same length of time.

There has been an unfortunate trend in documentary production to create the documentary out of interviews. As I wrote in *Making Documentary Films and Reality Videos: A Practical Guide to Planning, Filming, and Editing Documentaries of Real Events* (1997):

> Interviews may help define the point of view, but they are usually a terribly cumbersome way to get the documentary idea across. In spite of what you see nightly on PBS, interviews do not a documentary make, because they don't *show* the topic; they show people *talking about* the topic. (p. 4)

Presenting Abstract, Nonvisual Information

Video is generally poor at presenting abstract information that does not lend itself to some kind of visual treatment. For instance, commercials dealing with such abstract ideas as financial planning tend to go with an emotional appeal. They show the satisfying outcome of successful financial planning rather than getting involved with the what, why, and how of making a financial plan.

In general, economics has not been well treated on television. Nor has philosophy. These are topics that require a person to master a considerable body of ideas in order to participate at the most elementary level. There is a History Channel but no Mathematics Channel. History can be dramatized. Mathematics must be learned and practiced.

TV tends to deal with politics as a sporting event—which it knows very well how to handle—rather than getting caught up in the abstract ideas of political science and governance that require much more time and knowledge to cover well. On the evening news—and even on the political talk shows—you can get a clear idea of who is mad at whom, and even what they are mad about, but if you want the facts of the case, you have to read the transcript in one of the national newspapers.

Intellectual Argument

Any argument that can be made with visual evidence can be made well on video. But any kind of intellectual exercise dependent on prior knowledge and the manipulation of ideas has usually not been well handled using television. Video is a visual medium. That which is not visual won't show up on the screen.

THE COMING POWER OF MULTIMEDIA

The next generation of information media is interactive multimedia of the sort now found on CD-ROM and in Web sites on the Internet. Multimedia provides the opportunity to pull a variety of media together in one package—video for emotion and demonstration, print for intellectual argument, graphics to make the abstract tangible, and a series of levels of detail and option buttons that let viewers select the information they want to receive.

And the videomaker who has learned to record and organize visual evidence to inform an audience can be very much a part of the multimedia world.

PRODUCTION STORY—THE CEO WHO LOVED
THE SOUND OF HIS OWN VOICE

One of the production companies I work with had as clients a start-up cable shopping company that claimed to be well-funded and promised they would be sending a lot of production business our way in the future. But first they just needed this short information video about themselves that they could show to wholesalers to get products to sell and to investors to get money to operate. And they didn't want to spend a lot of money for it, so could we please just edit it out of existing footage that they would provide?

As that's one of my specialties, I was called in to review the footage, write the script, and direct the edit. The footage was twenty-two tapes of two-camera coverage of a day-long seminar the company had conducted for its staff and a few dozen close friends, suppliers, and potential investors, along with about fifteen minutes of edited video showing a few products and some scenes of the company in operation.

Unfortunately, what we had was a lot of videotape of something video doesn't handle very well. Most of those twenty-two seminar tapes showed the CEO talking.

And talking.

And talking.

I'm sure that in his head he was as polished a raconteur as Letterman or Leno. On the tapes, however, he came across as a person who would start a story, wander off into a digression, then into another, and with any luck eventually come back to the original story three to five minutes later. That sort of thing is devilishly hard to edit in order to make any sense. Even when you cut out all the digressions, the statement he started with and the one he eventually ended with may not fit together.

We also had some interviews with people who potentially would become vendors on the cable program, but they were conducted by a young man who obviously saw this as a chance to audition for a job on the air. So he kept interrupting with clever lines.

What we had on tape was talk. Hours of it. What we didn't have was visual evidence. I spent hours and hours going through the footage to find usable bits and eventually put together a twelve-minute script. It covered the ground the clients said they wanted covered using the existing footage and some graphics we could create in editing.

And then nothing happened. For one thing, each time we asked for the next progress payment to go into editing, we'd get put on hold. For another, I truly believe the CEO was appalled when he read the transcript of what he had said. He asked us to send him the VHS dubs so he could look them over, because he was sure there were better sound bites. In his mind he had been brilliant, while on paper his words seemed quite mundane. Here's an example.

> CEO
> I will assure you that more will happen in
> the next ninety days than has occurred in
> the last eight years. And what's occurred
> in the last year has been absolutely
> outstanding.

As it turned out, he was right. Ninety days later they were out of business.

3

CLIENTS HAVE THE MONEY

Making videos for money means that you have to have clients—people who need to have a video made and are willing to pay for the privilege. Clients can be anyone. If you're a freelancer or have an independent production company, then your clients are the people who call on the phone or come through the door with a message they want to get across. They are also people you have called on the phone or gone to see in the hope of marketing your services to them. If you're running an in-house video unit, then your clients are the other departments who give your unit some of their budget in return for the videos they need.

INEXPERIENCED CLIENTS

For some clients making a video is a new experience. They've done brochures or print ads or whatever, but they have never gone on the line for a full-on video. And that means they have no idea what it takes to make a video, their expectations may be unrealistic, and they may not really know what a production costs.

A man in an ad agency I work with called to say that one of his clients was having a demonstration of the use and installation of their home security product and would like to have it videotaped to make a training video for installers. The demonstration would take an hour to an hour and a half, he said, and the video would probably run forty-five minutes and certainly less than an hour. How much would it cost?

Based on what I was told, I put together a budget for a half-day, two-camera shoot with a minimum of postproduction, mainly just cutting back and forth between the two cameras to go in and out of close-ups.

And then the problems started.

- We had the crew ready and the lights set, but the audience hadn't shown up. I had to tell the client that the clock was running.
- The demonstrator spent the first half hour on sales information rather than installation, and his presentation ran long.
- The company hadn't provided a good mock-up of the product, so all the demonstrations were sort of slapdash.
- The client then decided the viewer should see the page in the installation manual as the demonstrator referred to it.
- The client also decided that the demonstrator had presented things out of order, and asked if we could rearrange them the way he preferred.
- Because of everything the client wanted included, the final version ran seventy minutes long, requiring more editing, longer mastering tapes, and ninety-minute rather than sixty-minute VHS dub stock.

As a result, we used more tape than we had budgeted for, ran two hours over the shoot time, and now required complex video editing and a complete editing script rather than simple cuts back and forth between two cameras in real time. The budget went up substantially. By then it was obvious to me that we would have been better off to start from scratch and make a training video than to try to turn a live presentation done for one purpose into a training piece with different objectives. But it was too late for that.

The client was pleased with the final product, but I wasn't.

In this case, the client knew what he wanted but not what he needed. I was working through the ad agency and doing essentially what they asked me to, with little or no opportunity to discuss with the client whether this was the best way to accomplish his objectives.

Because this was a product demonstration, I did a digital on-line so I'd have the best possible video master for making dubs. And of course I delivered a VHS copy to the client for approval. Then the agency asked for a price on making twenty copies. I called the dub house and got numbers on making a professional dub of a seventy-minute program from the digital master, put in my mark-up, and passed it on to the agency, which presumably marked it up again and quoted it to the client. But I never got a dub order.

Eventually my friend at the agency told me that the client had taken the VHS approval copy to a video store and had dubs made from it for substantially less than the quote we had given them. I didn't know whether to be upset that they had paid thousands for professional production and then tried to save a few bucks on duplication or to be proud that we had done such a good job that even dubbing from a VHS copy, they got a product they considered acceptable.

GOOD CLIENTS, GREAT CLIENTS, AND ALL THE REST

There are good clients, there are great clients, and then there are most clients.

A good client knows what he or she wants to accomplish with the video but relies on your expertise to determine how to accomplish it. With a good client, videomaking becomes a truly cooperative venture with everyone pulling together to make the best possible information video, commercial, or infomercial.

A great client commissions a video like a work of art, giving the videomaker total creative freedom. I have had only one great client, and I know of only one or two others. The best was the great client a friend of mine had—a religious denomination involved in social action. Each year they provided him with a budget and gave him a free hand to make a documentary of his choosing about a social problem. It was a good working relationship that resulted in a number of first-rate social documentaries.

But most clients are neither so experienced nor so enlightened.

And that means, in the absence of evidence to the contrary, recognizing right from the start that your clients—whether they have commissioned videos in the past or not—will probably be amateurs at video production. They think that because they've grown up watching TV (and, even worse, TV shows about TV) they know all about it.

They don't.

They shoot their home movies with a camcorder, handheld, panning and zooming to whatever catches their fancy. And they show the footage unedited. They often think of editing as either a nuisance or as a way of adding catchy titles and music to what has been shot— certainly not as a way of creating the structure of the video. They'll evaluate the way you shoot by the way they take their vacation pictures. They can't understand why editing should take so long or cost so much. And they'll judge the final print by whatever big budget feature film they've recently seen.

So you have to be the professional. It's up to you to let the clients in on the process by which a video gets made. Quite often, you have to teach them the fundamentals of communicating in a visual medium and at the same time teach them what makes a good video.

THE TROUBLE WITH CLIENTS

If clients would just put up the money and let us alone what a wonderful world it would be. They don't, of course. They want to be involved. They question our budgets. They give us "input." And that's their right. The client hires our skill at getting video projects made. And part of that skill is providing client service.

Our responsibility is to give them our best—if they'll accept it. And are willing to pay for it.

The world is full of problem clients. Here's a mixed bag of clients I've run into over the years:

The Penny-Pincher

Almost every client is concerned about the budget, but the penny-pincher either has a totally unrealistic notion of the cost of producing a video, or is convinced that you are padding the budget for your own profit. You have to take this client through the numbers very carefully.

And when you do, you'll also find yourself having to explain patiently why it's unlikely that "that pretty girl in accounting" can be substituted for a professional actress, why you need three days on location instead of one, and why the crew can't sleep in the van and cook their own meals.

Your toughest job with this client is to negotiate enough of a budget to do the job right. If the cuts go too deep you have to be willing to say no and walk away from the job. Otherwise, if you cut the lighting package, give up the dolly shot, and shoot on S-VHS to keep the costs down, the client could end up hating the final product for all the reasons you tried to explain as the budget was nibbled away. But the client won't remember that. If the product isn't any good, it's your fault. You didn't do a professional job.

Or if you decide to go ahead with a project that's had the guts sliced out of it, then you absolutely must write a protection memo that clearly states shooting available light with S-VHS—or whatever the client has asked for to save money—will not yield broadcast-quality video. Use terms such as "this will degrade the image," "the resulting production may be less than satisfactory," and so on.

Insist on listing the client as the producer in the production credits if you have to make the video this way.

Hollywood Wannabes

Hollywood wannabes are people who use their money—or their company's money—for a free trip to movie camp. They envision themselves as producers, have lots of ideas to "improve" the video, postpone their vacations to go on location with you, and are secretly hoping that you'll come down with the flu so they can take over. They figure that since they've been watching movies and TV all their lives, they know all they need to know about making a video. How hard could it be?

They'll meddle wherever they can, make changes capriciously, and may even try to take over and give directions to your crew. Because they don't know anything about production, they have no appreciation of the harm they can cause. If you labor mightily to bring in a first-rate video in spite of their "help," they'll never know it. They'll be convinced they did it all themselves with the aid of a few technicians.

But if the reviews aren't great, all the Hollywood wannabes will quickly disappear, leaving you alone in the spotlight to take the blame.

A tight script approved in advance, a contract that clearly spells out the lines of authority, and a firm hand during production are the only things that will save you from the Hollywood wannabes.

Credit Collectors

Credit collectors may be clients that you don't even know you've got. They're the upper-level bureaucrats and executives who are too busy to get actively involved with the sweaty part of production—that's what you were hired for—but when you do a great job, they'll be right there to take all the credit.

To make the hour-long documentary video *Defenders of Midway* on a contract with the navy, for instance, Tim Bradley and Mique Quenzer shot more than sixty hours of video in Hawaii and at Midway Atoll over the course of a year. Then I spent close to another year viewing and logging the footage and writing two drafts of the treatment and three drafts of the script. Peter Dawson and Forrest Cutright put in more months editing the show, and Jud Haskins and David Tucclarone composed an original score.

But at the world premiere of the documentary, held at the Arizona Memorial at Pearl Harbor, who got the credit? All the government bureaucrats whose initials had graced the funding proposal. Throughout all of their speeches, and all of the praise they heaped on each other, the professional videomakers who had done the actual creative work were almost completely overlooked. There was just a single reference to "the great job done by the navy film crew." That was it.

And the Oscar for credit collecting goes to . . .

You can't prevent credit collectors from hogging the spotlight. That's what they do. What you have to do is get a good video made so they'll have something to take credit for. To do that, be sure your contract spells out just one person with the authority to review and approve your work. Otherwise it could bounce around in the upper reaches of bureaucracy forever. Credit collectors take credit for successful finished products; they don't approve work in progress. In the bureaucratic jungle, that's dangerous.

The Cave Dweller

This client has spent most of his or her professional life in a cave (or an ivory tower) and has had little or nothing to do with communicating a message to an audience on film or video. The person may not even realize there's a professional skill involved, believing it's enough to "get out there and say what you mean, and if they don't understand, it's their fault."

If the cave dweller is a technical person, he'll usually respond well to a technical explanation of the communication process. Use formulae. Draw diagrams.

The cave dweller could also be a print person who is reluctant to give up a lifetime reliance on using words to carry meaning. In this case, try to show your most visual and least verbal samples, and if that doesn't work, do a comprehensive treatment that tells what the video will communicate without going into great detail about whether this will be done by words or pictures. Otherwise, you can find yourself spending a lot of time and money to get nowhere.

I had a cave dweller for a client, a print person who wrote and edited his organization's newsletter. And here's what happened after six months of work on a documentary that would play on public television stations across the state, which he had commissioned and I had made:

My client and I were sitting in the editing room, looking at the final cut. It was an acceptable program. The subject was strong and controversial and we had been given access to shooting situations that could have resulted in powerful imagery. But what we had too much of, unfortunately, was people talking about a problem, rather than a video that *showed* a problem.

It was, in fact, the program the client had insisted on months before, when I had originally proposed a stronger and much more visual documentary treatment. But the cave dweller had been adamant about what he wanted. And I had, somewhat reluctantly, gone along. But not completely. As I told my crew, "Constraints tend to melt away in the face of good footage." There were some strong, visually interesting scenes in the video. And virtually every one of them was a violation of the client's instructions.

When the program ended, the client dramatically leaned back in his chair, eyes closed, one hand on his forehead as if pressing out a difficult thought.

"What I would really like to have," he said, "is a video that shows more of the actual people in the community, as they really are—and that's less talky."

"Rick!" I finally managed to say. "That's the documentary I proposed in my original treatment. The one you turned down flat."

Working with a client is often a compromise between what you feel should be done and what the client insists on. When working with a cave dweller, you've got to teach the client what's really needed, or you'll have to live with what you're able to get.

The Comedian

I should put *comedian* in quotation marks because this client often is like the lieutenant played by Bruno Kirby in *Good Morning, Vietnam* —someone who thinks he or she has a great sense of humor, but who actually doesn't have any idea of what is funny and what isn't.

For instance, I was writing a recruiting video for a national organization and had sent off the first draft script—written from footage that had already been shot—to the communication director of my client's parent organization. After she had reviewed the script she asked if we couldn't work some humor into it. I asked what she had in mind. What she described was the kind of thing you might see in a skit night at camp—a lot of slapstick and inside jokes. She thought it would show potential members that the leadership of the organization was human. She didn't actually suggest the national officers take pratfalls . . .

But she didn't rule it out, either.

When dealing with a comedian, you have to listen politely, nod attentively, and then make the video the client needs, leaving out all the silly stuff.

Simple Simon

Simple Simon is usually an administrator who spends the working day in meetings far from the people who actually get things done and believes that whatever such people do is simple compared to the unending treadmill that is his or her professional life. That's because

Simple Simon sees creative work only in the final stage, when all the difficult and time-consuming stuff has been done.

This client has probably seen your sample reel, but doesn't realize that what looks easy and flows smoothly on the screen represents hours, days, even weeks or months of hard work.

I once had a Simple Simon client who would always start a request for me to write something by saying, "with your easy, flowing style, this shouldn't take you very long to write." I never could convince him that what reads easy often writes hard, that the perfect metaphor doesn't always spring to mind in the first draft, and that good, informative writing almost always rests on extensive research.

You have to take a Simple Simon through the entire production process, spelling out what happens at each step. And then do it again in writing as part of your proposal, which you make an attachment to your contract. Otherwise Simple Simon won't understand—and will never accept—your explanation of why you can't provide a print for the national sales conference the day after you finish principal photography.

Old Hard-to-Please

Old hard-to-please takes pride in being a tough administrator and proves it by rejecting most of your suggestions for the video. But when you ask what OHTP would like to see instead, he or she answers with the vaguest generalities, leaving it to you to fill in the specifics— which are then rejected again. This client likes to say, "I suppose if I want this done right, I should do it myself. I just don't have the time."

Or, one might suggest, the ideas.

Or the talent.

So stay away from old hard-to-please if you can. If you can't, add a sizable chunk of time and money to the budget for aggravation and get *everything* in writing.

The Snapshooter

Snapshooters put *too much* trust in pictures because they see only what they want to. They ignore bad composition, poor focus, or inadequate lighting if they can recognize what is going on and can identify the people in the scene. When they know what's in the picture, they block out everything except what they want to see. And they assume everyone who looks at it will see what they see.

I've had a snapshooter ask me why I didn't use "the shot with the CEO." And when I scanned through the footage trying to find it, he stopped me at a shot that included someone walking away from the camera, saying, "There he is. See?" He never did understand why I didn't use that shot.

Snapshooters, incidentally, are the people who take flash pictures of fireworks displays at night.

Snapshooters aren't difficult as long as you have the opportunity to shoot good video. They'll be happy with professionally made images, since they're prepared to accept so much less. And if they ask you to use a shot of the CEO walking away from the camera, tell them you'd love to, but technically it just isn't broadcast quality.

The Workaholic
This is a client who gave up keeping reasonable hours so long ago that he or she no longer realizes that some people—even videomakers—have a life. The workaholic will call you at any hour of the day or night and expect you to drop whatever you are doing to deal with his or her problems.

Some workaholics exist in a cloud of chaos, which is one reason that they take a ten- or twelve-hour day to handle what an organized person might do between nine and five. In their defense, some of the chaos is probably institutionally generated. I wrote and produced several videos for IBM as a freelancer working with a production company that handles a good bit of their convention work, and invariably the IBM executive with approval power would be on the road. I'd fax the treatment to one city, the revision to another, and drafts of the script to different cities. Sometimes the only way I could find the client was to send out a Skypage saying, "I have a draft for review, where are you?"

The latest of these workaholic clients was a woman who spent two hundred days a year on the road. I had faxed a first draft script to her and several of her colleagues on a Thursday. She was scheduled to fly in to record narration and sit in on post the following Monday. I expected comments on the first draft script on Friday, but of course they didn't come in until Saturday afternoon. I put the revisions into a second draft and faxed them out. Some time after noon on Sunday, the client called and said the second draft looked good. I figured we were home free. Foolish me.

That night I was in bed, reading, about ready to put the light out, when this client called to say that she and her colleague had been going over the script on the plane and had some thoughts they'd like to discuss with me. I said that was fine and I'd be glad to go over them with her in the morning.

They were late getting to the audio studio, and their "thoughts" turned out to be last minute revisions of several sections of the script. Therefore the audio session ran long. That meant we started the post two hours late and immediately began to fall further behind schedule because this client insisted on treating the script as a set of numbered suggestions rather than as an approved blueprint.

This turned out to be a long, bad process, exacerbated by a client who wanted to do everything herself and wouldn't admit—indeed may have had no idea—that she lacked the training, experience, and talent to do so.

When you sniff out that your client may be a workaholic, set firm deadlines up front for each milestone in production with penalties spelled out—in both directions—for failure to meet them. Workaholics tend to think that you should meet deadlines, but they don't have to. Then if the client wants to change the script after giving approval, you can say, "Fine. But as agreed, it's going to cost this much more, and all project activities will slip by three days to a week depending on when we can reschedule them."

And try to build an aggravation fee into the budget.

YOU'VE GOTTA TEACH THE CLIENT

My print of the talky video the cave dweller insisted upon before the fact and was disappointed in when he saw it, sits on the shelf gathering dust, a reminder that I hadn't managed to teach the client early enough what it would take to do the job right.

Don Sutherland, who was a contributing editor for *Photomethods* magazine at the same time I was, once wrote an article about an equally trying experience with an important client. Don ran into a series of technical problems in the course of shooting, and as he worked his way through them, the client became increasingly frustrated, until he finally canceled the production.

This client gave up on the project because he did not understand that the technical problems Don encountered were to be expected, and could be solved. As Don wrote in his article, he had gotten so wrapped up in the technology that he had neglected the equally important people problem—teaching the client what to expect.

"Don't Make It Serious—or Too Mysterious"

Some client-producer problems may actually be created by the videomaker.

Some videomakers try to mystify the client by using technical language, making the process seem more serious and complicated than it is, and generally keeping the client in the dark. Producing a video is not a magic act, and what the client doesn't know *can* hurt—you.

Other producers are guilty of oversimplifying and end up seeming to promise more than they can deliver, leaving the client dissatisfied.

Most of us are guilty, at one time or another, of underestimating how long the job will take, how difficult it will be, or how much it will cost.

And then there's the videomaker on an ego trip, whose attitude seems to be, "I'm a video artist. Don't tell me what to do." Even if this videomaker is the most creative person in the world, his or her professional life is going to be loaded with client problems.

What the Client Should Provide

Your client is putting up a hunk of money to commission a video and presumably has a reason for doing so. It is up to you to find out what it is. Clients may be amateurs about making videos, but you have to assume that your clients are experts on their business or their organization.

The client should be willing to commit in advance to the following:

1. A *statement of the video's purpose and intended audience*. What does the video have to do? Whom does it have to reach? About

how long should it be? Does it have to fit into a preset format, time slot, or training program?

2. *Schedule*. Where and when does the video have to be shot? Can it be done in the studio or will it require location shooting? How many different locations? Will location shooting require overnight travel? Will you have to shoot at a certain time of day (or night) or during a certain season of the year?

3. *Elements of the video*. What has to be included? Are there certain things or places that must be shown or people who have to be a part of the video?

4. *Special photography*. Will the video require video special effects, animation, slow motion, stock footage, or special expertise such as wild animal photography? Can the client supply stock footage, and if so, is it acceptable for use in a professional video?

5. *Special considerations*. If the client wants to use a movie star or a Nobel Laureate to narrate the video, you need to know about it well in advance, as it will probably require precise scheduling and added expense. The same goes for the use of special music or artwork, or acquiring the rights to a popular song.

6. *Dissemination of the video*. How many copies will the client need? What format will be used? Will it be distributed on VHS or will you need one of the broadcast formats? Will it be used only in the United States, or will you need to convert it to another format for use outside the country?

7. *Updates and other use*. Will the video need to be updated from time to time? Will footage used in this video also have to be available for use in future videos?

8. *Budget*. This is tricky, because it is a negotiable item. But it is important for you to know generally how much money the client expects to spend. There's no use proposing a video that will cost forty-five thousand dollars if the client can only afford fifteen thousand. And it's false economy to cut corners if the client wants, and can afford, the very best. It's important to determine, very early on, that the client actually has some money and isn't just window-shopping.

9. *Miscellaneous*. Who is designated as the client's liaison with the producer? Can you work with that person? Who has the right of approval at each stage? In other words, whom do you have to

please? Is there to be any collaboration in the preparation of script, artwork, or photography, and if so, who is to do what and when?

What the Videomaker Provides

Once you've gotten the client committed to these specifics, you've gone a long way toward defusing potential problems. At least you both know what your client thinks he or she wants. You've got it in writing, so you both can refer to it. And in working it out, you've had a chance to explain a lot about the videomaking process. Now it's up to you to commit yourself, in writing, as to what you can and will do.

The first step is a *treatment* of the video. A treatment is often called an outline, but it is actually an explanation of the video, in condensed form. It should explain the approach you are taking to the video, and why. It should suggest how the video will be organized, and what it will look like. And it should include all the scenes to be shot and tell where and when they will be shot.

At the same time, you might want to prepare a production guide which explains the process involved in the production of a video. This should list every step in your production process and explain briefly why the step is necessary, how long it can reasonably be expected to take, and where client approval is required. Once written out, this guide can be used, with minor revisions, in all future proposals. And if you've never gone through the process step-by-step before, it can be a help to you in planning your production schedule and budget.

Next is a *budget*. If the video is an independent production for an outside client, budgeting becomes a tactic in negotiating the overall sale of the video. The cost of the video should be broken down into broad categories so the client can tell, generally, where his money is going.

If the video is an in-house production, the budget should be a reasonable estimate of costs, including not only those items charged to the client's department but also listing separately the items charged to overhead such as salaries, cost of equipment, and so on. Let your in-house client know he or she is getting a thirty-thousand-dollar video for an out-of-pocket cost of seventy-five hundred dollars. More on budgeting in chapter twenty-two.

Finally, you should prepare a written *letter of agreement* or contract spelling out your responsibilities and those of the client—even for in-house productions. Do a first draft yourself, then get legal help with the final version. He who writes the contract gets to slant things in his favor, so don't leave this to the client. Remember, a contract only becomes important when things start to go wrong. More on contracts in chapter twenty-one.

Positive and Negative Strokes

In addition, you're going to have to continue to teach the client about video production in general and about this video in particular.

Fairly early on, prepare a list of titles and credits for approval. This is a help in planning your own title photography and it's a place where you can stroke the client's fantasy life.

At the first sign that things are going wrong, or that the client is being difficult, write a protection memo. This gives you the chance to state the problem in your terms. Write it down, be specific, and keep a copy.

Finally, if you find yourself in a head-to-head apparently irreconcilable disagreement, threaten to remove your name from the video. I discovered the power of this tactic when I used it, quite honestly, with a client who wanted changes that I totally disagreed with. I said I'd make them if he insisted, but would have to take my name off the video. The next day we compromised, but he told me later he hadn't slept all night. That was when I realized that most bureaucrats and administrators, which is to say most clients, are always trying to get their names *on* things. So when you threaten to remove your name, they'll be convinced that the changes they want are ten times worse than you think they are. But only try this when you are actually prepared to take your name off the video if the client doesn't relent.

In making videos for money, you'll find that you can turn most clients into good clients if you'll take the time to teach them what you're doing and what their responsibility is. And you'll learn that great clients are hard to come by and should be prized above all things when found.

PRODUCTION STORY—SOME CLIENTS AREN'T WORTH IT

When you are running as hard as you can to make the payment on your equipment and keep food on the table, it's hard to turn down business even though the prospective client looks like trouble. But there are times when the worst thing that can happen to you is that you get the job.

Sometimes you can figure out how things are going to go right at the start. The owner of a one-man agency called me about doing some writing for a prospective new client who had moved to our town and bought several bakeries. He suggested I figure out what the fee should be and call the client. I did.

The client's first words were, "How much?"

I'd kept the writing fee fairly low since this was new business for the agency and I didn't want to be responsible for scaring the client away. I told the number, and he said, "That's way too much. In Miami I had the whole thing done for a couple hundred dollars."

I told him he had been very fortunate, but that I couldn't do the job for that, and the conversation ended.

I called the agency, reported the conversation, and said, "This guy is going to be nothing but trouble. He wants to haggle. He wants everything on the cheap. And he's never going to be satisfied."

In spite of my warning, the agency went ahead and put in a lot of time on a creative campaign on spec, which the prospective client said he liked. Until the budget was presented. Suddenly the client wasn't that crazy about the work the agency had done, and besides, he had some other people he wanted to talk to.

Okay, I spent a half hour doing an estimate and two minutes on the phone and bailed out. The one-man agency spent at least a day on creative work and had two or three meetings with the prospective client and never made a nickel. Yes, you have to put in some time to get new business. But you also have to develop a sense of when it's worth it and when it isn't.

Because some clients aren't worth having and some jobs aren't worth doing.

. . . .

4

IT HAS TO SELL THE AUDIENCE

Making videos for money means creating programs that will persuade the viewer to do something: buy a product, call an 800 number for information, sign up for the company 401(k) plan, vote for a candidate, or have a favorable opinion toward one side of a controversial subject. Most of the time, in short, you're selling something.

Clearly, commercials and infomercials are selling tools. So are most information videos. Only the length of the program and the approach to the subject changes from genre to genre. So let's see what goes into making a successful media sales pitch.

SET CLEAR OBJECTIVES

In setting the objectives for your video, you have to be very clear about what sort of behavior you are trying to produce in the viewer. And always think of it that way. You're communicating with the viewer, and your goal is to get the viewer to do something.

You also have to be very clear about what a video can accomplish, and what it can't. The client's goal may be "to sell more widgets." But that goes several steps beyond your responsibility in creating a video to help the client sell more widgets. For a retailer holding a sale, you might create a commercial with the objective of delivering potential buyers to the store. But if your only involvement is making the commercial, you certainly can't guarantee that people *will* buy the store's products. That depends on factors beyond your control.

For example, there's a home furnishings store in my city that puts out beautiful four-color inserts in the Sunday paper and runs really great looking commercials. Several times they've offered furniture items we were interested in at very attractive prices. But when we got to the store we found that what looked like hardwood in the ad was actually flakeboard with a thin paper veneer; no matter how low the price, the items simply weren't worth it. The communication people had accomplished their objective. They got us to go to the store and look at the merchandise. And not just the first time. We came back to check out other items a couple of times even after we really knew that this store didn't deliver quality merchandise.

You may make a good spot, but the store may be offering shoddy merchandise, unattractively presented, and overpriced—even though "on sale." Or the salespeople may be surly and uncooperative. Or there may be a dozen other things having nothing to do with your video that will turn off potential buyers.

So you need clear objectives, worked out in conjunction with your client. In some cases, of course, you as the videomaker are hired by the client's ad agency to make a commercial or program to their specifications—in which case the selling objectives are the agency's problem. But you still need to know what they are, so that you tailor the video to meet them.

In general, selling objectives are:

- immediate action
- influencing the next buying decision
- delayed action
- attitude formation

Immediate Action

Anything that has to do with retail selling has immediate action as its goal. Retailers advertise to bring people to their stores *right now*. Many an advertising agency account executive has received a call from a store owner saying, "What's wrong? My commercial ran five minutes ago and nobody's come in to buy."

Direct marketing also looks for an immediate response. The objective of all those offers for Ginsu knives, music albums, tarnish removers, salad makers, and exercise machines is to motivate the viewer to pick up the phone and dial the 800 number right then. Because if the viewer goes back to watching the movie, he or she won't call. Infomercials work the same way. Most run a call to action several times during the half hour, at which point they show the 800 number and beg the viewer to call now.

What the viewer is calling for may vary. In most cases it's to order the product. But sometimes it's to request additional information—a video about the exercise machine, a packet of materials about the insurance offer or inventor support program, or a free offer from an encyclopedia publisher (delivered to the door by a salesman).

Influencing the Next Buying Decision

Much advertising on TV is aimed at influencing the viewer's next buying decision—either by asking viewers to try a new product or, if they already use the advertiser's product, reinforcing that decision so they'll continue to buy it. Coca-Cola, McDonald's, Nike, and other national advertisers want the viewer to like their products and either start or continue using them. The objective of the video might be stated this way:

> If on their next shopping trip viewers are going to buy a product in this category, they should want to try ours. And for viewers currently using our product, they should feel that they've made a good decision—and should stay with it.

In areas where the products may be very similar—Coke vs. Pepsi; McDonald's vs. Burger King; Nike vs. Reebok; beer, laundry products, toilet paper, and anything else sold in supermarkets—the objective is to have the viewer feel that the advertiser's product is in some way the viewer's product. The shopping list on the refrigerator in our house says "Coke" and "Taster's Choice" not "soda" and "coffee," because those are *our* products. Your list may read "Pepsi" and "Yuban."

In highly volatile areas, hair care or shaving products, for example, the advertiser aims to drive a wedge between the viewers and their current product. Advertisers know that women are usually just a little dissatisfied with the way their hair looks and are susceptible to an appeal to try a new product which promises to do more for their hair. Similarly, men have to get up and scrape at their faces with a sharp blade every morning and are always hoping to find an easier, more convenient, and more comfortable way to do it.

Delayed Action

Some sponsors, such as Maytag and Century 21, recognize that at any given moment most of the audience will not be in the market for their goods or services. Their spots do prod the tiny percentage who, at the moment, want to get a new washing machine or buy or sell a home to make a decision in their favor. But their main objective is delayed action and might be stated this way:

> Whenever in the next few years the viewers have a need for our kind of product or service they should think of our company as the best way to satisfy that need.

Most information videos do not involve delayed action selling. This is generally reserved for big-ticket national commercials. Information videos usually want to influence a buying decision or are aimed at attitude formation. And infomercials, of course, aim for an immediate response.

Attitude Formation

Many information videos and some commercials—political ads, institutional spots, and public service announcements (PSAs)—want to influence the viewer's attitude on some issue or toward or against some company, institution, or political entity.

Attitude formation is very tricky. The research literature seems to take the commonsense approach that it is easier to generate a positive or negative attitude in areas where the viewer now holds no strong opinion than to change the person's established attitude. Attitude change is tricky stuff. For a long time social activists and social scientists clung to the belief that if they could produce a change in attitude, for instance toward a minority group, this would result in a change of behavior. The results, unfortunately, weren't very promising. Researchers could get subjects to agree that the minority group certainly was just as good as anyone else and deserved equal treatment. But the subjects' behavior toward the group didn't change at all.

Then along came the theory of cognitive dissonance and a series of experiments that indicated that if the researcher could, without undue coercion, get the subjects to alter their behavior, this would be followed almost immediately by an attitude shift so that their attitude would be consistent with their behavior.

In short, attitude formation is easiest in a vacuum. The time to get people to believe a petroleum company cares about the environment is before it has a humongous oil spill at sea, not after. Political commercials are aimed less at the faithful than at the undecided voters in whom an attitude for or against the candidate or issue may not yet have been formed.

In this area of attitude formation, it is especially important to be specific and wherever possible to state the objectives in measurable terms. Here are some examples taken from the entry forms for information videos viewed during my week as a festival judge:

The main objective of the video is to increase membership in the National Leadership Coalition on AIDS through conveying the urgency and impact of HIV and AIDS in the workplace.

After viewing the video, viewers should:

1. Know that Ventura County has an air quality problem.
2. Understand how smog is formed and what impact it has on their environment.
3. Be able to list three things they can personally do to help improve the air quality in Ventura County.

Our objective was to encourage teenage grocery store employees to help create a friendly store environment by demonstrating the fundamentals of good service.

After viewing the program, new employees should have a general knowledge of USAA's Vanpool program and have a clear understanding of the many advantages of using the Vanpool service as opposed to driving a personal vehicle to and from work every day. Ultimately, the video should motivate employees to call the Vanpool office to obtain more information and hopefully sign up for the service.

After viewing the program, the audience will agree that social workers in healthcare:

1. are distinctly professional
2. are fiscally prudent and use resources appropriately
3. have multidisciplinary knowledge, skills, and functions
4. play an ever increasing role in ethical decision making
5. facilitate problem solving among professionals, patients, and families

TARGET AUDIENCE

Equally important is to be absolutely clear about the target audience for the program. Whom does your client want to reach and where are they to be found?

In-house communications may be directed to new employees, all employees, supervisors, and so on.

Commercials may be targeted to the general public, to women of child-bearing age, to sport fans, to senior citizens, to kids who go shopping with their parents, or to any other target group.

An infomercial will define its target audience very tightly and must be carefully tailored to attract that audience, because few people will watch a half hour about a product or service they're not interested in. One of the strengths of a well-done infomercial is that it appeals specifically to its defined target audience, therefore everyone viewing is a potential buyer. And that's why infomercials can make money for their clients even with very low viewership ratings.

ELEMENTS OF A SELLING VIDEO

What are the things that go into a video to make it a persuasive, selling communication? Most people who have been watching commercials all their lives think it's obvious. But it may not be. After all, there are many different kinds of commercials, and many different communication objectives.

Get the Viewer's Attention

The first thing a selling video must do is attract the attention of the viewer. With commercials this is not easy when spots are clustered four or six or more to the break, each clamoring to be noticed. This is why we now have black-and-white spots—to differentiate them from the five spots in color in the same break. And why we are suddenly finding spots with no sound track, just silence. Most of us have learned to do other things while the TV set blathers on. But when it goes silent, we look up to see what is happening.

So commercials need to cut through the clutter. The truly memorable spots find a way to do this, to do something unexpected or intriguing or mysterious or shocking so that the viewer has to watch.

Infomercials must maintain a high level of interest in every scene because they have to capture the channel surfer before he or she can click off to something else. After all, when your listing in the TV section simply says "paid program" you don't get many people tuning in on purpose.

Information videos, because they are shown under somewhat different circumstances, don't require the intensity of attraction of commercials and infomercials, but they do have to capture the interest of the viewers to keep them watching. If they don't, the viewer will turn them off, either literally or figuratively.

Benefit, Benefit, Benefit

The effective selling video never gets very far away from demonstrating benefits to the viewer. What do the viewers get for their investment of time or money? What sets this product or service apart from others that are similar? What can you promise the viewer that the client can deliver? Stressing benefits is an excellent way of attracting and holding the viewer's attention.

Demonstration

We're working in a visual medium and what it has done well, from day one, is product demonstration. Who can ignore the little man with the mustache who quickly cleans handkerchiefs in cold water for Cheer laundry detergent? Or the various ways of showing how this antacid or that one coats your stomach?

Then there's the infomercial for a sandwich maker in which a woman prepares breakfast, lunch, dinner, hors d'oeuvres, snacks, and dessert using the sandwich maker—all in a half hour, and all in real time.

A demonstration is visual evidence of the benefit to be derived from whatever it is you're selling in the video.

Essential Information

Every now and then I see attention-grabbing commercials that somehow failed to tell me what they were selling or how to buy it.

Essential information includes the name of the product or service, the price if that's a factor, shipping and handling costs if it's a direct marketing item, credit cards accepted if that's important, and whom to contact or what the viewer must do to take the next step toward realizing the benefits you've been demonstrating.

"At a theater near you" tells the viewer where to see the movie.

"Call for details" tells how to get started.

The address or location of the store or office tells the viewer where to go to receive the benefit.

Call to Action

In my college days, I spent a summer as a door-to-door salesman, and one thing I learned is that you have to ask for the sale. Otherwise you've spent a pleasant hour or two in someone's living room, had some coffee or lemonade, shown your samples, and accomplished nothing. "Close early and close often," my sales manager would say.

The call to action is the point at which you ask the viewer for the sale:

> "Call now, operators are standing by."
> "Don't delay, you'll never see prices like this again."

"To begin your journey to wealth and comfort, complete the form that came with your packet."

"Vote for _____."

STRAIGHTFORWARD VS. "CREATIVE" APPROACH

I love a selling video that gains my attention and interest, amuses me, and when I'm relaxed and receptive suddenly reveals that all this time it has been persuading me to try its client's product or service. This is the "creative" approach. I put the word in quotation marks because true creativity rarely calls attention to itself. It simply seems to be the most natural way to organize the video or tell the story.

When the benefit is strong, a straightforward approach is often the best way to present the information.

If a store is having a 50 percent off sale, and the merchandise is good, all you really need to do is to announce the sale and tell when and where it is being held.

If the company 401(k) plan offers real advantages to employees, all you need to do is demonstrate the advantages and tell how to sign up.

On the other hand, Maytag has stepped away from all the competition by dramatizing the dependability of their washing machines through showing the Maytag repairman with nothing to do. The implication is that Maytags never need repairs. The fact is that most washing machines are dependable and last a long time. But if everyone claims that, the winner will be the one who makes you believe it. Maytag has done it for years with the repairman with nothing to do.

Make It Memorable
If you can remember the spot—the little drama it played out, the people, the funny line, the zaniness, the thing you thought was clever or creative, or beautiful or whatever—but you can't remember what the spot was selling, it was not an effective selling video.

The first job of any selling video is to meet the client's objectives. It can hardly do that if the audience can't remember who the client is.

This doesn't mean you have to repeat the client's name every five seconds. But it does mean that the client's message should never get lost in the attention-getting devices.

VISUAL PRESENTATION

Start with a visual idea and build the video as a visual argument. Remember the amazing Ginsu knife. The spots show that knife cutting through everything! The visual argument was that this knife does it all, never gets dull, and is absolutely worth the price.

In spots, today, it's the Dremel, which is shown doing almost every task in a shop except hammering nails.

Or how about the water sealer commercials that show a wooden deck with rain on it?

The more you can do to organize the elements of the video in terms of visual presentation, the more effective you will be.

PRODUCTION STORY—
MEET THE CLIENT'S NEEDS FIRST

A savings bank mounted a series of highly effective commercials using two local celebrities. They started out parodying the James Garner–Mariette Hartley Polaroid commercials that had created a lot of viewer interest and media comment in the '80s. The bank spots were cleverly written and fun to watch, and they nailed the bank's selling objectives. Good, award-winning spots that sold the client's product.

But after a year or so, the spots changed and began to parody popular feature films. The cast, crew, and director were having a great time making little 60-second movies. But inevitably the message got lost. Everyone could remember the spots, and they still won awards for creativity, but almost no one remembered the product or service they were supposed to be selling.

The purpose of a selling video—commercial, infomercial, or information video—is always to do the job for the client, never to win the accolades of your peers. If you can do both, great. But you have to be sure you are meeting the client's needs first.

A WEEK OF NOTHING
BUT VIEWING VIDEOS

What makes an award-winning video? That's the question that seven of us gathered for a week in the Holiday Inn in North Dallas to try to answer. We were there as judges to pick the winners in the annual International Video Festival conducted by the International Television Association. Each of us had extensive production experience in corporate, academic, or independent video production. We didn't always agree on what we liked or why we liked it—although usually we did; excellence has a way of capturing everyone's attention.

What a week! We watched videos ten hours a day for seven days. And by the last day of our video marathon we had viewed a hundred videos and had designated Golden, Silver, and Bronze Reel award winners in nine categories ranging from external communication to videoconferencing. With the exception of a couple of student entries, all of the videos were sponsored projects made to communicate the sponsor's message to a target audience. So they were not—as some short films often are—produced for the purpose of winning awards in competition. They had work to do.

BUDGET WAS NOT THE IMPORTANT FACTOR

The cry of every videomaker in every production office in the country is, "If I'd only had the budget, I could have done something great." In North Dallas we gave the awards to people who had made the most of the resources they had available. One project, from a major Holly-wood production company headed by a marquee name, must have cost close to a million dollars. It had specially constructed sets, actors, aliens, and special effects—and it simply missed the point. As you read this, it may still be playing to school field trips, providing forty minutes of entertainment to fifth through ninth graders, but in the opinion of the judges it didn't do much to accomplish its stated objective of inspiring young viewers to learn more about high technology. It was just Saturday morning TV.

By contrast, the video that won all the major awards that year—"Synergies," made for the Hewlett-Packard Company by Tyee Productions in Portland, Oregon—does far more to champion emerging technology in fourteen minutes than the other video ever accomplished, and does it in such a mature way that even fifth through ninth graders would be impressed. Yes, "Synergies" had a good-sized budget. But more important, the producers used the money well.

So did the producers of "Bridging the Gap," another video about a high-tech computer application made for Wall Data Corporation by Seattle writer-director Jim Gulian. This video explores the sponsor's philosophy of database technology as a way to prepare the audience to "be ready to learn about the company's new product." This is a beautifully realized, eleven-minute video which focuses on Dr. David Kroenke, chief technologist for the SALSA business unit at Wall Data, discussing what he has learned about the needs of end users for database technology, illustrated with a series of apt and interesting visual cutaways. For instance, at one point Kroenke talks about the nature of information, and asks, "If I take information, write it on a piece of paper, and put it in front of my dog, is there information there?" The video cuts from Kroenke to a close-up of an appealing shaggy dog looking bewildered. It's a nice cut, and it makes the point beautifully. This is a video requiring only a modest budget. It depends for its success on a good idea, well realized, not on expensive sets or visual effects. And while I am against talking heads on principle, this is a talking head video that works, because the person speaking is the best visual evidence the videomaker has to present to the audience.

HERE'S TO THE LOSERS

All of the videos we screened had been finalists in various regional competitions. So they had already survived at least two tiers of preliminary judging. Some were good, hard-working products that put their sponsors' messages out in public in an interesting and well organized way. Some were simply delightful—fun to watch; easy to understand. And yet many of these finalist videos had obvious flaws. And that made us wonder about the hundreds of videos that hadn't made the cut. Were they worse? Or just not something that would appeal to volunteer judges at an ITVA meeting?

It's often easier to learn from a flawed product than from a successful one, because it's usually fairly obvious what's wrong with the video that doesn't work, while it can take a lot of detailed analysis to determine exactly what makes a good video successful.

Problems with Objectives

The North Dallas judges—ITVA calls each year's group the "Blue Ribbon Panel"—were unanimous in our belief that the first thing an information video must do is accomplish the task at hand. We saw videos that were—or tried to be—funny, charming, beautiful, or provocative, but in the process did a less than first-rate job of communicating the sponsor's message to the viewer. A video that fails to meet its own stated objectives is hardly on its way to achieving its sponsor's purpose, let alone to winning an award.

Admittedly, the ITVA judging form is skewed to reward videos which have clearly stated communication objectives and which meet these objectives. This would seem to penalize videos whose reach exceeds their grasp and to reward those that pretend not to be trying to accomplish much. But the judges usually know better, so it all evens out. One problem with festival entry forms is that while they ask the entrant to state the program's objectives, they don't insist—nor would there be any way to police this—that the entrant list the objectives as he or she understood them prior to production.

I do think there is a correlation between poorly stated objectives and poorly realized videos. A producer who isn't clear about the video's purpose going in will very likely have problems in accomplishing that purpose. It's enough to state here that a sponsored video should never be made without first being clear about why it's being made, who will view it, and the message it means to communicate. We'll look at how you define the purpose, audience, and message of a video in chapter six.

Chasing Fads

Some videos suffered because the videomakers seemed not to understand the difference between a convention, which helps to make a communication understandable, and a cliché, which may have been a good idea when someone else thought of it, but has been used too many times by too many other people. Chasing a fad is doing what others are doing, rather than what the video's communication needs require.

The Black-and-White Fad. We saw a lot of videos released in black and white or with a large number of their scenes shown in black and white, usually for no discernible reason. Look, Alfred Hitchcock shot *Psycho* in black and white in 1960 because he thought the audience in those days would be too shocked by the stabbing scene in the shower if they saw red blood flowing down the drain. The point is, he had a reason. And it wasn't just because Otto Preminger had made *Anatomy of a Murder* in black and white the year before and it did well.

The traditional reasons for using black and white in film productions were:

- black and white was cheaper to shoot and process than color
- black-and-white film was faster and could be shot in lower light conditions than color film

But neither of these reasons applies to contemporary video production. Video production cameras *are* color cameras and they *can* shoot in relatively low light conditions. The only use of black and white in video production that makes sense to me is the convention that scenes from the past may be shown in black and white. And that is not because the past was lived in black and white; it wasn't. But it may have been recorded on film or video in black and white and this convention allows the videomaker to intercut stock historical footage with scenes that have been recreated for this production.

Fake Documentary Style. The use of black and white—and, even worse, shaky camera work—to suggest a documentary style is a slap in the face to every serious documentarian. The evolution of documentary is a history of constantly striving to present the best possible image to the audience. We shot black and white when that was all we could do, and when fast color film became available we shot documentaries in that. When video cameras began to approach the quality of 16mm color film, and video editing became as versatile as film editing, we switched to video. The one thing a true documentarian wants to do is show the visual evidence to the audience, not obscure it with a shaky camera or out of focus or badly lit shots.

In today's production world, good color is so easy to do that it makes no sense to release a documentary in black and white except for a very good reason.

Chasing a fad is never a good reason.

Slow Motion for No Reason. Because I think of what is shown on the screen as visual evidence, I believe that when you slow the picture down or speed it up, you should have a sound communication purpose. The main reason to go to slow motion is to help the audience see something that otherwise would go past too quickly to be recognized and understood.

In a dramatic video or film, two conventions have evolved for the use of slow motion:

- To impart a dreamlike quality to a dramatic scene.
- To suggest that something is happening so quickly that it has to be slowed down for the audience. This might be used to imply that a man is running at superhuman speed.

And that's about it. I'm willing to accept any other use of slow motion that helps me understand the video better. But not slow motion for no reason.

We're seeing a lot of historical documentaries in which soldiers in uniforms of the Revolutionary War or the Civil War sort of lope past the camera in slow motion. Since these same shots are used over and over again, I suspect that the documentarian either couldn't or didn't shoot enough of this footage and has gone to slow motion for no reason other than to make the shot last longer. Since it's unmotivated, it looks dumb.

I have never seen a good reason to show someone walking down the street in slow motion. It just looks like bad videomaking.

Funny Business

There's an old show business story about the young actor who goes to pay his respects to a famous director, who is on his deathbed. Overcome by a sense of imminent loss, he says, "Dying is so hard . . ."

"No, no, no," the director replies. "Dying is easy. Comedy's hard."

Making a funny information video for a sponsor is much harder than making a group of friends laugh at skit night. It takes a writer, director, and actors who know how to do comedy well. And it requires a producer and client who understand humor.

Several of the videos we judged were parodies of old TV shows such as *Dragnet* and *The Twilight Zone*. A good parody is a work of art. But a bad one is like listening to a drunk trying to tell a joke. *He's* having a great time, but no one else is laughing.

Lack of Visual Evidence

In spite of the fact that video is a visual medium, some videomakers have the idea that they must *tell* the story rather than show it. So they put a spokesperson on camera walking around and talking about whatever they should be showing. Yes, there are times when a person speaking *is* the best evidence. And, yes, there are times to use a spokesperson. But not if you can get good footage that will tell the story in pictures.

For instance, the Job Corps commissioned a video with the twin objectives "to inform and motivate potential recruits to the program and to prompt a positive response from the community." To accomplish this, the videomakers put a perky young woman on camera as their spokesperson, and videotaped her walking up steps and through buildings, talking about the program. In eleven minutes they covered a lot of factual information about the Job Corps program. What they didn't do was show us the program in action. Oh, we got glimpses— quick MTV cuts with cameras tilted at a weird angle of kids doing job stuff. And we got testimonials—more talk!—from a Job Corps center staff, as if they were going to say anything bad about the program, and from a handful of employers. But what we never got was a sense of seeing the program in action. My notes on first viewing included these thoughts:

> We are not seeing Job Corps members in the program. We are seeing the spokes and the faculty and the students talking. This had all the credibility of a Department of Labor pamphlet.

A Good Video Knows When to Stop

On a number of occasions we saw a very nice little video stuck inside the awkward framework of a program that simply went on too long. For instance, Tandy Corporation did a fourteen-minute video about the marketing strategies, research, and long-term goals behind a new advertising campaign for Radio Shack. The video got off to a slow start with some scenes of top management that did nothing to advance the plot, and then suddenly took off. My notes said that at that point "this video grabs you by the nose and leads you seamlessly through the story for about eight minutes." The point was made and it seemed to close out, by showing the logo, but instead it went on for another five or six minutes, running the new commercials and repeating itself. The judges voted the video a Silver Reel award. Without its several endings, it might have won the gold.

Bookend Opening and Closing

Many videos were made with a bookend opening and closing that could have been eliminated completely, leaving a nice little piece that accomplished the objectives quite well. Too many get off to a bad start by having the CEO or someone from top management introduce the video and sometimes even return at the end to close out the program. Having the CEO tell about the video before it's shown can make the video itself an anticlimax. The CEO's comments almost never make the program more interesting. The CEO opening is most often a sin committed by in-house units who either don't know any better—they may even think it's a good idea—or they don't know how to say no to the boss.

A bookend structure means the video has two openings and two closings—and that's one more of each than a good production needs.

Talk, Talk, Talk

I wrote notes on my judging sheet for several videos in which I said my guess was that the narration for the program was written first, and then they went back and decided how to illustrate what they'd written. Wall-to-wall narration is almost never a good idea. I've done it. I actually have a client who insists on it. And he's paying the bills, so I give him what he wants. But I would never enter one of the videos I've done for him in a competition for excellence.

A well-structured video has a rhythm and pacing that allows time for the pictures to speak for themselves. When narration is written first, the entire message of the video goes into the audio channel instead of striking a balance between information carried visually and information that needs to be heard. When I show a video like this in a class or seminar, I'll block off the screen and ask the students if they can still follow what's happening. If they can get the message from the audio alone, it's not a well-made *video*.

Videomakers whose first thought is to go shoot interviews with everybody are not far from those who write the narration first. They're looking for words to tell the story, not pictures. Reliance on interviews yields a talky video. The curse of videotape is that it allows video-makers to record long interviews on camera cheaply. And, unfortunately, when they've got all those interviews on tape, they sometimes feel compelled to use them.

I started out in documentary, and I do long interviews for just one reason: the hope that out of a half hour of talk I will find a few seconds of absolutely great stuff that can be used in voice-over—or occasionally on camera. I tell the interview subjects up front that we are doing a lot of interviews and we don't know which ones will be used. And I make it clear that if an excerpt from their interview is used, it will undoubtedly be very short. That way the subjects have no reason to expect that they'll be featured in the video. And I don't feel pressured to use a poor interview just to keep from hurting someone's feelings.

WHAT MAKES A SUCCESSFUL VIDEO?

In general, a winning video states its objectives well and then meets them. It is a well-organized visual event that integrates audio elements — including interviews or the use of a spokesperson — into a visual structure. And it is a high-quality production within the limits of its budget; it puts the money available up on the screen.

Demonstrating Imagination

"Imagine," an eleven-minute video meant to introduce "3M to a worldwide audience of customers, suppliers, distributors, and visitors," uses strong visual evidence to do the job. It sets the tone in the opening scene, showing a jumbo jet on takeoff as the narrator says, "Imagine . . . an adhesive so strong it's used to hold airplanes together." Making the point that 30 percent of 3M's business comes from products introduced within the last four years, the video chronicles the company's dedication to innovation while showing new products and customer satisfaction vignettes.

The visual evidence is there. We see the antiglare screen developed for an automobile navigation system in Japan. There's participation in a project to bring the former East German telecommunications system up to the standards of western Germany. In a hospital operating room we see 3M products aiding in health care. And there are many other examples, all well-shot, well-edited, and well-shown. In my judge's notes I wrote, "This was a very slick corporate piece with lots of excellent shots of products in use around the world." The other judges obviously agreed, because collectively we voted it a Golden Reel award in its category.

An Award-Winning Award Introduction

When JCPenney Company gave its Juanita Kreps Award to Marian Wright Edelman, founder of the Children's Defense Fund, it commissioned a seven-minute biographical video as an introduction. Its objective was to communicate "to the audience who attended the ceremony some of the achievements and personal characteristics of Mrs. Edelman that qualified her to receive this award."

The video is charming. It uses all the usual elements—photographs, stock footage, and an excerpt from an interview with Mrs. Edelman—to get its message across. And where the videomakers had no photos or footage, they used childish drawings to show scenes from the life of a woman who has dedicated her life to children. The narration sounds like it is read by a child and maintains an engaging childlike quality:

> Mrs. Edelman is a friend to children. Mrs. Edelman is an important person. She works in Washington, D.C., where the president works. She has a real important job. Marian Wright Edelman is her whole name. She was born June 6, 1939. She grew up in Bennetsville, South Carolina. Her daddy was a Baptist preacher and her mommy played the organ. Mrs. Edelman grew up in rural America. Back then people who had different color skin couldn't eat together or go to school together or anything . . .

What emerges is a powerful biographical portrait told in pictures and words. It works, because videomakers John Grable, Ben Giddings, and Rochelle Langford gave thought to what they were doing. This is the kind of routine assignment that faces every in-house production unit. And the temptation is to say we're too busy, we don't have enough budget, and do the usual. The JCPenney team found an exceptional way to accomplish the assignment. We gave it a Golden Reel award in its category.

By contrast, a production group in Chicago had a similar story to tell about a school and its leader. "In the second most violent neighborhood in the country," they said, this school "has been sending 99 percent of its kids to college for each of the last sixteen years." The video was intended for PBS broadcast and, unfortunately, never rose above that. I wrote in my notes, "You had a great subject, a terrific character, and I want there to be something more than a PBS documentary." By that I meant it should be better than the sort of production that tells too much and shows too little. The judges were unimpressed. It wasn't a bad program, but it fell short of being an award-winning one.

Talk to Promote Discussion

In a video called "Don't Let It Slide," made for the Job Corps, "designed to promote discussion among Job Corps students about the causes and consequences of sexual harassment and to suggest appropriate and effective ways to respond to harassment," the videomakers used Job Corps students talking about harassment. This is a case where talk provided the best evidence, because there was enough controversy to spark discussion when the video ended.

For instance a young man says, "Nobody's going to see this girl walking down the street in high heels and no underwear on and a real short miniskirt on and no bra and a little tank top and not say nothin' to her."

One of the young women replies, "Wait a minute. No. I totally disagree. I cannot believe that you'd even say that. A woman has the right to wear anything she wants to wear. That does not give you the right—or your little vulgar friends the right—to harass her. Nobody can make you do anything . . . No woman puts a gun to your head and says, 'Say perverted comments to me.'"

To which the young man replies, "I can say anything I want. It's freedom of speech."

That's a discussion starter—conflicting rights.

And most harassment either is, or starts with, talk. So in this video, talking heads are appropriate.

The video also includes several dramatized vignettes of harassment, including an excellent role reversal in a weight room in which several young women make harassing comments to a good-looking young man who is working out.

What it does so well is to accomplish its objectives. I wrote in my notes, "Must be *dozens* of ways to do this badly. You *avoided* all of them. The vignettes were well-made and believable, the discussion well edited and controlled."

The judges gave this a Silver Reel award.

Presenting the Evidence about "Seat Belt Safety"
"Seat Belt Safety," a Golden Reel winner in the category of training made by Wetherell & Associates for New York Telephone, used the two things video does best—making an emotional appeal and demonstrating visual evidence—to make a compelling case for the use of seat belts. The video opens with the dramatic re-creation of a crash involving a New York Telephone employee. He was not wearing a seat belt, and he was killed. We see the demolished car and hear the rescue crew saying that if he had had his seat belt on he would have survived.

Following that, we see a series of demonstrations of test crashes using crash dummies that present the evidence for seat belt use. Then a group of employees ride "The Convincer," a car seat sliding down a short incline at five to seven miles an hour with a sudden stop at the end, simulating a crash. The visual argument is overwhelming.

This is simply a well-made video that any professional videomaker could make on a modest budget. Its goal is to help send "employees home safely to their families at night," and it does the job.

PRODUCTION STORY—"SYNERGIES"

We talk all the time about something or someone being on *the cutting edge of technology*, as if this were a ride in a futuristic theme park or the crest of some virtual wave surfing inexorably into the future. But where *is* the cutting edge of technology? What's it look like? And how will you know when you're there?

These are questions Hewlett-Packard Company may have asked themselves, their customers, and their consulting visionaries before commissioning the fourteen-minute video, "Synergies." They intended it to be a springboard for discussion with customers, the public, and colleagues and co-workers within the company.

The video from Tyee Productions, Portland, Oregon, written by Kevin Cole, produced by Mary Jane Wood, and directed by Roger Thompson, dramatizes a natural disaster—like the January 1994 earthquake in Northridge, California—offset into the near future. It shows how improved tools of information handling and communication—essentially the next generation of computer applications—translate into a much better ability to deal with the practical problems of working through a disaster. And by implication, it suggests these same tools will be valuable in everyday situations.

I talked with the executive producer of the video, Dr. Jan Smith, creative director at Hewlett-Packard Company, who said the video shows fifty-three separate technologies, all of which were either available at the time of production or were under development. Production was preceded by a long period of planning and thought.

What is brilliantly done in this video is that each piece of gee-whiz technology is treated and used by the characters in the story simply as a working tool — without comment or elaboration. The script is tight, dramatic, and underplayed, keeping the focus always on the people and the problem. Dialogue is terse and believable. The characters are well cast and superbly directed. Music, lighting, set construction, visual special effects, and a mixture of re-creation with actual disaster footage all contributed to the credibility of the video.

"I was captivated," one judge said.

"It was visually imprisoning," another commented.

"Synergies" was a major production with what had to be a substantial budget, but that is not what made it an award winner. The judges viewed more than one big-budget production which missed the mark completely. "Synergies" received a Golden Reel award because every element of the video was painstakingly thought through and flawlessly executed. As Smith said, "Everyone involved worked at the top of their craft."

"Synergies" went on to win the top award, the Grand Prix, at the 4th Annual ITVA International Video Festival.

PLANNING

. . . .

6

YOU ALWAYS START
WITH RESEARCH

Years ago someone wrote a great little article called, "You Can't Write 'Writing.'" Its point was that the act of writing is not an exercise, like penmanship or memorizing multiplication tables, but is a way of communicating with an audience *about* something. Therefore, in addition to a piece of paper and a pencil, a would-be writer needs content—something to tell the audience.

The same is true in making an information video. Just as you can't write writing, you can't videotape video. Before you turn on a camera, you ought to have some idea—a clear one if possible—of why you are recording whatever you are shooting and what you hope to get. Those of us who started out in film always kept this in mind, because film was expensive. Just to shoot a four-hundred-foot magazine of color film cost a lot of money. You had to buy, process, and print the film. You had to record the sound on audiotape and then transfer it to magnetic film. And you or an editor had to sync the picture and sound on an expensive sync projector or editing table in order to play them together. When all of that was done, you had eleven minutes of footage at a cost of about fifteen to twenty times what we pay for professional videotape. Only the independently wealthy and a few certified geniuses could afford to shoot promiscuously. The rest of us had to know what we were doing.

And that's the reason for the research phase in planning a production.

MAKING A START

Your work always starts with an assignment, either one that comes from a client (or your boss), or one that you give yourself.

It can be stated in general terms, such as, "We need a way to get message A across to audience B. What do you recommend?"

Or it can be more specific, such as, "We need a ten-minute sales video on the new model 1900 by February 15."

Your research for the project will be highly focused. In a short time you have to become a sufficient expert about the subject—whatever it is—that you could take a pop quiz on it. Or go on talk radio and discuss it. Because that is essentially what you do when you make a video for a client. You bring to the audience the knowledge you have gained about the subject in a highly organized and purposeful way.

Your research for an information video will be mainly gathering background information. This is what writers and producers call research and scientists call gossip.

Start with Questions
Before you rush out to gather information, ask yourself what you need to know. Make a list of questions, starting with the journalistic five W's and an H:

What	What is the project about? What is happening? What do I need to know? What information exists? What footage, photographs, or illustrations are available? What is the budget for the project?
Who	Who is involved? Who will I need to talk with? Who will I need to show doing something?
Where	Where is this happening? Where are the people who are involved? Where will we need to shoot the video? Where can I get the information I need?
When	When is this happening? Is time an element? Is there a deadline or other critical time which must be met?
Why	Why are they doing this? Why is it important? Why should an audience care?
How	How does it work? How can it be shown?

Be as specific as possible. Write your questions down. Then ask them to the people who should have the answers.

Questions Lead to Questions and Answers Lead to More Questions

If you don't get answers to the questions you are asking, it may be because they're the wrong questions. Or because you are asking the wrong person. So keep probing to find out what you should be asking about or whom you should be talking with.

And the answers you do receive will often lead to a new set of questions as you define the project better and refine your research approach. I always think of the research phase as a trial-and-error process. The more I learn about the kinds of things I need to know to handle the project, the better I become at getting the information I want. And the better I become at getting the information I want, the higher the quality of the information I have available to work with in developing and producing the video.

The Central Question

All through the research process you are seeking the answer to the central question which is:

> What is there about any of this that will interest the target audience?

THE MAGNIFICENT SEVEN

My students have become accustomed to my referring to a checklist of planning items they call "the magnificent seven." Six of these refer to the research that needs to be done before you can begin to write or produce something for a client. They are:

1. What is the *purpose* of the project?
2. What is the desired *audience*?
3. What is the *message* you want to communicate to the audience?
4. What are the other *main copy points* you need to communicate?
5. What is the *benefit* you can offer to the audience?

6. What is the *call to action* you need to make in order to evoke the desired response from the audience?

The seventh has to do with *organizing* the material for presentation to the audience and is dealt with in the next chapter.

Purpose
Why are we making this video? Is there a problem we're trying to deal with? Is there a solution we want the audience to know about?

What do we want the audience to do? Is our purpose to inform? To teach? To motivate? To sell?

If we're doing a commercial or an infomercial, the ultimate purpose is to sell the client's product or service. But the immediate purpose may be to have the viewers call an 800 number for more information so that the client's sales staff can have their names and addresses. Or it may be to create a strong positive attitude in the viewers toward the client's product or service, so that when they need that product or service they'll think of your client.

The more specifically you can state the purpose, the better chance you have of designing a video to meet it. A well-stated purpose would be:

Increase the walk-in traffic at ABC Art Gallery by 15 percent.

A poorly stated purpose—although this is often the form in which such objectives are written—would be:

Make the public more aware of the art values at ABC Art Gallery.

The first tells exactly what needs to be accomplished. And it immediately suggests that any approach which does not deliver art lovers to the door of the gallery won't achieve the purpose.

The second is one of those warm, fuzzy, feel-good objectives that actually can be met without necessarily accomplishing the ultimate purpose of selling the client's products. You may be able to produce a video that will make an audience "more aware of the art values at ABC Art Gallery." And you may even be able to measure an increase in such awareness. But that is no guarantee that the viewers will ever set foot inside the gallery. And the client can't make a sale if you don't get potential customers there.

Increased awareness may indeed be a legitimate purpose for an information video. But usually your client will also want some kind of action on the part of the viewer. Awareness without action is what you get from afternoon talk shows. They raise a problem and talk it to death without ever coming close to an action plan for dealing with it. I mean, what *should* we do about mothers who date their daughters' boyfriends?

Clients want action. I wrote an information video for a bank about changes in its pension and profit-sharing plans. The bank certainly wanted its employees to be aware of these changes. But that was primarily so that they could make an informed decision about how to participate in the new plans.

After viewing the video, what should the audience know? Think? Feel? Do?

Audience

You need to define the target audience for the video as clearly as possible. This means asking specific questions as you do your research to find out whom your client wishes to reach and where they can be found.

If the audience for an information video is the employees of the client's company, then you need to find out as much as you can about the typical employee and whether you will be trying to reach all employees or just some of them, such as:

- those in branch offices
- or in the manufacturing plants
- or just new hires
- or just senior management

Most clients will be clear about the audience. They know who buys their products and whom they need to inform. Beware of clients, especially those in a business start-up situation, who say they want to reach "everyone."

As you begin to ask pointed questions, you will find that they don't mean *everyone*. If they are selling something, they might mean everyone who can afford their product or service. Depending on the price of the item, that could immediately eliminate children under twelve, or people with an income of less than one hundred thousand dollars a year.

So make them be specific, because you'll make a different video to sell investment opportunities to senior citizens than to sell CDs to teenagers.

Primary and Secondary Audiences. A client may want a video made to reach a specific audience—the primary audience—but would also like to use it for other audiences as well. As I write this chapter, I am completing a script for a resort hotel and theme park. The client asked for a video that could be used for orientation of newly hired theme park personnel and for training of personnel throughout the resort to make them knowledgeable about what the theme park contains and to give them the information to answer guests' questions with enthusiasm. So the primary audience for the video is employees of the resort.

But the client would also like to use the video as a tool for their sales department to show the park to potential clients and also might like to use it as an in-room video playing to hotel guests. So the secondary audience will be guests and potential guests of the resort.

Conflicting Audiences. Sometimes the client wants to reach target audiences that not only are different but also may be in disagreement on the issues involved. What one audience sees as a benefit another audience may perceive as a negative.

For example, I wrote a video about a corporation's new employee time-tracking system. The video was to be used to make a report to top management about the success of the pilot project. One of the advantages of this system was that it eliminated a lot of ways in which some employees had been padding their time or goofing off without getting caught. I wrote this into the first draft of the script as a benefit to management. But at the script review I was asked to tone down this section. The reason given was that they now planned to show the video not only to top management but also to union officials and possibly even to workers. So the company didn't want to seem to be implying that workers were cheating, even though that was a main reason for going to the new system in the first place.

Unconscious Audiences. In addition to the primary and secondary audiences, there also may be unconscious audiences. These are people who will have access to the video but are not part of the intended audience. For instance, when a company puts on a big presentation for its customers there are usually at least two unconscious audiences listening in. One is its competition; every company wants to know what its competitors are doing. The other is its own employees; sometimes the way they find out what their management plans to do for them—or to them—is to monitor what the company tells its customers and stockholders.

Message
What is the *message* you need to communicate to the audience? Message often is similar to purpose, although usually not the same. For instance, the purpose for making an information video about a client's charitable activities may be to demonstrate to the audience that the client's company is a warm, caring organization. The message of the video, however, may be that the company took a bunch of kids to the circus.

Can you reduce the message to a single, simple idea? If not, you may be trying to communicate too much. Clients and bosses often hate to narrow the message—or the audience, for that matter—for fear that they'll leave something or someone out. That's when I tell the client that when you try to be all things to all people, you can end up meaning nothing to anyone.

Main Copy Points
What are the main things you need to communicate to the audience? These main copy points, whatever you determine them to be, will become the content of the video that you make. When you start the research, you may not know what is important—and your client may not know, either. Clients often have a simplistic view of what it takes to make a successful video. So you have to dig it out. You have to ask,

"What are the important things we want to get across to the audience?"

Gather all the information you can. Ask what information exists, and where it can be found. Be a pack rat for paper. Ask for project descriptions, newsletters, catalogs, proposals, reports—anything and everything that has to do with the content of the video you're going to make.

Ask your prime informant for the names of other people you should talk with. This is a way of narrowing the information to focus on the main copy points. For instance, if you were given the assignment by the marketing director, you'll probably get the marketing slant on the project. But if your purpose is to document a company research project, the marketing slant may not be the correct one. So you'll need to talk with the project director and possibly some of the scientists and technicians doing the work. You may also need to talk with the research director. And you may need to visit the facility to see what actually goes on.

You also should find out what outside information you may need, in order to broaden the information and put the video in context. Again, if you're documenting a research project, you'll want to know how this project fits in with needs and activities in the world outside the company. And you may need to know something about previous attempts to create this product or solve this problem.

Be meticulous about details. Do you have the correct names and titles of the people involved, the address and hours of operation of the client's store or office, and the client's 800 number or other response mechanism?

Always, you are looking for ways to gain the audience's interest and to keep them interested. For instance, is there a human interest angle—a compelling human story you can use to tie the main copy points together?

Benefit

Benefit is certainly one of the main copy points, but I've broken it out to remind you that this is something you always should be looking for.

Benefit is the primary way to interest an audience. Show that they will gain something they want, and they'll stay with you to find out what it is and how they can have it. So always ask, "How will this benefit the audience?" or "What benefits can we offer the viewers?"

Some common benefits are:

- enhances the viewer's image
- makes the viewer richer, smarter, more attractive, more popular
- helps the viewer do something better
- saves the viewer money
- saves the viewer time
- offers higher quality (than the competition)
- offers lower price (than the competition)
- offers reliable service and support
- offers a product not available in stores
- provides safety and security
- prevents something bad from happening

Call to Action

The *purpose* of the video usually tells us what we want the audience to do. In the *call to action* we ask them to do it.

The incredible thing is that I have seen advertisements that caught my attention, offered a benefit and then failed to tell me what I had to do to take advantage of the offer. So be aware that you have to ask for the desired response.

Almost every information video, commercial, and infomercial will have a call to action of some sort. If you want employees to make a decision about their new pension benefits, then you need to tell them to stop in the human resources office and fill out the appropriate form, or to call the Pension Hotline. If you want viewers of an infomercial to call for more details, you have to tell them to call the 800 number, *now*.

THE RESEARCH INTERVIEW

The research interview serves two purposes. The first and most obvious is that it's a way to get the information you'll need to write and produce the video, regardless of whether it's an information video, infomercial, or commercial. In the section above I've repeatedly said you have to *ask* for this or that piece of information. You do this in the research interview.

The research interview is also an opportunity to take a look at the person you're interviewing to see if you might want to use him or her on camera in the video you'll make. Part of the brilliance of "Bridging the Gap," described in chapter five, was writer-director Jim Gulian's realization in the research phase that the best possible representative of Wall Data's product and its philosophy was Dr. David Kroenke.

Conduct the interviews face-to-face if possible. If you can't, do them on the phone. But face-to-face is better, because you get a lot more visual information. You see the facility, you see the person, and you meet others who are involved—any of which may lead to a scene in your video.

Talk with the Key People

Interview the key people who have information about the topic of your video. It doesn't have to be a long interview; a half hour may do it. What is important is to get the story from each person's unique point of view and have the chance to ask specific questions. Each person you interview will put his or her own spin on the information. By talking with several people you'll often turn up contradictions which have to be resolved. And each person you talk with becomes a resource you can go back to for more information.

Sometimes there is someone between you and the people with the information who doesn't want you to interview them. "Just tell me what you need," this intermediary will say, "and I'll get it for you."

In some cases this may be the account executive of the agency hiring you, trying to keep you at a distance from the client. There can be a variety of reasons for this, but the primary one will usually be that the account executive—or someone else at the agency—is worried that you may try to steal the client. And there is very little you can do to crack through that kind of paranoia other than to keep assuring them that your only interest is in doing a good job for them. And then to build up a track record that bears that out.

Sometimes it is someone at the client organization who is standing in the way, either through an exaggerated sense of his or her own importance or through a misplaced desire to save others from having to take time to deal with you. I was working on a project for a hospital which had a successful drug and alcohol treatment program. Most of my information was coming from the marketing director at the hospital and the account executive at the ad agency which had contracted with me. The agency had brought me in, in the first place, because they were having a difficult time getting the hospital to approve copy and concept, and I had worked with this hospital in the past before it ever had an agency.

I insisted that in order to plan the project properly I needed to talk to the directors of the two programs. When I did, I learned that much of the information I had been given was not quite right—which was probably why the agency had trouble getting anything approved—and in one critical area it was dead wrong. I knew the hospital had been operating a substance abuse intervention program, but the marketing director had indicated to me that the hospital had dropped it. When I finally talked with the director of the in-patient program, he said, "Not true! It's one of our most successful programs."

Incidentally, when the information is filtered through an intermediary, and it later turns out to be wrong, guess who will be blamed? Don't expect the intermediary to take the heat. People who can't take the time to provide you with accurate information always seem to be experts at coming up with bulletproof excuses.

Be Prepared

In anticipation of the interview, review whatever background information you have gathered to become as familiar as possible with the topic. Find out all you can about the person you'll be talking with, his or her organization, and whatever the video will be about. Your list of questions will give you a checklist to work from. But don't be a slave to it. The point to a checklist is that you have it to refer to when you're not sure what to ask next or you're not certain if you have covered everything.

The way you get good material in an interview is by encouraging people to tell you stories, not by interrogating them. You avoid leading questions because you want the person being interviewed to tell the story in his or her own words. The important thing is to follow up on *whatever* the person is most interested in talking about, not just to check off the questions on your list.

I wrote the script for a documentary about a group of veterans of the Battle of Midway who returned to Midway Atoll for the fiftieth anniversary of the battle. The producers of the video shot long interviews with all of them. Unfortunately the interviewer, who worked for the government, acted as if his list of interview questions was a government form, and if he didn't check off each item in order, he'd be fined or go to jail. When any of the veterans got excited and started to tell a story about something not on the checklist, the interviewer would often say, "We'll come back to that, but first I want to ask you about . . ." And he'd go on with his prepared list of questions, often forgetting to follow up on the topic that had excited the veteran.

He didn't understand that the reason you can go with whatever the subject is excited about is precisely because you have your checklist questions written down. You can *always* get back to them. The most important thing after you ask a question, is to listen carefully to the answer and then follow up on the answer. Let the person you are interviewing know that you are more interested in what he or she has to tell you than in the list of questions on your clipboard.

If You Can't Be Prepared, Be Ready

Sometimes the person you need to interview is available right now or not at all. You have to do the interview with no time to prepare. That's when you call on the first six of the magnificent seven. Keeping those six items—purpose, audience, message, main copy points, benefits, and call to action—in mind, you can conduct an extensive interview with almost anyone at almost any time and come away with the essential information to make the video.

Treat the Interviewee as an Expert

I always assume the person I'm interviewing is an expert on his or her business, but not necessarily an expert on communication. They've hired me to handle that. I've made a good living for years listening carefully to what clients and their employees have told me, writing it down, and then typing it up in an organized fashion and calling it a script. Quite often the client will say, "It's amazing how much you've learned about our business in such a short time."

Even though you've done preliminary research prior to the interview, don't assume you know what the interviewee wants, does, or intends to say. Always ask.

Tell the Story in Pictures

Look for things that can be shown. Even when the interviewee gives you a verbal concept, try to follow up to find out how that might be shown to the audience. Remember that you are going to organize the information in the video into a visual argument, not an oral story *illustrated* with images.

Identify Obstacles

Are there any obstacles which must be overcome in order to produce an effective video? These could be physical obstacles—the model of the new product won't be available to be photographed for several months. They could be budgetary—you think the best way to show the new plant would be with helicopter aerials, but the budget won't permit it. They could be people problems—the person who developed the process now works for a different company and is no longer available. Or existing footage showing that person can no longer be used. It could be an audience or perception problem. For instance, an organization which is too closely identified with one side of a controversy will probably have difficulty convincing an audience that it is making an objective presentation.

The Last Two Questions of Any Interview

Once you have listened to everything the interviewee has to say, and have gone over your checklist to make sure you've covered everything you planned in advance, you still have two questions left to ask. These are designed to leave no stone unturned. Most interviewees will tell you if you are off the track, or don't have your facts straight. But they may not volunteer information that you didn't know to ask about. So ask. The first question is:

> Is there something that I should have asked you that I just didn't know enough to?

The people you are interviewing may also have some things they would like to tell you. It's quite possible that from the time the interview was scheduled, they've been rehearsing statements in their minds. But, again, these may never come out unless you give them the opportunity. The second question is:

Is there anything you would like to tell me that you haven't had a chance to?

Nine times out of ten, if you've done a proper job of planning for the interviews, the answers to both questions will be no. But every now and then you'll hit a responsive chord, and the answer can be pure gold.

Listen, Listen, Listen
The critical ability in interviewing is to listen carefully to whatever the person has to say, even if it seems to have no relevance to what you are doing. Maintain eye contact as much as possible, even though you are taking notes. And always take notes, even if you're using a tape recorder. Recorders have been known to fail, so the notes give you both a backup system and a kind of quick index to what is on the tape.

Nod and make affirmative noises—uh-huh, umm-hmm—to encourage the speaker. And when you come to the end of the interview, summarize what you have learned in a feedback statement to the interviewee to be sure you've gotten it right.

Be sure to go over your notes within an hour after the end of the interview to clean them up while the interview is fresh in your mind. You'll often find you have incomplete sentences and words that make no sense. But by reviewing the notes immediately you can figure out what you meant and fix it before you forget. If you wait a day or two before reviewing your notes, you may find that those ambiguous sections have slipped out of your consciousness like a dream that seemed unforgettable when you woke up, but was gone by the time you stepped out of the shower.

CLIENT-SUPPLIED MATERIALS

Preproduction research is also the point at which you may learn about—and have to evaluate—anything that is to be supplied by the client. Be cautious with this. Unless clients are very experienced at video production, they may think they're offering something of value, when all they're giving you is another headache.

"We've Got Lots of Slides"

When the client offers you visuals, reserve judgment until you get a look at them. The first time a client offered slides, I visualized professional color slides, possibly 2¼ by 2¼ or 4 by 5, properly lit and artistically composed. What I got was box after box of tiny 110 Instamatic slides shot by somebody's relative. I had to try to make a professional program out of amateur snapshots.

"We've Got Plenty of Video"

Same song, different verse. One of the worst traps you can find yourself in is trying to make a video using existing footage that was shot for some other purpose. You may find that you've got hours of close-ups of a product that means nothing to the program you're writing. And that every time the camera gets close to the stuff you are interested in, it moves on to something else, *because what you are interested in was not the purpose for which the footage was shot.*

The client may not have any idea what is there. He just knows there are five hours of videotape in the vault that he paid several thousand dollars to have shot. For instance, we were doing a recruiting video for a national organization and our contact gave us VHS copies of two videos that had been done previously, to use both as background information and as a source of footage. But when we got the script finished, we found out that the information—and therefore the footage—in the benefits video was hopelessly out of date. And when we asked for scenes from the other video, national headquarters could not find either the edited master or the raw footage that had been shot.

"We'll Provide the Talent"

Clients always like to save money, and one of the ways they sometimes try to do it is to cut out the talent fees by providing their own employees as on-camera talent. Even a large corporation will sometimes make this mistake. If you can, get a look at their candidates on-camera before agreeing to use them.

The worst I've had was a situation in which the executive I had been dealing with in putting together the script for the presentation confided to me that she would like to gain experience doing voiceovers. She sent me a tape she had done which sounded flat, emotion-less, and not professional. I suggested we would be better off using professional voice talent. But she insisted and I was stuck.

Logos and Music

Usually you'll want a good color copy of the client's logo in a size large enough to reproduce well on video. If the client has an animated logo on video you'll want a copy of that. And if there is any kind of theme music associated with the client or the client's products, you'll want that.

These are the sorts of things you usually will get in professional quality. But not always. I remember asking one client for a color logo and receiving by messenger the corner of an envelope with the logo printed on it. All I could do was hand it to the Paintbox artist who recreated it in production quality, with a bit of animation thrown in.

Don't Agree Until You See

The important thing to realize is that clients often can't tell good material from bad. They don't know what makes good video—that's why they've hired you. All you can do is be very cautious about accepting these gifts from the client before you've seen them.

PRODUCTION STORY—THE QUESTION
THAT MADE THE VIDEO WORK

My partner Sylvie Hampe and I were asked to produce a series of short, informative vignettes for use on the annual Children's Miracle Network telethon. Our videos would be two-and-a-half to three-minute stories showing seriously ill or injured children who had been helped through the pediatric services of the local hospital, which was supported by donations to the telethon. We were working on the story of a young woman, six months pregnant with her first child, who was hit by a drunken driver, knocked out of her car, dragged more than a hundred feet along the highway, and left for dead.

Through what will pass for a miracle until the real thing comes along, the accident was witnessed by an off-duty policeman, who immediately phoned for an ambulance. The young mother was rushed to the trauma room at the hospital in cardiac arrest with paramedics keeping her body functioning in hopes of saving the baby. The baby, weighing just three pounds one ounce, was taken by cesarean section and rushed to the hospital's neonatal intensive care unit. His mother was resuscitated—and lived.

We wanted to shoot the finish of the story on a day the mother and her baby, now a healthy nine-pound little boy named William, returned for a visit to the pediatric unit. It was a day I managed to come down with the twenty-four-hour flu and wasn't allowed anywhere near patients, especially small babies. Sylvie took the crew in and set up while I sat outside in a family waiting room. She asked Rebecca, the mother, one question, "Tell me what happened that morning," and in one take got the whole story of how the hospital staff saved her and her child. Then, before shutting down, Sylvie looked around at the crew, and the camera operator asked Rebecca, "Would you like to thank them?" That question gave us the ending of the video.

Rebecca looked directly into the camera and said, "Without them, I wouldn't be here. I mean, you know, yeah, God was smiling on me that day, but if it wasn't for them he wouldn't have smiled very long. So I'd like to say thank you. If it wasn't for you all, William wouldn't be the little boy that he is today. [At this point her voice became husky and started to break.] He probably wouldn't be here if it wasn't for you all. So I'd like to say thanks, and [her voice almost a whisper] you guys are so wonderful."

No one has ever watched this video with dry eyes.

7

SCRIPTING IS CRITICAL

The script for a video is an architect's blueprint, a general's battle plan. It is the point of commitment at which you declare you are going to do this and not that. You're going to show this and not something else. You're going to say these words and not some others. You're going to organize the video from this opening, designed to catch the attention of the viewers, through this series of images and statements to this closing that should provide the viewers with a sense of satisfactory completion and should motivate them to do whatever it is that you want them to do.

The script is also the point at which you go to the client or sponsor putting up the money for the video, tell them that this is the video you plan to make, and ask for their approval to go ahead.

The script is inextricably tied to the production budget. Either the budget is developed from the approved script, or, as is all too often the case, the budget is set ahead of time and the script must be written to fit the funds available.

THE FEW TIMES YOU WON'T HAVE A SCRIPT

With very few exceptions, an information video, commercial, or infomercial will be completely scripted prior to production. The exceptions are a documentary-style information video with the outcome in doubt or a project in which, for one reason or another, you have to start shooting before a script can be written.

Documentary-Style Information Video

For an information video that is a documentary of behavior or of a unique event, I believe you should plan as carefully as possible prior to production, but should write the final script as late in the production process as you can manage. The reason is that you simply won't know in advance what you are going to get on video. So all you can do is plan as thoroughly as you can to have the camera operating at times and places where there is a high probability of recording the sort of things you're looking for. As both a documentary director and a documentary scriptwriter, however, I am convinced that the writer should be involved from the start of the project even though the full script will not be written until much later. The reason is that a good scriptwriter will bring skills of research, organization, and visualization to the project that may very well be needed as preparation for shooting.

On more than one occasion I've been called in to write a script from footage that had been shot "documentary style," which often meant that a camera crew had gone someplace, turned the camera on, and recorded whatever happened in front of it. In those cases, preproduction planning had, unfortunately, been more about plane tickets and hotel accommodations than about developing a strategy that would define the sort of thing the camera crew should be looking for and giving them the best chance to record it on videotape.

The prime example of this was an information video I became involved with that was intended to document the opening and dedication of five fast-food restaurants. Originally, the public relations firm which handled the restaurants was going to write the script. But after the footage was shot, they asked the producer to bring in a writer. When I got a look at the footage, I found out why.

The production company had sent two camera crews along with a group of executives to cover the ceremony at every one of the five restaurants. But they obviously went off without a plan, because at the first restaurant—even with two cameras operating—they failed to get complete coverage of the dedication ceremony, they failed to record the special activities going on at that location, they failed to get a complete statement of the purpose of the event by someone from restaurant management, and although they were traveling with a Dixieland band, they failed to record a complete song from the band.

Well, that was just the first restaurant, I thought. They're just getting their feet wet. They'll figure out what they've missed and do better the next time. But they never did. With five chances to cover the events of the day, they made the same set of mistakes five times.

I wrote an editing script that organized the footage into a reasonable presentation of information and wrote a couple of new scenes to cover the missing pieces that could be shot inexpensively in the studio. And we made a video that satisfied the client and got us paid. But *any* competent scriptwriter could have spent less than an hour prior to shooting with nothing more than the written background information I received from the client and put together a treatment—or at least a suggested shot list—that would have eliminated *all* of the problems I found in the footage.

A really good scriptwriter might well have spent a little longer and come up with some suggestions of concept and coverage that would have made this into an exceptional information video.

No Time for a Script

Occasionally you have to go into production before there's a script because you have to shoot while you have the opportunity. Clients sometimes contribute to this when they don't make up their minds to do a video until the last minute. Sometimes a client doesn't have the money for a full production but decides to record an event while it is happening with the idea that they'll raise the rest of the money to finish the video later.

This happened with First Night Honolulu. First Night is a nationwide movement to develop a nonalcoholic alternative to the traditional New Year's Eve celebration. When it was tried in Honolulu, the organizers thought that a video of the first year's events would be a terrific vehicle for fund-raising and for recruiting volunteers, and they approached a production company about making one. But when they got the budget, they didn't have the money to go forward. Then on the thirtieth of December, the day before the event, they had a windfall. They called the production company and asked how much it would be just to shoot what was happening. It turned out they had enough money for that.

Two crews took to the field, using the published program of events as their shot list, and managed to record a good bit of what went on. Months later, when First Night received their preliminary funding for the next year, they went back to the producer and told him to go ahead and get a script written and finish the video. The resulting information video was well received not only locally but also nationally. But it wouldn't have been made at all if they had waited to shoot until they had the money to finish the show.

Last year I worked on a recruiting video for a labor union that was having its national convention in our town. They contacted a production company I often work with about creating the video—including interviews with officials and members who would be at the convention—and completing it so that they could hand out copies to the delegates as they left to go home. We presented a budget and said if we could start well ahead of time with research, writing, and gathering all the footage we'd need other than the shots and interviews at the conference, we could do it. Time passed and we didn't get a go-ahead. Given the original idea, that they wanted something to hand out at the end of the convention, when it got to be too late to do the preliminary work before the delegates arrived, both the producer and I assumed the project had gone south. Two days before the convention, the union official who had contacted us originally called to ask if we would come to a board meeting the day before the convention began to make a presentation about the project to the board. We said sure, but there's no time now to complete the video before the delegates leave. We were assured that was no problem, went to the board meeting, and got an immediate go-ahead. I spent the next day on script research, wrote a quick, tentative outline and shot list, and we started two days of shooting the following day. The actual outline is shown in figure 7.1. From the outline I put together a list of interview questions designed to cover the various content areas, which we used in shooting. When the convention ended I sat down with copies of the video we had shot and my outline and wrote the script.

Figure 7.1

Script Outline

I. Purpose.
    A. New employee orientation and recruiting.
    B. Have 15 minutes to present the union story to new employees. Show the video and answer questions.
II. Brief Content Outline.
    A. Opening.
        1. Fast cut quick statements of union benefits from members.
    B. Union background.
        1. Union seal.
        2. Founded in 1968.
        3. Relation to AFGE and AFL/CIO.
        4. Relation to government agency.
            a) Fast growing service; fast growing union.
    C. What the union does (current president).
        1. Represents the membership to the agency.
            a) Reviews changes in workplace and management policies.
            b) Total Quality Partnership.
        2. Input to Congress.
        3. Input to new administrations.
    D. Protection for new employees on the job.
        1. Recovered millions in back wages.
            a) Got the largest settlement ever.
        2. Saved hundreds of jobs.
        3. Has the trained people and willingness to fly national officials wherever they are needed to represent an employee.
    E. Benefits program through AFGE.
    F. What your dues are for:
        1. Stories of union representation (from interviews).
    G. Where we're going (incoming president).
        1. Statement from John Sturdevant, AFGE.
        2. Statement from President Clinton.
    H. Closing.
        1. It's in your own interest to belong.
        2. Look over the information and see your union representative.

SCRIPT STRUCTURE

Structure is crucial to creating a successful script. An information video will suffer more from bad structure than from bad writing, bad cinematography, or bad acting. A poorly organized presentation can cost you your audience almost before you start. And you will *never* know why.

Beginning, Middle, and End

Most informative and persuasive writing, including the scripts for most kinds of sponsored videos, will have a *beginning*, a *middle*, and an *end*. We all know that. What may not be clear is what those words mean, what we have to write to make a good beginning or a good ending. And what precisely we have to put in the middle.

The Beginning—Attracting Attention. The beginning is always an attention-getter. In a video, regardless of whether it's a 30-second commercial or an hour documentary, time is critical and you can't waste it. You have to grab the audience's interest right away or you may lose them, either literally—they don't like your commercial and switch to another channel—or figuratively, when they continue to sit in the audience, but are playing a video of their own making inside their heads instead of watching yours.

A good beginning might pique the audience's curiosity, promise a benefit of some kind, or tell a story. If at all possible, it should be built with compelling images rather than talk. In her excellent guidebook for screenwriters, *Making a Good Script Great*, Linda Seger, writing about the opening of a screenplay, says that most good films begin with an image. "We see a visualization that gives us a strong sense of the place, mood, texture, and sometimes the theme. . . . Films that begin with dialogue, rather than a particular visual image, tend to be more difficult to understand. This is because the eye is quicker at grasping details than the ear." (p. 21)

Sometimes, of course, all you have are words. And when that's the case, you have to make them count. You're trying to grab and hold the viewer's attention. For the opening of a fund-raising video on prevention of child abuse, I didn't have—and didn't want to show—images of abused children. So I opened with a montage of shots of attractive, appealing children under the age of five and a strong statement from the spokesperson, who was a highly respected news anchor:

> SPOKESPERSON
> (Voice-over)
> These are the tragic facts . . . four out of
> every five cases of severe child abuse
> requiring hospitalization happen to
> children under the age of five. What is
> worse, in a study of *deaths* from child
> abuse in Hawaii, *all* the victims were
> under five . . . and more than half were
> younger than two years old.

Documentaries often open with a series of controversial, attention-getting statements from people who will be seen and heard throughout the program. This works. But starting with good pictures is always better.

Try not to start with the CEO. I have seen far too many corporate videos that open with a statement from the boss. Someone is out there shooting one right now. Unfortunately, this is almost always the poorest way possible to open a video. Unless your CEO is a media star, equally at home in company commercials or trading stories with Letterman, the president's message is likely to be formal, sleep-inducing, and unnecessary. The CEO almost always tells the audience either why what they are about to see will be good for them or why it's an example of the enlightened management of the current administration. Invariably it gets the video off to a brisk trudge. If you have to have the CEO in the show for political reasons, try to do it somewhere other than the opening in a way that moves the video forward.

The Middle—Presenting Visual Evidence. The middle presents the main copy points in a series of strong images. These are the visual evidence for the rhetorical argument that makes up the content of your video. As with the opening, it is important to make each scene as strong visually as possible. Your audience will follow your argument more easily if it is composed of an understandable visual sequence. The visual argument may be backed by dialogue or narration which explains the information that doesn't come through visually. But spoken words should never take primacy over visual evidence. The audience is most likely to believe what they see, rather than what they are being told. When the sound track is in control, there is an understandable tendency to use *visuals* that *illustrate* what is being said.

Illustrative visuals are usually not visual evidence. Often they are not much more than visual wallpaper; something to put on the screen while the narrator talks. Which is hardly the most exciting thing you can do for your audience. Sometimes the visuals may be a metaphor for what is being said. In a script I reviewed for a video about pharmaceutical software, the writer used the visual metaphor of a jigsaw puzzle, and showed each component of the program as a piece in the puzzle. This got across the idea that all the components fit nicely together. Unfortunately it got it across in the first shot or two, but went on for several more shots before the puzzle was complete. And while the puzzle metaphor was apt, it was hardly compelling. It was another way of telling what was already being said on the sound track, rather than showing the audience evidence of the ways the components worked together.

The one exception to the rule of visual evidence first, words second, is the situation where words coming from the mouth of a person on camera constitute the best evidence for your rhetorical argument. It would be poor usage to have the CEO say, "This is going to be a great year for our company," because that's not evidence; it's his opinion. You may have other things you can show that will bolster the statement, but the statement itself is weak. It's the sort of thing CEOs are expected to say. On the other hand, when the CEO says, "This year everyone in the company is going to get a five percent bonus and an extra week of vacation," that's probably the best evidence you'll ever get of that promise. Use it.

The middle of a video must stay on message and not go wandering off the theme. In a sponsored video the middle will almost always stress a benefit of some sort to the viewer. And it will tend to focus on the life and needs of the viewer rather than on the hopes and dreams of the sponsor. Narration will talk about *you*, the viewer, and not *we*, the sponsor.

> You and your family deserve a better way to [do whatever it is] and XYZ company is helping to make it happen.

not

> We're giving people a better way to . . .

As part of the evidence in the middle, you may also want to answer negatives—if they can be replaced with a positive. Visual evidence can work wonders here. If you have footage that contradicts the negative assertions of the opposition, show it and make the point.

The End—A Satisfying Conclusion. The end of your video should do three things:

- Reinforce the theme of the video.
- Make a call to action, if appropriate, and tell how the viewer can or should respond.
- Wrap up the piece in a way that is satisfying to the audience.

The Structure of a Commercial

A commercial, even though it is short, can serve as a model for almost any kind of information video. A well-made commercial is a mini-movie, complete in thirty or sixty seconds. Properly conceived, it will have a beginning, a middle, and an end.

The beginning sets up what is to follow. It may ask a question that the rest of the spot will answer in terms of benefit. Or it may simply show something that attracts the viewer's interest. A good opening makes you want to see what will happen next. And that's important because, as we all know, when the commercials come on is when we go to the kitchen or bathroom—or go channel surfing.

The middle is all about benefit. It may be implied benefit, as in the Maytag repairman spots that tell the audience the appliances are so dependable the repairman has nothing to do. The spot may offer the benefit of high quality or low price. Or a spot may open with a problem and then show as a benefit how the client's product or service will solve that problem for the viewer.

The ending of a commercial is almost always a call to action. It tells the viewer what to do to get the benefit and how to do it. Or it may end with the campaign slogan, which stands in for the call to action. The award-winning commercials from "America's Dairy Farmers" end with the slogan, "Got milk?" and the implied call to action, *if not, get milk*. Nike's "Just Do It!" campaign shows athletes going all out while wearing Nike sport shoes, and each spot ends with the slogan and the implied call to action, *do it wearing Nikes*.

The Structure of an Information Video

In many ways, an information video is very much like a commercial with the structure expanded to accommodate a longer length. It too has a beginning, middle, and end. And it too generally aims to motivate an audience to some kind of action, even if it is just to feel good or bad—or to think—about something. But an information video is not a commercial, and I have written more than one information video that was badly mauled by commercial directors who thought they could treat the longer form exactly the way they made 30-second spots.

A commercial has to move quickly through setup and benefit to the satisfactory conclusion. An information video, while often fairly short, is measured in minutes rather than seconds. So the pacing will be different and the possibilities for development can be much more complex.

The Opening. The opening of an information video should engage the interest of the audience and set the rhetorical argument that will be carried on in the middle and resolved in the ending. Unfortunately, the opening is often the weakest part of an information video. It's as if the videomaker, whether writer, producer, or director, doesn't understand that as far as the audience is concerned, the opening begins with the first image that appears on the screen. So it had better be a good one.

The CEO introduction, for instance, is an example of the "before I start my presentation, I'd like to tell you something" school of communication. It can put the audience to sleep long before what the videomaker thinks of as the first image of the *real* video ever gets to the screen. You get only one chance to do it right. But some information videos will try to hedge the bet by having two and three openings—something for everyone. First there's the CEO statement, then a little history of the company, and then something that sets the topic for the video. It takes a dedicated audience to wait through all of that to see if the videomaker actually has anything to show them.

The Middle. The middle is made up of everything the audience needs to know about the topic—and nothing more. It should flow smoothly out of the opening and deftly into the ending, presenting your argument to the audience in a sequence of compelling images that makes the case as strongly as possible. The most important structural consideration in the middle is to get it organized properly. Usually there will be several copy points or topics to be covered. The most economical way to handle this is to raise a topic, deal with it completely, and move on. Anything other than that is like the person telling a joke who gets to the punch line and says, "Oh, I forget to tell you. First she . . ." which breaks the flow of the story and often gives away the fun of the ending.

So the scriptwriter has two main concerns in writing the middle of an information video:

1. Determining what must be included—and what can be left out.
2. Establishing the sequence in which to present the copy points and their visual evidence in order to keep the video moving easily and logically from the end of the opening to the start of the ending.

The End. The closing of an information video will usually tell the audience what they need to do to receive the benefits promised in the middle—or to prevent the dire consequences of negative benefits threatened there:

- Visit the human resources office to select your pension program.
- Take the time to make a friend of a customer and watch your commissions go up.
- Show your concern about global warming by joining the Coalition for the Future.

If it is a sales video it will urge the viewer to try or buy the product or service:

- Take it out for a test drive. You may never bring it back.

Sometimes the ending will tell the audience how the sponsor is working to make things better for them:

- This new state-of-the-art product line promises an increase in sales and commissions in the year ahead.
- Leaner, stronger, and better organized, your company is ready to meet the competition head-on—and win.

The Structure of an Infomercial

As its name implies, an infomercial is a hybrid combining elements of an information video with elements of a commercial. An infomercial is usually a television half hour that offers the audience help in dealing with some problem in their lives—anything from being overweight and out of shape to being broke from not having enough income to wanting to catch bigger fish. But within the half hour running time an infomercial is actually a series of sales pitches—part commercial, part information video—each of which starts with a promise, demonstrates benefit, and ends with a call to action. An infomercial has to be designed to trap channel surfers whenever they show up and hold them through at least one full pitch.

The Beginning. An infomercial starts with a bang. Ideally you would like to keep interested viewers from the previous program. So you've got to grab their attention right away with strong visuals, good music, celebrity talent where appropriate, and, most important, a promise that if they will keep watching, they'll learn something that can change their lives for the better.

The beginning may also function to suggest that what the viewer is watching is an informative television program. For that reason it may open like a talk show or a documentary or a cooking, fitness, or travel show. The host is introduced, who proceeds to inform the audience of the problem for which this infomercial is the solution.

An infomercial consists of a series of five- to eight-minute pitches, each of which has its own beginning, middle, and end. The beginning of a pitch will usually state the problem that the product or service in the infomercial will solve.

The Middle. Each pitch presents various aspects of the problem and demonstrates evidence that the product or service shown in the infomercial is effective in solving the problem. Each pitch shows the benefit of using the product or service. If it's an exercise system, we see attractive-looking people using it. If it's a kitchen appliance we see more and more ways that it can be used to make cooking better, easier, and more nutritious. If it's a product or service, we see how successful users—"people just like you"—have benefited by taking the course, ordering the home study materials, or viewing the video.

Each pitch should be a little stronger than the one before, in the hope of tipping the viewer from undecided to buyer. Unlike a TV show or even an information video, an infomercial can never take a breather. It must be either detailing a problem, promising a solution, demonstrating a benefit, or explaining how to participate. Each pitch must be high energy, highly visual, and highly interesting in order to catch and hold channel surfers.

The End. At the end of each pitch there is usually a break to a commercial which tells how the viewer can order the product or service. This use of a commercial within the infomercial serves to maintain the fiction that it is a program. Just before going to the commercial the host will promise something spectacular in the next segment to keep the undecideds watching:

- Stay tuned, because when we come back we'll meet a couple who bought two hundred thousand dollars worth of real estate with no money down and went from unemployment to a net worth of half a million dollars in just eighteen months.
- When we come back, you'll learn how you can preserve all the natural vitality of fresh fruits and vegetables for years right in your own kitchen.
- When we come back, you'll meet a woman who lost thirty pounds in one month by using this system.

If the convention of breaking to a commercial is not used, then each pitch ends with a call to action which tells how the viewer can take the next step, again with the promise that something spectacular is coming up in a few minutes.

The infomercial itself essentially ends with the last and strongest in the series of pitches. This is the one that pulls out all the stops and tries to convert the undecideds before the infomercial goes off the air. If commercials are used, there will be one last commercial. After that, it's closing credits just like any other TV show, although the 800 number and ordering information may be kept on the screen throughout.

PLANNING THE VIDEO

It is possible that there are a few creative geniuses who can skip all the preliminary steps and—like those mathematical wizards who solve giant equations instantly in their heads—go directly and effectively to script. Most of us can't. We have to take the research that we've done, organize it, see if there's anything missing, and follow up if there is.

Finding an Approach to the Topic

Then we have to come up with an approach to the topic, a unifying concept that helps us fit all the elements into a structure that will carry the message to the audience. That takes some time, thought, and trial and error.

To people who read scripts, but don't write them, it all seems so obvious when they sit with fifteen or twenty pages of manuscript which lay out the progress of a video that is still to be made, from its opening fade-in to its closing credits. But for a scriptwriter starting with a set of notes and a blank computer screen, nothing is obvious. Your first ideas may go nowhere, the material you've gathered may seem unconnected and devoid of structure, and all that keeps you going is the knowledge that you've been lost in these woods before, and you always got out alive.

For a recent ITVA international conference, Chris Jones, an award-winning writer-producer-director, put together a panel of three video scriptwriters who all agreed to take on a pro bono project for the United Way of Greater Minneapolis—research it, write a treatment, and write a first draft script. The United Way would then select the script they wished to have produced.

The writers agreed to appear on a scriptwriting panel at the conference where they would show the scripts they had written, tell why they had taken the approach they chose, and answer questions. I was one of the writers and this was the project I mentioned in chapter two—on the need for affordable housing in the Minneapolis–St. Paul area.

Purpose and Audience. In my treatment for the project, I stated the purpose and audience as I understood them:

A. Purpose
   1. The video will be used to motivate corporate leadership and top management to become more directly involved in the creation of affordable housing.
   2. It will show how current housing costs coupled with a shortage of rental housing are significant barriers that prevent working families from obtaining safe, stable, affordable housing.
   3. It will show that a "living wage" in the eight to ten dollars an hour range is not adequate to afford decent housing in the metropolitan area.

4. It will show that affordable housing is a community problem not a commodity problem.

5. And it will make the point that the people in need of affordable housing are not just the highly visible "street people," but are primarily families with children and with one or more family members employed.

6. The video will argue that it is in the corporate interest to help provide safe, stable, affordable housing for its workers and the people in the surrounding community.

B. Audience

1. The audience for this video will be corporate executives and upper-level management people, both male and female, generally over the age of forty. Audience members will be generally affluent and ten or more years removed from any concern about finding adequate housing for their families.

2. The audience will view the video in groups, with a trainer.

Three Writers—Three Approaches

The other writers were Tyson Greer of Seattle and Susan Steger Welsh of St. Paul. We each started with the same general background information supplied by Chris Jones. We then went our own way in researching the project and writing the treatment. We got a certain amount of feedback on the treatment from the client and then wrote the script. What I think is interesting is that leaving the same starting line at the same time, we came up with three different approaches.

Susan Steger Welsh—An Emotional Approach. Welsh elected to focus on families. Her script, "Homestability," was an emotional appeal centered on caring for our children and on the almost Jungian significance of a house and home in the life of a family and a community. In the opening her narrator says:

HOUSING IS A BASIC NEED. IT UNDERPINS OUR
FAMILIES AND OUR NEIGHBORHOODS. YET, IN OUR

COMMUNITY, TODAY, A WIDENING GAP BETWEEN
WHAT MANY PEOPLE CAN AFFORD, AND THE HOUSING
AVAILABLE, IS MORE THAN A BAD DREAM. IT'S A
NIGHTMARE THAT DOES NOT FADE WITH THE DAWN.

She personalized every aspect of the story in terms of specific families and their needs. She shows a two-income family averaging a total of seventeen dollars an hour or twenty-nine hundred dollars a month. But when she takes out a big slice for child care, since both parents are working, and transportation, the usual medical expenses with children, and so on, there suddenly is very little left for housing.

Her script ends with an unabashed emotional appeal:

29. Children's house pictures and children playing.
    A HOUSE.
    A HOME.
    A SAFE PLACE TO GROW UP AND TO LEARN IN.
    A NEIGHBORHOOD THAT IS HEALTHY AND PLEASANT.
    ALL CHILDREN DESERVE THIS.
    THEIR FUTURE, AND OURS, DEPENDS ON HAVING . . .
    HOMESTABILITY.

30. If we have one last heart-tugging child sound bite,
    use it here. Otherwise, music up full and slow
    motion to freeze frames of the children.

Tyson Greer—Dramatization with Humor. Tyson Greer's approach was a play within a play, including a star turn by Minnesota's own Garrison Keillor—if that could be arranged—or by his evil twin (a look-alike actor) if it couldn't. The setting is a Garrison Keillor–style minidrama, the sort of thing he does so well on *A Prairie Home Companion* on National Public Radio and occasionally does on PBS when he puts his radio show on TV. His character, Willard Gateless, is a busy executive whose staff measures his valuable time in half-minute bites.

As the scene unfolds, Gateless learns the sad statistics of the lack of affordable housing in the Minneapolis area. These are presented in a humorous way that has fun with the Gateless character while not making fun of the plight of those who can't afford decent housing. He learns of the "gap"—housing costs increasing faster than wages—and the "trap," which is a family trapped with too high a rent or mortgage payment relative to family income, so that any financial problem at all can mean they lose their housing. And he learns that the families affected may be his own employees. In fact, his executive secretary, even though her income provides adequate housing, has had to take in her sister and her family, after they fell into the "trap" and lost their home.

Greer puts the call to action in the form of a surprise ending in which the audience learns that this has just been a rehearsal, and the real event is yet to come.

> DIRECTOR
> Good job everyone! Good job! We'll finish
> tomorrow. (to Gateless, his real self)
> Nice job _____ (actor's real
> name).

> GATELESS
> Thank you. Just one thing, though. I
> haven't been given the final pages of the
> script—the ending! What does Gateless do?
> I need the script. Doesn't the writer . . .

Arm around actor's shoulder he shepherds Gateless off the set, and reassures.

> DIRECTOR
> (soothing his race horse)
> No, no, no. It's coming. We've got good
> people working on it . . .

Empty set. The lights click off, leaving working lights, and the credits roll.

In Greer's production notes she writes, "In the final scene with the director, the director needs to convey that 'good people' refers to leaders in the community—not procrastinating writer gnomes chained up in the basement until they get the pages done."

My Script—A Documentary Approach. I tailored my script to the primary audience of "corporate executives and upper-level management people." I used a documentary approach with an on-camera spokesperson, and I noted that, "if possible, this should be a respected news anchor or businessperson who is well-known in the metropolitan area." My idea was to present the facts about the lack of affordable housing as a serious problem, and to make the argument that it was in the best interests of the businesspeople in the audience to come up with a solution. At the same time I used dramatic visual evidence to make an emotional appeal. For instance, this is the opening:

1. Stock footage of a winter blizzard in Minnesota.

                    SPOKESPERSON
        How would you like to be looking for a
        home for your family on a day like this?

2. Spokesperson on camera.

                    SPOKESPERSON
        I'm _____. More than
        eighty thousand families in the
        metropolitan area can't afford the
        minimum cost of safe, stable, low-cost
        housing. These are not "the homeless"—
        single individuals pushing shopping carts
        with their belongings or sleeping in alleys
        and culverts—although they are the small
        but visible part of the problem.

                                        DISSOLVE TO:

3. Some cute small children.

> SPOKESPERSON
> We're talking about families. A quarter of
> a million people. Maybe more. These are
> your employees. They may even be your
> relatives.

The script goes on to give several examples of good people who can't afford good housing. It then presents the elements of the problem. Jobs are in the suburbs but low-cost (although often rundown) housing is in the city. Single family homes have been overbuilt, while there is a serious shortfall in rental housing. It takes a minimum income of twelve dollars an hour to be able to afford a decent basic rental unit in the area—more if there are other major expenses such as child care, transportation, or medical problems.

Then it turns to some solutions, including showing some programs that have worked, but points out that only about a third of the people in need of low-cost housing are being helped. The close suggests some things the audience might do, starting with using their political influence, and offering management expertise to the nonprofit organizations working in this area to help them build and manage low-cost housing more effectively.

41. A clogged expressway at drive time.

> SPOKESPERSON
> For instance, you might look at the
> interrelationship of jobs, housing,
> transportation, and day-care services.
> They have to work together or nobody
> works.

42. Construction site.

> SPOKESPERSON
> You also could bring some results-oriented

analysis to identifying artificial barriers
that hamper the creation of housing that
people can afford.

43. City building being rehabilitated.

SPOKESPERSON
Are regulations and hidden agendas adding
to the cost?

44. Spokesperson on camera.

SPOKESPERSON
This problem of housing is large and
complex . . . and it has serious
implications for the future of our
communities and the health of your
businesses. As we've seen, a good start
has been made. But there is still a great
deal to do. We need your help.

There you have three different approaches—one heavily emotional, one dramatic and humorous, and one documentary—each presenting the same basic factual information. And any one of these
approaches would do the job just fine. The bottom line is that the
United Way officials told Chris Jones that if they had received any one
of the scripts—alone—they would have been delighted to have it produced.

Pick the Approach That Works for You

The approach you choose should be one that you are comfortable
with, and that will adequately convey the message to the audience.
For instance, if you can jolly the audience into a good mood—and a
positive attitude toward your message—with humor, go ahead and
have fun. But if you're not good at humor, or if humor is inappropriate to the subject, pick a different approach.

If you don't have a lot of visual evidence, you may want to use an on-camera spokesperson. But if there is a lot of good video available, then an on-camera spokes will just slow things down.

GETTING ORGANIZED

So how do you go from a couple of tablets full of notes and a portfolio stuffed with the memos and brochures you've collected to a realistic plan for writing the script?

Make an outline.

The trouble with outlines is that we were all taught some cumbersome outlining system in seventh grade, had to outline something that didn't need outlining to prove that we had learned the system, got graded on how well we did, and swore off outlining for life. Oh, sure, we tried the outlining program that goes with our word processor, but it all got too complex to be useful.

And that's the point, isn't it? An outline has to be useful.

The Existential Outline

In *Video Scriptwriting: How to Write for the $4 Billion Commercial Video Market*, I describe how in desperation I stumbled onto what I now call the *existential outline*. I had contracted to write an hour-long information video and had never done a script longer than ten minutes. I knew I couldn't hold it all in my head. So as I went through my notes and the paper I had collected, I wrote each copy point on a separate three by five index card and taped it to the wall of my office. I tried to keep things that were similar clustered in the same place so I could find them easily. When I had everything I could think of that might go into the video written on a card and taped to the wall, I got down to the business of organizing the script.

First I looked for something that might make a good opening and taped the cards dealing with that in a clear space on the wall. From there, I proceeded to put together the segments that made up the middle, following my own rule of dealing with a topic once and moving on. As I decided what segment should come next, I would take all the cards dealing with that topic, select the bits that I wanted to use, tape them on the wall in order, and return the discards to the cluster they had come from, where they would be available in case I changed my mind.

And that's how I built up the outline for the script. No Roman numerals. No capital letters. No small letters. No worrying about seventh-grade rules. Just a series of clear statements of content topics organized in sequence from the opening of the video through to the close. Did I get it right the first time? No, of course not. As I'd be putting the cards for, say, sequence number five on the wall, I might realize that some of the information wouldn't make sense unless the audience was aware of something contained in a cluster I had planned to use later on. And I'd have to reshuffle the cards, moving that information into an earlier sequence so that the video would flow smoothly and the audience would understand what was going on. But because all I was doing was moving around index cards on a wall, it never seemed like outlining.

With this system, I could keep track of everything that needed to go into the script because I could see it in front of me. Information still in notebooks or file folders is not really accessible. And as every writer should know, ideas in your head are nothing but vaporware—they have no validity until they've passed the test of being able to be written. This way, nothing important could be left out. The cards on my wall became a paper edit of a video that had not yet been shot. And when I liked the way it played out on the wall, I wrote the script.

When it came time to take the cards down, I discovered the only flaw in the system. The cards had been taped up there for several weeks, and when I removed them, a lot of wallpaper came with them. To get around this I went to Post-it Notes in place of index cards and stuck them on artist's foam core display boards instead of on the wallpaper.

Sure It Seems Like a Lot of Work, But . . .
The function of a script is to organize the information that must be covered and present it to an audience in an interesting way. You must have a way:

- to know what information you have available,
- to choose from this the information to be used—and that to be ignored—and

- to place the information in a sequence that will convey the message to the audience.

You can take the time to do this before you start writing. Or you can write a draft and then take the time to revise it, afterward, when the draft doesn't work. I've used both systems and, frankly, I much prefer to know where I'm going before I start writing.

I use this system for everything. Every script is organized this way. Each chapter of this book goes up on a board and is shuffled around until it offers an organization that covers the information economically and organizes it logically. Do I write the manuscript exactly as it is outlined on the presentation board? Not on your life. Every writer knows that the work takes on a life of its own. What seemed like a good idea days or weeks ago when I was constructing the outline sometimes doesn't seem so great when I've written my way up to it. No problem. I just shuffle the Post-its until I find something that works. That's what I love about this system. It's out in front of you where you can see it. That's why I call it an existential outline. And it always maintains its flexibility. A Post-it on a piece of foam core presentation board is not very intimidating. It can be moved easily. So you are not being controlled by some arbitrary outline. You are in control of what you write.

This is simply one way of planning your work before writing. It's certainly not the only way to do it, and if you have another, use yours. If not, try mine. I teach this system to the students in my writing class, most of whom have never made a plan before writing. Some use it; some don't. Those who use it are generally writing better by the end of the semester. Those who don't, generally aren't.

PRODUCTION STORY—
THERE'S ALWAYS MORE THAN ONE APPROACH

There is never just one good way to tell a story. There are as many good ways as there are good writers to come up with them.

My teacher and friend, the late Sol Worth, would ask his documentary film students what their films were about. And usually, being graduate students in communications, they would come up with some fairly abstract statement, such as "I want to make a film about anger."

Sol would say, "Fine. How are you going to show that?"

The students would think about it and laboriously come up with a series of images that portrayed anger.

"That's good," Sol would say. "Very good." And just as the students began to look pleased with themselves, he'd ask, "And how else could you show it?"

. . . .

GETTING IT WRITTEN

Syd Field tells in his book *Screenplay: The Foundations of Screenwriting* how as a writer-producer for David L. Wolper Productions and as head of the story department of Cinemobile Systems, he read thousands of screenplays, rejecting 99 percent of them. And he ponders the reason so many were not worth producing, asking himself, "What is a screenplay?" and answering:

> A guide or outline for a movie? A blueprint? Diagram? A series of scenes told with dialogue and description? Images strung together on paper? A collection of ideas? The landscape of a dream?
> What is a screenplay?
> A screenplay is a STORY TOLD WITH PICTURES. (p. 7)

It was Field who wrote the definition in capital letters. But if he hadn't, I might have been tempted at least to put it in italics. For what makes a script work—for commercials, information videos, and infomercials as well as for the feature films Field writes about—is how well it gets its message across to the audience through images on the screen.

And that starts with the job of the scriptwriter, even though there's an unfortunate trend in documentary, which has filtered down toward the world of information videos, to let interviews on camera replace the planning and organization of a well-visualized script. I flinch whenever I hear a producer or director talk about shooting lots of interviews and then having them transcribed so he or she can work from the transcript to organize the video. Because what will result is another dull, talk-talk show—something that may be more than a Q & A magazine article, perhaps even more than the sort of thing you might hear on talk radio, but it definitely will be something less than a story told with pictures.

A Story Told with Pictures

Writers who come to scriptwriting from the print medium often have a hard time in the beginning learning to trust storytelling through pictures, because for so long they've depended on words to tell their stories. One way around this is never to write narration before picture. First line up a sequence of images that tells the story, and when that seems to be working, go back and put in the least amount of narration you can get away with. When in doubt, ask yourself: Have I written a script for a video, or a script for a narrator who is going to tell us about the video? If you can cover up everything in the script except the audio portion, and a reader can still understand what the video is about, then you've done the latter and you need to rewrite.

THE TREATMENT FOR A SCRIPT

You'll almost never write a treatment for a commercial. A commercial is just too short. Once I have a concept and plan for a 30-second spot, I can often write two or three variations in finished form in a matter of hours. And that means there is no need for a treatment, because I can give the client a choice from among several finished scripts.

For an information video or an infomercial, however, I like to do a treatment for clients, because a treatment gives me a chance to show the client where I think the video is going before I commit to a formal script. If you show your clients a single finished script and they don't like it, you're in trouble. Because they'll start to question whether they've hired the right writer, and whether you really do understand what they need. But if you show them a treatment and they say it isn't what they want, you can just tell them that's why you do a treatment first—to make sure you've got everything right before going to script.

And they'll buy it. With a treatment, you're saying to your client, "Here's a first cut at what I think should be in your video; how close did I get?" And that puts the focus where it belongs—on how much you got right the first time.

A *Treatment Describes the Video to Be Made*

A treatment is a description of the video to be made, written without going into detail and without crafting all the dialogue or narration. It's sometimes called an outline and sometimes called a summary, but you'll never go wrong if you'll think of it as a description. If a script is like an architect's blueprint, then a treatment is like an artist's rendering. It shows what the building will look like but doesn't bother with the specifics of how and where each brick and girder is placed.

From a good treatment, a producer should be able to make a fairly realistic budget for the video. So a treatment should be complete enough to tell what images will be shown and what people and things will appear in the video. From the treatment the producer should be able to estimate how many people and how much equipment will be needed for how many days, which is always the foundation for making a budget. And words in the treatment such as "aerial view" may alert the producer to a potentially budget-busting helicopter shot in time to make changes before the clients fall in love with an idea they can't afford.

Treatment Style and Format

While there are enough rules about script formatting that several writers have published books on the subject, there is no single format for a treatment. The International Television Association published its *Handbook of Treatments* in 1993, and the one distinguishing feature of the fourteen treatments included in that book is that each tells its story in its own way. Some use an outline, some go back and forth between sentences and bullet points, and some stay with straight narrative in sentences and paragraphs.

If there is a common denominator, it is the use of subheadings to help keep the reader on track. When I first started writing treatments for clients, I thought that if I described scenes dealing with the major copy points, the client would immediately recognize that I was covering the important stuff. Not so. Many clients have no experience in imagining how the written description in a treatment will play on the screen. So I've learned that if the new air conditioning system, for example, is a big thing with the client, I need to put in a subheading, "Improved Air Conditioning," before describing the scenes dealing with that topic. That way the client knows the hot buttons are being pushed and feels more confident in the treatment and in the script that is to come. Incidentally, that subheading is strictly for the client to read. It is not intended as a title on the screen when the video is made—and will fall out when the script is written.

Purpose, Audience, Copy Points

I begin a treatment by reviewing the purpose for the video, the intended audience, and the major copy points to be included based on my research. These were discussed in detail in chapter six. By listing my understanding of purpose, audience, and message, I have a chance to build the client's confidence that I understand what is needed and that I am on track to deliver it.

By the same token, the treatment is a reality check. If I've misunderstood a point, left out something that should be included, or included something that should be left out, we can deal with it at the treatment stage when no real damage has been done. Most clients are so amazed that a writer can absorb so much about their business in so short a time that they will cheerfully forgive the occasional minor error. And when they point out a mistake in the treatment, I always say something like "Good. Thank you for catching that. That's why we do a treatment before going to script."

Style of the Video

Next the treatment describes the way the video will present the information. An information video may be shot in documentary style, it may be a little drama using actors, it may be a parody of a television show, it may take the form of a newscast or a talk show, it could tell the story through animation or special effects, it could be a guided tour conducted by a spokesperson, or it could be something else altogether. The important thing is to explain the style sufficiently for the client to understand what you intend.

You should include the expected length of the video and mention any production considerations which may be pertinent, such as the use of stock footage, specially composed music, computer animation, or special visual effects.

Outline of Content

The final section of the treatment is the description of what will be seen on the screen, along with a suggestion of what will be heard.

As far as I'm concerned, I've done most of the creative work on a script when I've created the existential outline. At that point I know pretty much what the video should look and sound like. So writing this part of the treatment is just fleshing out the outline in sentences and making sure that the proposed structure seems to work.

Here's an example from the treatment for an information video which was a report to investors on renovation and expansion of a hotel and casino. The section starts with the subheading, "The Construction Plan," and then tells what the audience will see and hear.

The Construction Plan

1. We see more construction activity.
   Narration talks about: Three phases to construction . . .
2. The hotel/casino sign.
   Narration talks about: Phase one—renovation and erection of the hotel/casino sign.
3. Construction in the casino interior.
   Narration talks about: Phase two—creation of a two-story, 78,000-square-foot casino with some seven hundred slot machines, a number of popular table games, a race and sports book, and a lounge.
4. Renderings, if available, of the facilities on the second floor.
   Narration talks about: The second floor will include convention and banquet facilities, a delicatessen, and a six-hundred-seat buffet.

In the next scene, the owner talks about the project. His words are taken from an interview already shot, so they are given verbatim.

5. We see the Coney Island theme of the facade on the
    rendering.

   The owner says: "We've got about 7,000 square feet worth
    of rentable space in front, as a facade of a Coney
    Island, to be adjacent to a boardwalk. I think we'd
    like to carry out a theme and put one or two of our
    security officers in the uniform of Keystone Cops.

    "We want to create nothing but a fun
    atmosphere. We're building a clown entrance. You
    have to walk into the clown's mouth to get in."

6. We see a rendering of the hotel tower.

   Narration talks about: Phase three—construction of a 472-
    room tower, bringing the total number of rooms to
    672.

I've broken this out into specific scenes in this treatment, but it
could as easily be a single descriptive summary of the three phases of
construction, mentioning the things that will be shown and suggesting
the audio.

Treatment Length

How long should a treatment be? Like any other written work, a
treatment should be exactly as long as it takes to do the job and not a
word longer. The treatment I write for a short video may actually be
longer in pages than the eventual script. That's because I start by
defining the project in terms of purpose, audience, and message or
important copy points. The copy points are then repeated in the section on the outline of content, so they appear twice, although not
necessarily in the same form in both places.

The idea that a treatment should be only a couple of pages long is
nonsense. It will usually take a couple of pages just to detail the
purpose, audience, and message. Remember that the treatment has to
convince the client that you know what you are doing and that it's
okay to go ahead with the project.

Approval of the Treatment

If the client requests substantial changes and additions to the treatment, I'll write a second draft, incorporating these changes, which will

go back to the client for approval. That's because I want to write the script from an approved treatment. If the client's changes are minor, I'll usually request approval to go directly to script, incorporating the changes in the first draft script.

THE SCRIPT

I appeared on a panel on writing information videos with several other videomakers a few years ago. I expressed the opinion that by the time I had organized the material and written the treatment, I had done most of the creative work, because I then knew what the video would look and sound like. In my innocence, I suggested that the other writers would probably agree with me. They didn't. One said he didn't really get into the creative work until he began writing the script. He liked to do dramatizations, and it wasn't until he got to the script stage that he began to deal with what his characters had to say. Another disagreed, saying that creativity was in the clever way the narration was written.

Nevertheless, I stand with Richard Walter, screenwriter and UCLA professor, who says in *Screenwriting: The Art, Craft and Business of Film and Television Writing*:

> While all the elements of a screenplay are important, and none exists independently, the most important component of all, and certainly the most difficult to craft is story.
> The three most important facets of story craft are: (1) structure; (2) structure; (3) structure. (p. 37)

Once you've found the structure and organized your material within it to tell your story, the rest is easy. My fellow panelists to the contrary notwithstanding, if you put too much reliance on being *creative* with the words said by your characters, spokesperson, or narrator, you probably haven't organized the script to make a visual argument.

A footnote to this story is that some time after that writing panel, I was hired to analyze and eventually rewrite a script that the director declared was unshootable. The problem was lack of structure. The original scriptwriter was my old friend who didn't get creative until he got to the script. Most of his experience had been with very short videos—primarily commercials. When he got into a piece running almost an hour, his lack of structural concern caught up with him. He had lots of clever dialogue, and I kept most of it. But his script lacked an organized framework on which to hang his cleverness.

Script Format for Information Videos

Script format is a big deal in the world of feature films and television programs. Every book on screenwriting assures the reader that unless his or her script is correctly formatted, it will never make it out of the slush pile. It may be for this reason that the first screenplay I wrote and entered in a competition received an A in formatting from the judges, who unfortunately then gave it a C for content. Back to making videos for money.

In writing the script for an information video or infomercial, format really hardly matters at all. The most important thing is to use a form that can easily be understood by the client, who has to approve the script in order for the video to progress, and by the director who has to realize your concept on the screen.

Commercials—Last of the Two-Column TV Tradition

The scripts for most commercials are written in a two-column format. Each scene is shown with video and audio side by side, video in the left column and audio in the right. This is the way scripts were done in the early days of live television and many TV directors have grown up in this tradition.

Figure 8.1 shows a traditional two column TV script for a 30-second commercial I did for the Aladdin Hotel and Casino. Scenes are numbered on the left. Audio sources are shown in capital letters on the right, with a slight indent to make them stand out. Since one voice-over announcer does all the talking, the announcer is identified at the start of the narration and not again. However if there had been sound effects in the middle of the script, then the announcer would be identified again for clarity when the narration picked up after the sound effects:

The Oasis is always open—
serving breakfast any time, and

Figure 8.1

Two-Column TV Script

VIDEO	AUDIO
1. The Aladdin glistens at night.	MUSIC: Aladdin theme established, two seconds, then fade under narration. ANNOUNCER: The Aladdin . . .
2. MALE GENIE among slot machines.	Magical days and nights . . .
3. Tracking shot along buffet salad bar.	Las Vegas is known for its great buffets. And the Aladdin all-you-can-eat buffet is superb!
4. CHEF carving beef.	
5. Buffet desserts.	
6. Oasis Coffee Shop, COUPLE having breakfast.	The Oasis is always open—serving breakfast any time, and terrific lunch and dinner specialties.
7. Cascade of money and chips. Montage of slot play. *Superimpose:* **Next to MGM Theme Park**	When you want to play, it's all here. And the Aladdin is next to the new MGM theme park.
8. Marquee with Aladdin's lamp above. *Superimpose:* **Call 1-800-RUB-LAMP**	For Aladdin reservations, call one, eight hundred, rub lamp—or your professional travel agent.

```
            terrific lunch and dinner
            specialties.
        SFX: Sound of roulette wheel.
        ANNOUNCER: When you want to play
            it's all here . . .
```

Similarly, if several people were speaking, they would be identified each time they spoke.

Put Narration in Upper- and Lowercase Type. You may see script examples that show the narration typed in all capital letters. Like the two-column format itself, this is a leftover from an earlier time, when scripts were typed on typewriters, and capital letters were used to make the type seem larger when shown on a TelePrompTer. We now know from readability studies that large blocks of capital letters are hard to read because all the words are the same shape. Lowercase letters give each word its distinctive, easily recognizable shape, and are therefore much easier to read. Besides, narrators usually don't use TeleProimp-Ters. They read directly from the script in an audio recording booth. And dialogue has to be memorized by the actors, so they don't use a TelePrompTer, either.

Actually, only a very small amount of any of the speech in a script is actually played on a TelePrompTer. Today scripts are written on computers, and a TelePrompTer, when used, is loaded directly from the computer. So it's an easy thing to format speech going into a TelePrompTer in a larger font if necessary while maintaining upper-and lowercase letters for ease of reading.

Formatting for the Client

Clients do best with scripts that read straight down the page. When faced with a two-column format, they have a deplorable tendency to read the audio side and ignore what you've written on the left. Even though you may have written a brilliant scene covering an important topic visually, your clients may think you've left that important something out of the script if they don't find it in narration. Note that the three script fragments from the United Way project shown in chapter seven are all formatted differently, but all read straight down the page.

In each case the description of the visual scene comes first, followed by sound, narration, and dialogue.

Clients actually do best with storyboards, which, like little comic strips, show a drawing of the visual information with the narration or dialogue typed in below. But storyboards are an added expense because you have to pay an artist to draw all the little pictures, unless you use desktop publishing and generic clip art to create ready-made storyboards with illustrations.

Screenplay Format

For a long time I used the screenplay format for client videos. This reads straight down the page with scene description in wide paragraphs and dialogue or narration in indented paragraphs in the center of the page. An example is shown in figure 8.2.

Actually figure 8.2 is a modified screenplay format since the first line of a new scene in a screenplay is written in capital letters and tells whether the scene is an interior or exterior, where it is located, and whether it should be lit for day or night. This is used in developing the shooting schedule and budget for a feature, but not usually for a video. The description of the scene follows on the next line.

> 22. EXT. APARTMENT BUILDING—DAY
> Family piling belongings into a pickup truck or van.

Scene Numbering. Scenes are not numbered in the screenplay for a motion picture until the film goes into production and the shooting script is typed. The reason for this is that a screenplay often goes through so many changes and rewrites that the numbers are meaningless until the final script is approved. For a sponsored video, however, I take the position that the project is in production when the script is assigned, and I number the scenes in the script. This also makes it easier for the client to read and understand the script and to suggest and make changes.

If a new scene is added, for instance after scene 11, I change scene 11 to 11A, and make the new scene 11B. If a scene is deleted, I retain the number but put "Scene deleted" for the description.

Figure 8.2

Screenplay Format

22. Family piling belongings into a pickup truck or van.

> SPOKESPERSON
> Unaffordable rents and the housing
> shortage can result in a family
> moving two and three times a year
> in search of reasonable, safe
> housing. As costs climb, they go in
> search of a smaller unit, which may
> not be appropriate for the family, or
> for the same space at a lower rent,
> which may mean a more dangerous
> neighborhood.

23. Parent and small child enter a schoolyard.

> SPOKESPERSON
> Children may change schools two or
> three times in a year . . .

DISSOLVE TO:

24. Small child alone in a room, in shadow, isolated, staring out window.

> SPOKESPERSON
> (continues)
> . . . becoming isolated from friends
> and relatives, and losing touch with
> learning.

25. Family carrying belongings into new apartment.

> SPOKESPERSON
> Unfortunately, lurching from crisis
> to crisis tends to reinforce short-
> term decision making. It seems
> simpler for the family to pack up
> and move again and again rather
> than to make a long-term plan to
> secure safe, stable, low-cost housing.

Video Script Format

Some time ago, I developed a format that combined the visual separation of a two-column script with the straight-down-the-page readability of a screenplay but without the screenplay's finicky rules and tricky formatting. I was pretty proud of myself until I discovered that a number of other videomakers had done much the same thing. Figure 8.3 shows an example of this script format. This is actually the next page of the United Way script shown in figure 8.2, reformatted as a video script.

Scenes are numbered and all visual information, including titles, subtitles, graphics, and supers, goes on the left, extending about two-thirds of the way across the page. All audio information, including narration and dialogue, music, and sound effects, goes on the right, starting about a third of the way from the left margin and extending to the right margin. Speakers or other audio sources such as music and sound effects are identified in capital letters above the audio copy block. Any parenthetical information goes in parentheses directly beneath the character name or audio source identification.

Running Time. In a video script timing can be critical and I like to keep track of scene-by-scene running time as I'm writing. I put it in brackets at the end of each scene:

$$[S = :05 \; // \; RT = 8:27]$$

S equals the approximate length of the scene in seconds. This may be the reading time for the narration or dialogue. It may be a close estimate of how long a visual scene will play, or it may be a combination of both. RT equals the approximate total running time in minutes and seconds from the beginning of the video to the end of this scene.

USING NARRATION

You can hardly go wrong if you write narration as if you were being fined ten dollars a word. The purpose of narration is to tell the audience the things which they need to know and may not be able to pick up from the footage on their own—and nothing more. Think of narra-

Figure 8.3

Video Script Format

26. Spokesperson on camera. (Or a person
    from a social service organization.)

> SPOKESPERSON
> These families live on such tight budgets
> that almost any problem soon translates
> into a money problem. Illness means lost
> work and that means lost wages and a
> payment missed. And this can turn into a
> downward spiral of increasing problems
> and increasing stress on the family.
>
> [S = :15 // RT = 8:10]

27. We see again the isolated, lonely child
    staring out the window.

> SPOKESPERSON
> (off camera)
> You may be looking at the next generation
> employee or customer for your business,
> now a child, poorly educated, and lacking
> the security of a stable home. The truth is,
> the well-being of your business depends on
> the well-being of the community.
>
> [S = :12 // RT = 8:22]

28. Horror shot: dilapidated building.

> SPOKESPERSON
> (off camera)
> And a community lacking adequate
> housing is a community in decline.
>
> [S = :05 // RT = 8:27]

tion as a precious resource. You have the potential for between one thousand and fifteen hundred words of narration in a fifteen-minute video. That's all. So treat narration as a valuable asset and don't waste it.

Keep It Simple
If the footage is good, the narration can be straightforward, in easy-to-understand English. Keep the language simple and the sentences short. Be prosaic, not flowery. Yes, narration can be clever. It can be humorous. It should always be interesting. *And it should never get in the way of the pictures.*

You don't tell the audience what they are looking at:

Natives fishing in the lagoon

> NARRATOR
> Here we see the natives of Tula Tula fishing
> from their canoes . . .

unless the audience won't know what it is if you don't tell them.

From the lanai atop the Reef Tank, showing the water tower and the Rocky Shores tanks and area.

> NARRATOR
> The Rocky Shores area replicates the
> conditions of a shoreline intertidal zone.
> About every ninety seconds, six hundred
> gallons of water is dropped from this
> tower . . .

Surge of water rushes through the exhibit.

> NARRATOR
> simulating the crash of a wave against the
> rocks . . . sending water surging into the
> various tide pool tanks.

Pictures First

As a documentary writer-director, I always liked to write narration as I was editing the final cut of the documentary. By that time I had a good idea of how well the images carried the essential information and where narration would be needed. I knew how much space was available for narration, and I could make the words and pictures merge the best possible way. In doing a commercial video, however, you rarely have the luxury of waiting until you're editing the video before writing the narration. You usually have to complete the script—and that includes the narration—before the video goes into production.

But the scriptwriter who writes the narration before fully visualizing the images to be used is borrowing trouble. In the first place, the lazy person inside all of us is likely to look at a well- (but prematurely) written narration and select pictures to illustrate it. Which inevitably results in a talky, "show-and-tell" script instead of a blueprint for an evocative video. In the second place, the images have to be able to stand on their own. Even when narration is the major element in the audio track, the rule remains pictures first. If the scene is well visualized in the initial organization and in the treatment, narration will follow picture as it should.

WRITE NARRATION FOR THE EAR, NOT THE EYE

Narration is written to be heard, not read. Which means that in writing you need to think about the sound of the narration.

How Does the Narrator Sound?

Is your narrator a man, a woman, or a child? Or is the narrator the characterization of an animal, such as Smokey the Bear; an abstraction, such as the Voice of Liberty; or an object such as a school bus? I once did a safety film for children in elementary school called *Stanley the Friendly School Bus*. Stanley narrated, talking directly to the children. Which brought up the question, what does a school bus sound like? Our Stanley was vaguely adolescent, the knowledgeable voice of an older brother.

Will you use one narrator or more than one? Most of the time one will do. But sometimes it makes sense to use two—or more. For instance, in one video where I had both a lot of technical information and a lot of warm, fuzzy-feeling stuff to go in the narration, I used a male and a female narrator. And because I like to cast against stereotype, I had the female voice do the technical stuff while the male voice handled the warm fuzzies. Under other circumstances it might have made sense to use two women or two men or an adult and a child. The point is that your narrator or narrators can be whoever or whatever you need to help you do the job of informing the audience.

Listen to the Words as You Write Them

Read narration aloud to yourself as you write it. I mean it, *out loud*, not in your head. If you find you are stumbling over words or phrases, change them. If you can't read the narration correctly—when you wrote it—how can you expect a narrator to read it?

Then read it aloud to someone else to be sure they can follow the thoughts expressed. If they're having trouble understanding the meaning, tell them what it means, as simply as possible. *Then write that down and use it for the narration.*

Rhythm. Spoken language has its own rhythm, which makes the words easier to say and easier to understand. You'll feel it as you read out loud. Some sentences are easy to say; some aren't. If you find a passage you seem to stumble over each time you read it, the reason may be that it breaks the rhythm of the narration. Taking out a word—or adding one—may be all that is needed.

Write Out Numbers and Symbols. Write out numbers the way you want them read. If you write 1,500, the narrator may read it "one thousand five hundred" or "fifteen hundred." Decide which you want and write it that way. Spell out common symbols such as dollars, cents, and percent. Write "seven million dollars" or "eighty-nine cents," not "$7 million" or "89¢." When you write out numbers and symbols, you maintain the relative correspondence between the physical length of the passage in the script and the running time on the audio track.

Give a Phonetic Pronunciation to Names and Foreign Words. In your research you've found out how to pronounce the names of the artist who is interviewed, or the correct pronunciation of a foreign phrase you have to use. So make life easy for the director and the narrator by giving the pronunciation phonetically in parentheses after the name or phrase.

Use Conjunctions. Some English teacher, somewhere, probably told you not to begin a sentence with *and* or *but*—or any other conjunction. That's because, according to grammatical rule, conjunctions connect simple sentences into compound or complex sentences. But readability formulas such as the Flesch Reading Ease Scale or Gunning's Fog Index count a conjunction as the start of a new sentence, even when it's in the middle of a compound sentence. That's because the reader or listener treats it functionally as the start of a new thought. So break up those compound sentences. And don't be afraid to start a sentence with a conjunction. It can make the thought easier to understand.

Keep Reading Directions to a Minimum. We all have the desire to direct the narrator by remote control by putting little instructions in parentheses. But you have to fight against it. You don't really need a lot of stage directions telling the narrator how to read your words. If you put them in, you'll just annoy the director. And the narrator will ignore them anyway.

Use a Stopwatch. Nothing cures overwriting like a stopwatch. Get one and time each scene. Read the narration with dramatic emphasis while you time it. But don't just time the words in the narration. Visualize the action that occurs without narration and time that as well.

Using a Spokesperson
A spokesperson is a host for your program. The difference between a spokesperson and a narrator is that a spokesperson appears on camera, while a narrator is heard but not seen. There are several reasons you might want to use a spokesperson:

Authority/Credibility. The person you have selected as a spokesperson is a recognized authority on the topic of the video and adds credibility to the message. In a medical video, you might plan to use a well-known doctor.

Celebrity/Attention. You might choose to use a celebrity as your spokesperson to draw attention to the message.

Abstract Content. If the information you must present in the video does not lend itself to concrete imagery, one solution is to place a spokesperson on camera and have that person tell the audience the information.

Demonstration. An on-camera spokesperson can demonstrate a product or take the audience on a guided tour of an area.

Movement. An on-camera spokesperson can often add a sense of movement to an otherwise static video by walking or riding through the location.

Dramatic Effect. Some statements are more powerful when we can see the person making the statement than they would be in voice-over narration. Especially when you don't have strong visuals to go with the strong statement, the reaction of the spokesperson to the words he or she is saying may make the most dramatic appeal to the audience.

The Cost of Using a Spokesperson

Before choosing to use a spokesperson you should realize that there are costs involved. One is screen time. Having someone stand up and tell the story will take longer than showing it in pictures. The other is budgetary. The use of a spokesperson may add to the cost of the production. You have to pay the spokesperson as an actor. You may need a makeup artist on the crew when the spokesperson is used. You may want to use the spokesperson in several different locations, which may mean you pay the spokesperson and the makeup artist for several days of shooting. And shooting on-camera voice is far more time consuming than recording narration.

DIALOGUE

It's hard enough to write good, believable dialogue in a fiction film where you have a story to tell. It gets even harder in a sponsored video, where you can find yourself trying to put words in the mouths of actors about a product, process, or service to please a client who doesn't really *care* how people talk.

The Difference Between Conversation and Dialogue

Conversation *maintains contact* between two or more people and sometimes carries information. It is made up of incomplete ideas and fragments of sentences. The parties feel free to interrupt each other, to talk at the same time, and to change the subject capriciously. As long as the conversation is working for the parties involved, they pay little or no attention to its form. They may lace their utterances with repetitions, y'knows, interminable pauses, mistakes, and mispronunciations.

Dialogue, on the other hand, takes place between two or more characters for the purpose of informing a third party—the audience. Dialogue is artificial speech which must be accepted by an audience as believable. When the lights go down and the video comes up on the screen, you get the benefit of the doubt from what theater people call the willing suspension of disbelief. But the audience will give you only so much slack.

Good dialogue, therefore, has to fall comfortably between two extremes. On one side is the stilted language of corporate, legal, and bureaucratic English—very often the sort of thing you'll find in the memos and reports you've collected during the research phase. At the other extreme is the muddy sound of realspeak, full of *ums, uhs, likes,* and *y'knows.* Thoughts are not completed. Antecedents to pronouns are left out. Repetition runs rampant. Grammar is abused. And often the point of the conversation is never even stated, because the speakers already *know* what they're talking about.

But you just can't do that in a script. Truly realistic dialogue will come across as bad writing. You have to write the dialogue the way people *think* they are talking and not the way they actually speak.

Why Use Dialogue?

If dialogue is so difficult, why not just use a narrator or a spokesperson? There are several good reasons to use dialogue in a commercial video:

To Increase Audience Interest. Most of us would rather watch a little dramatic scene than sit still for show-and-tell with a narrator. Using actors to carry the information can often increase interest—if the actors are good and the dialogue is well written.

To Stage a Demonstration. If you want to show the audience what happens in a particular situation, you might do it with an enactment. In a video on workplace safety, I showed the audience what actually could happen during an occupational safety and health inspection.

For Credibility. Audiences understand that the off-camera narrator speaks for the client. When you want to praise the client's work or products, you might prefer to have it done by someone other than the narrator. A spokesperson may be one way to increase credibility. Another way is to have people who seem to represent the viewer talk about the client's work or services. People in a store can talk credibly about the store and its products while they seem to be shopping.

To Make the Information Easier to Absorb. For some reason, most of us seem to absorb and retain the information better if we receive it while apparently eavesdropping on people who are talking about it. When there's a lot of information to impart, and it's not very visual, having two or three people discuss it can often be better than using a narrator or even a spokesperson.

To Add Human Interest and Humor. Scenes with actors and dialogue open up the possibilities of the script. You can bring in a piece of the outside world and use it as a reference point for your audience, as a point of human interest, or even as the focus for some humor.

SUGGESTIONS FOR WRITING DIALOGUE

Decide Who the Speakers Are

Dialogue begins with characterization. Who are the people in the scene? Why are they there? What do you know about them? It may help you write better dialogue if you do a back story on your characters the way screenplay writers do. This is a brief biography which you make up that tells you more about the person who is speaking. Even before you get into characterization, you'll need to decide how many of what kind of people are in the scene. Do you want a man and a woman? If so, are they strangers, lovers, friends, married? Are a man and a woman best for this scene in this video? Would it be better if you used a mother and her two daughters? How about two nine-year-old boys?

Who Says What?

Once you've decided who the people are, you have to determine what they do, what they say, and how they say it. Quite often in an information video, one person has the answers while other people need to ask questions to find out what they (and the audience) want to know. Be very clear about who can talk about what. Don't have your questioner suddenly giving answers or vice versa. And *never* have the parties to a dialogue recite the client's message back and forth like a bad radio commercial. In real life two people who share the same information don't recite it to each other unless they're cramming for an exam. They talk about something else.

Keep It Short

Good video dialogue tends to consist of short speeches that bounce comfortably among the characters. A long speech by any character is a monologue and the character becomes a spokesperson—while all the other characters in the scene slowly die of nothing to do while the camera is on them.

Say a Name Once and Move On

You identify characters by name, and the way the audience knows what the names are is for each character either to introduce himself or be called by name by another character. Inexperienced dialogue writers keep tucking the names into dialogue, either for emphasis ("Well, Joe, this is serious . . .") or because they are afraid the audience didn't get the name the first time it was said. In a short commercial video the names usually aren't very important, anyway. So mention them once and move on.

Watch Your Grammar

Don't let the rules of grammar drag down your dialogue. Use sentence fragments. Use one word sentences. Start a thought with one character and let another complete it. When in doubt, follow social rule rather than grammatical rule. In print I might actually find an opportunity to write "It is I." In dialogue I would always use, "It's me," unless I wanted to use overly correct grammar for characterization.

Understate

On stage, actors project their voices so they can be heard in the last row. And when stage actors come to video or film they have to learn to understate, to speak softly for the microphone. Similarly, the best language for video and film dialogue will be simple words in simple form. Simplify, simplify!

Don't Say What You Can Show

Just as you don't have narration describe what the audience can see is happening, you don't have dialogue talk about something you can just as easily show.

Give Your Characters Something to Do

You don't just stick two or three people on an empty sound stage and have them talk. Get them busy doing something that relates to the video, and they'll have something to talk about. If you reach the point where your characters don't have anything to do, you may want to ask yourself whether a dialogue video is the right way to go.

PRODUCTION STORY—THE CAPRA TOUCH

In *Screenwriting*, Richard Walter tells a story about the great director Frank Capra who made *It's a Wonderful Life* and *Mr. Smith Goes to Washington*, among others.

> [Capra] was asked in an interview to explain precisely how he achieved that special quality known as "the Capra touch." For page after page he rambled on about this technique and that one. At great length he discussed how he had lent "the touch" to this film and to that one. And in all these pages nowhere was mentioned Robert Riskin who had merely written the films.
>
> The day after the interview appeared in the press, there arrived at Capra's office a script-sized envelope. Inside was a document very closely resembling a screenplay: a front cover, a back cover, and one hundred and ten pages. But the cover and the pages were all blank.
>
> Clipped to the "script" was a note to Capra from Robert Riskin. It read: "Dear Frank, put the 'Capra touch' on *this*!" (p. 4)

9

OFF TO A GOOD START:
PREPRODUCTION PLANNING

It seems to me that most bad videos—certainly the ones I've been asked to analyze and, occasionally, try to fix—have suffered from poor planning. There's a school of documentary production, for instance, that says, "We'll just take the camera and go shoot whatever's there." That yields a lot of "whatever's there" footage, most of which is unusable for human communication.

The more complex the production, the more important it is to have a well-worked-out plan before you start. When you're juggling actors and musicians and stock footage and volunteers and a location that will be available only at certain times, while trying to create a decent program for your client, you'd better have a clear idea of what you're doing. And a fallback plan when things go wrong.

You do realize that things will go wrong.

REVIEW OF THE PRODUCTION PROCESS

This section provides a comprehensive overview of the video production process. Many videomakers, who have learned production on the job by doing a part of the process, should find this helpful in tying together a lot of loose ends. Students and newcomers to video production should find this section especially useful and informative. For those who want more detail, I cover the process for both video and film in *Video Scriptwriting* and in *Making Documentary Films and Reality Videos*.

Preproduction

The preproduction phase for a sponsored video begins with the assignment for the video, followed by content research to determine what has to be included. The research material is organized into a treatment and then a script. If the budget was not set at the time of the assignment, it must be calculated and approved along with the script.

If it's to be a location shoot, the location or locations must be scouted—and in some cases selected. Crew members and the equipment that is to be used in the production are chosen, and if actors will be used, a casting session is held.

Then a production schedule is created to make the most effective use of cast, crew, equipment, and location availability, and you are ready to go into production.

Production

The production phase may be the most complex and difficult of the three stages in making a video, but it is the simplest to describe. This is when you record the images and sounds that make the video.

During the production phase it's a good idea to view—or at least spot check—the tape you've shot to be sure that your equipment is working properly and the crew is getting what you need. Viewing the scene on a monitor as it is shot won't tell you what has actually been recorded on tape—or even if it has been recorded. You need to see a playback.

The time to learn that a microphone isn't recording properly or a camera is picking up RF interference is while the lights are set and the actors are still in place, not in an editing room, days, weeks, or months later.

Postproduction

In postproduction you do all the things that are necessary to deliver the best possible final product to your client. This includes recording or rerecording voice, music, and sound effects; editing the footage into a pleasing sequence; adding stock footage, graphics, animation, and computer enhanced images; even altering the look or running speed of the images where appropriate.

The postproduction phase usually begins by making a windowprint dub of all the footage and then viewing and logging everything that was shot. This lets you eliminate the bad takes and select the good ones for editing. It also yields a comprehensive log of all the footage to be used during editing.

Sometimes an editing script will be written at this point, especially if the video has been shot from a treatment rather than a finished script.

If any stock footage is needed, it must be found and made available for editing. Similarly, any computer graphics, animation, Paintbox, or other effects must be prepared. Narration must be recorded and music selected.

Off-line Editing. When everything is ready, you take all the footage, logs, scripts, audio, and other materials into an off-line editing bay and do a first cut of the video. You'll probably do this on a nonlinear editing system where all the footage and sound is stored digitally on a computer hard drive. All editing is done digitally by computer. Some nonlinear systems are fairly low resolution, giving you more storage space on the hard drive — and therefore more editing possibilities — in return for a less than perfect picture. Other nonlinear systems will output broadcast quality digital video.

Once you have an edited version of the program that satisfies you, you'll need to show it to your client in order to get approval to complete the video.

On-line Editing. The next step in editing is to create an edited master of the completed program with everything in place. This could be the output you'll get from a broadcast quality nonlinear system. Otherwise you'll do an on-line edit, which brings all the parts together onto the highest quality video master.

Again this is a client review point, because the on-line master will be used to make copies for the client's use.

Distribution. The final step in postproduction is making copies for distribution. If only a few will be used, they may be dubbed directly from the on-line master. If copies in quantity will be needed, then a dubbing submaster should be made from the on-line master. The dubbing submaster takes the wear and tear of making copies, while the on-line master is preserved in pristine condition and stored in the vault to make additional submasters when needed.

CONCEPT, RESEARCH, AND SCRIPT

Preproduction planning could be said to begin with research and scriptwriting, as detailed in the three previous chapters. I've separated research and writing from preproduction planning, however, because the project usually must be defined through the scripting process before operational planning can take place. But obviously there's going to be some overlap. For instance, on-site script research may also serve for location scouting. So the division is arbitrary and useful, but hardly cast in concrete.

DETERMINING LOCATION AND SET NEEDS

Where are you going to shoot the video? Can you do it all at a small studio at a video production company? Do you need a sound stage? Does it have to be done on location?

Does the video need a specific type of set? Is what you need available near you?

In Los Angeles you can rent standing sets to meet specific needs, such as an airplane interior, a train, or a town in the old west. It may be more economical to take your production to L.A. and use those sets than to try to recreate that sort of thing in your local area. Especially as the costumes you need and actors and extras are readily available there also.

Location Scouting
If you'll be doing the production on a practical location, you need to check it out before you bring cast, crew, and equipment there to start shooting. Why are you using this location? Is it to give the video a certain look, such as the interior of a home for a family scene? Or is it because this location is where the action is? Perhaps it's the headquarters or research lab or manufacturing plant of your client, and it's where you have to shoot. Whatever the reason, be sure to scout the

location at a time similar to whenever you'll be filming. If you scout a plant when it's closed on the weekend you may be in for a shock when you bring the crew in on a noisy Monday and find that there's no way you can record legible audio with the level of ambient sound that exists.

Lighting. What will the available light be like at the location when you'll be shooting? If you are shooting exteriors, where will the sun be and how will the shadows fall? Can you shoot the setups you need before the sun moves enough to change the look of the location? Can you provide fill light for the scene with shiny boards or will you need to bring in additional lighting? Will you have access to adequate electricity or do you need to bring along a generator?

If you're shooting interiors, what are the sources of light? Do you have overhead fluorescents? Wall-mounted incandescents? Windows flooded with sunlight? Will you have to live with mixed lighting or can you turn everything off and bring in your own lights set the way you want them? If you have to shoot in a large area, is there enough light? Again, is there adequate electricity available or will you need to make your own arrangements?

Sound. What are the conditions for recording sound at the location? Is it quiet or noisy? Are there intermittent noises such as trucks going by or planes taking off from a nearby airport? Is the interior lively—full of hard edges and bouncy echoes—or dead, with sound muffled by carpet, curtains, and upholstered furniture? Will you have to put up with the hum of appliances, the drone of air conditioning, or the whoosh of a heating system? Is there a public address system or piped-in music and if so, can it be turned off?

Location People. Will you need a licensed electrician to tap into the electricity at the location? Will you need a police officer or park guard in order to be able to shoot? Will you need a guide or host who knows the location? When I go to an out-of-town location, even if I bring my own crew and equipment, I try to hire a local person as a driver or production assistant. This person also functions as a guide and source of information about the town and its people and knows where you can get twenty D-cells at five in the morning or steaks for the crew at midnight.

When I shot for several days in a hospital, I asked for and received a full-time liaison person who was available to explain who we were and what we were doing, and also to help us find props and volunteer extras when we needed them.

Use of Film Commissions

All states and most major cities have film commissions or film offices whose job is to promote the state or city as a location for filming. They can help by providing stills and video of locations you might like to use. They can point you toward a location coordinator, who will help you find what you are looking for. And they may be able to advise you of a source of stock footage that might give you all you need without your actually having to go there and shoot. One shot of the Statue of Liberty or the Empire State Building says "We're in New York," leaving you free to shoot interiors in your hometown.

Set Construction

If you'll be shooting in a studio or on a sound stage, you need to construct whatever set you are going to use and outfit it with set decoration, props, and furniture. Once you've built a set, you have to decide what to do with it after principal photography is finished. The choices are to store it or destroy it. Your call—either will be at your expense.

CREW AND EQUIPMENT

If you own or work for a video production company you already have access to the crew people and equipment you'll need.

If you are an experienced independent producer, then you know where to find the people and hardware to make your video.

The third possibility is that you are an amateur who has gotten involved with a video production either by choice or because you've been assigned to get a video made by a boss who doesn't know any more than you do. In that case, you're in over your head. You need a guru or a consultant or at the very least a friend to help you find the people and things you need.

Here are some suggestions on finding and choosing a production crew, offered with the thought that the people you choose will either provide or point you toward the equipment you'll need.

One way is to go to a film or video production company. You'll find them listed by the dozen in the Yellow Pages of any metropolitan phone book. Almost all of them will tell you that yes, they can do *whatever* it is that you need. They're in business, after all. But that doesn't automatically mean that they can make the video you need. I recently wrote the script for an information video for a videomaker who specialized in weddings but was trying to expand into corporate work. The video was a disaster. The videomaker simply didn't have the experience to do the job that was needed.

Another is to look in the directories of organizations such as the International Documentary Association or the International Television Association.

Another way is to look at lots of videos. Make a habit of writing down the production credits when you see a video you like. Then contact the person or the production company.

The Selection Process

It's quite possible that early in your search you may find a producer, production company, or individual crew members who can do exactly what you want. If so, sign them up. You would probably end up hiring them anyway. Otherwise narrow your list as quickly as possible to a small number of candidates.

Don't Hold a Competition. In dealing with production companies, I *do not* recommend holding a competition or sending out a request for proposals (RFP) as a first step. You are likely to eliminate the very people you would most like to talk with, because many excellent videomakers will avoid this kind of competition, for several reasons:

- They feel that an important part of their job is to understand and interpret the needs of your project. This requires the kind of personal contact that is generally eliminated by an RFP.

- They regard a competition involving a large number of production companies as little more than a lottery. It requires a lot of work for which they will not be paid unless they win.
- The best people, once they have established a reputation and a body of work that shows what they can do, are unwilling to do any creative work on speculation. And that is what an RFP usually asks for.

Good people are certainly willing to present themselves and their work for your inspection. And they *will* make a proposal and discuss costs when they feel they will be judged on the quality of their existing work, not on how well they guess what you want from an RFP.

Do Look at Their Work. If you are talking with a production company, be sure to find out if the person you are dealing with is in sales or production. Withhold judgment until you've met the production people and seen their work. The best way to find the people you need is to look at the videos they've made, because their skill and the nature and quality of their work are the *only things that count.*

Look at complete productions; a composite reel of highlights or best shots tells you nothing about the ability of the crew to sustain a quality effort over a complete production. If you are planning a longform information video or infomercial, you won't learn much by looking at samples of short works. The planning, pacing, and editing of a long video is quite different from that of a short production.

Look at the Technical Quality of the Work. If the color is off or the sound is bad, don't accept an explanation such as this is a nonlinear off-line edit and all the flaws were corrected in the final version. After all, they are choosing to show you this copy and not the final version. And be very leery of anyone who tries to tell you that you have to expect some technical problems in shooting documentary-style or on location. That may have been true some time ago, but it is far less true today. Bad picture, bad sound, or bad editing are most likely evidence of a bad production company. Look elsewhere.

When you see a video you like, find out:

- how much it cost in current dollars
- who directed, shot, and edited it
- whether or not these people are still working there
- if they will be available for your production
- if you can see other work they've done

Contracting with a production company is one way to find the crew for your video. Another is to build the crew yourself, by locating the key individuals you need. You might find a director or camera operator whose work you like and ask him or her to recommend other people to fill out the crew. In general, good people choose to work with other good people. So finding one key player may lead you to everyone else you need. Nevertheless, look at their work, ask for their credits, and check their references.

CASTING

As with crew and equipment selection, your approach to casting—whether it's for a narrator or spokesperson or for actors for dramatic roles—depends on your experience and what you've done in the past. If you or your production company do a lot of work with actors, you may have your own files and audition tapes and know right where to go to get the people you want to consider for the part.

If you don't handle casting as an in-house function, then you will either work through a talent agency or use a casting director.

Using a Casting Director

My preference is to use a casting director. This is a person whose livelihood depends on keeping up-to-date information on the actors and models available in your locale. A casting director has no special loyalty to any specific actors or talent agencies and can call on anyone, from anywhere, to audition for a part.

The casting director should know what is a fair rate to pay for the talent you want and should help in negotiating with the talent or his or her agent. In this way the casting director works for you just as a talent agent works for the actor. You pay the casting director—either on a daily or hourly rate, or on a flat fee for the production.

Using a Talent Agency

In most metropolitan areas, you'll find a list of talent agencies in the phone book. In my town, they're in the Yellow Pages under "Modeling Agencies," "Professional Talent Management," and "Theatrical Agencies." There are also some schools for models and actors—which may be run by a talent agency—listed under "Dramatic Instruction" or "Modeling Schools." These are always a potential source of talent for your productions.

Like a casting director, the agency will make all those phone calls to line up talent for an audition. But unlike a casting director, an agency usually will not make any direct charge to you for its services. It gets paid a commission by the talent you hire. However, if the agency supplies special services, such as videotaping auditions, there may be a charge for these. Ask.

In my opinion, using a talent agency is far better than trying to set up your own casting department. But there are drawbacks:

- Every agency likes to give its newcomers experience. Not just experience in front of the camera, but experience in an audition. So you may find that in order to see the few really qualified candidates for a part, you have to sit through some poor auditions by inexperienced neophytes.
- The agency may not have people for all the parts you want to cast. So you face a choice between accepting someone who is not quite what you had in mind or starting all over with another agency.
- An agency casting session won't tell you much about an actor's overall experience or how he or she will do on the set as you go through take after take. Unlike a casting director, the agency will want to play up each actor's assets and minimize any liabilities.

Holding Auditions

Your casting director or talent agency will handle getting the people to the audition, but it will be up to you—or your director—to select the people you want for your video. Don't allow yourself to be talked into someone you're not comfortable with.

Videotape the auditions. This gives you a chance to see how each person behaves in front of the camera and how they come across on camera. The camera likes some people, making them look wonderful, exciting, and appealing. And it doesn't like others, making them look heavier than they are, turning their teeth into fangs or their smile into a grimace. So audition your characters on camera.

Some of the things you want to find out in an audition are:

- Can the actors remember their lines? Ask them to memorize a short speech and see if they can do it.
- Can they deliver the lines? It's one thing to repeat the words that were written. It's quite another to say them as if one had just thought of them and were saying them for the first time. That's acting.
- Can they follow directions and adjust their delivery? Some actors are one trick ponies. They get a certain way to do a scene in their heads and that is the only way they can do it. So ask for a change and see if they can make it or if they simply give the same performance without realizing it.
- Can they replicate? Once you have gotten the actor to give you the reading you want, can he or she deliver it consistently, take after take?
- Can they handle props? Can they walk and talk at the same time?
- Do they have any bad habits? Inexperienced actors tend to wave their hands about and bob their heads on camera. They have to learn to use their bodies minimally in order to appear natural.
- Do they seem real or seem to be *acting*? Do they seem natural? Believable?
- Finally, how do your top choices work together? It's not enough that as individuals they give you a good reading. Do they give you what you're looking for as an ensemble? If not, try different combinations until you find what you need.

If you are casting a spokesperson and will be using a Tele-PrompTer, try to have your candidates read from a TelePrompTer if possible or from a cue card placed close to the camera as though it were a TelePrompTer. Reading from a TelePrompTer takes experience to look natural. Amateurs bob their heads from side to side while their eyes never waver from the line of type. Pros look as if they are just talking to the audience, not reading.

SCHEDULING

It's best to be a pessimist in making up the production schedule. Allow a little more time than you think you'll need. If the shoot is complicated, allow a lot more time than you think you'll need.

Be Realistic in Scheduling

Productions have budgets, and scheduling affects the budget. If the budget will pay for five days of shooting but the schedule indicates you'll need six, you either have a scheduling problem or a budget problem. If you have to make cuts to accommodate the budget, it's better to cut out whole scenes or consolidate scenes from two or three different location setups into one setup rather than to try to shave minutes off setup and shooting time. A rushed production is a production prone to errors, and errors ultimately waste even more time.

Discuss the schedule with the key people on the production. Ask your director of photography how long it will take to set the lights and be ready to shoot. Talk with the director about how long it should take to shoot each scene. Check with your sound person about any problems in recording sound at the location.

Never go into a production with a schedule that has to work perfectly. It never does. There will always be problems you haven't anticipated. I used to shoot a lot of golf shows—outdoors on beautiful golf courses in out-of-the-way places. Shooting outdoors you know you may have weather problems. And they are not limited to whether it's raining or not. If you start shooting under clear skies, and then some clouds roll in putting your set in shade, you have to decide whether to wait for a break in the clouds to continue, to accept the changed look, or to start over and reshoot the sunny portion under the clouds. So you expect that. But one morning I was at a golf course in a remote, quiet area twenty miles out of town, shooting my golf pro giving a lesson on camera. Suddenly a couple of military airplanes showed up and began a noisy dogfight about a mile away. And we were dead in terms of recording sound until the planes left. Who could plan for that?

Schedule Rehearsal Time

If you are working with actors, schedule time prior to the production for rehearsal involving the actors, the director, and if possible the scriptwriter. This gives you a chance to find out what the actors can do and to work out any problems in advance in a rehearsal room, where thinking time is cheap. You don't want to have to iron out acting, script, or delivery problems on the set with a lot of expensive people and equipment standing idle.

Shooting Out of Sequence

Schedule the hardest things to do first and get them out of the way if you possibly can. The ideal production schedule should move you always in the direction of scenes that will be easier to shoot and take less time than what has gone before.

- Schedule exterior shooting early in the production so that you can reschedule in case of bad weather. Try to have an interior backup that you can shoot if you lose the exterior to weather.
- Schedule critical people as early in the production as possible so that you can reschedule them if they have to postpone their appearance.
- Schedule all the scenes at a given location to be shot while you are there so you don't have to go back.
- Try to cluster together all the scenes with the same people so that you can bring in the people, shoot the scenes, and let the people go.
- Try to allow some time for pickup shooting—reshooting scenes that you aren't happy with or picking up scenes that couldn't be shot for some reason at the time they were scheduled.

Be Truthful

Be honest with actors, volunteers, and the people at the locations where you will be shooting. The unfortunate tendency is for video-makers to minimize the time it will take in order to get cooperation.

But if you've said it will only take a few minutes and you're still not finished going into your third hour, you're going to have cooperation problems anyway. I've found it's better to say it will take a little longer than I think it will, and to gain cooperation by promising we'll try to keep the distraction to a minimum and work around the needs of the people at the location.

If You Fall Behind Schedule

It happens to the best of us. You think everything's going all right and suddenly you have a problem and the schedule starts to slip. What do you do?

Don't panic. If you've planned the production properly you have some pickup time in the shooting schedule and some contingency money in the budget, so that, if necessary, you can go back later and pick up a scene or two.

Inform everyone that you've had a problem and you're running behind. Let the people at the next few setups know that you are likely to be delayed, so that they are not waiting around wondering where you are.

Consider leapfrogging one or two setups to get back on schedule and then picking up the missing setups at the end of the day.

Slow down. Haste can lead to more problems and more delays. You need to take the pressure off. Call a break if you think it will help. Work deliberately without rushing and you will often find that you start to pick up some of the lost time.

Remember That Your Crew Needs to Eat and Sleep

Video crews put in long hard hours, but they don't like to be taken advantage of. Be sure they get meal breaks at reasonable times. Having a caterer bring in a meal will usually cost you less time than having the crew go out to a restaurant. Be sure any problem days in the schedule, such as a late night shoot followed by an early morning call, have been explained to cast and crew in advance, and they have agreed to this.

Be courteous to the crew. Never assume that the people you've hired to do a job are as committed to saving time and money as you are.

PRODUCTION STORY—LIGHTING AHEAD

Shortly after I moved to Las Vegas I got a subcontract through a local TV station to write and direct two information videos for the Aladdin Hotel and Casino. We had to shoot everywhere on the property and we had to do it on a fixed budget with a tight schedule that allowed for four-and-a-half days of shooting plus a half day of pickups if needed. During that time we had to cover 105 setups, some of which were simple—a sign in the slot machine area for instance—but some of which were complicated, involving actors or performers, sound recording, and camera moves.

We had promised the client lush, professional lighting to give every shot a look of quality and luxury. I was working with the crew from the station, fortunately not a news crew, but the crew that normally shot commercials, so they knew about things like using a tripod—and even a dolly—and lighting for a specific look, the sort of thing not taught in Newsvideo 101. The shooting schedule averaged twenty-four setups a day or a little over three an hour, since one hour in the day's schedule was set aside for a crew meal. It is almost impossible to move from one setup to the next, set lights, and record any kind of a decent scene in less than twenty minutes.

My solution was to augment the basic crew of camera operator, sound operator, and grip with a lighting director and one or two gaffers, and to order twice as many lighting instruments as I'd normally use. To stay on schedule, as soon as we'd light a setup, I'd send the lighting crew on to the next setup while the camera crew and I shot in the one we'd just lit. For simple shots—signs, graphics, displays—we could often move in and shoot in five to ten minutes, banking the spare time for the more complicated scenes involving tricky stuff. And it worked. Not perfectly; we had to pass some shots by for one reason or another and pick them up later, and we managed to eliminate a couple of shots and combine others into a single, longer take.

We had superb cooperation from the hotel. Whatever we needed, they delivered. We had a security guard with a walkie-talkie with us at all times, who could call and have an electrician meet the lighting crew at the next setup if we needed it or send out a message from some volunteer extras. We had planned the work carefully to accomplish what we needed to on location, with some allowances for the inevitable problems that develop. You never know what these will be.

In the middle of the last day's shooting, with thirty-one setups on the schedule, a hotel executive who had been helping us began to exhibit the symptoms of a heart attack. My partner, Sylvie, who in another life had been a registered nurse, was right there and offered some first-aid suggestions. And eventually, at the hotel's request, she left the shoot for two hours to accompany the executive to the hospital in the hotel limousine.

And still we finished on time.

. . . .

10

THE PEOPLE WHO MAKE IT HAPPEN

Some production crews work together day after day, year after year, until they can almost read each other's minds and in a pinch can do each other's jobs. Other production crews are brought together to do a specific project, which they work at for a few days or weeks and then go their separate ways. Either way can work and both have their drawbacks. The close-knit crew has its own way of doing things and sometimes may not be open to new ideas—or to outsiders. The pick-up crew has no natural cohesion and may need firm control from the producer or director in order to work as a team.

This chapter is a brief look at the key players on a production—the people who make it happen—and what they do. If you're doing production every day, you may want to fast-forward to the next chapter. But if you're just getting started at making videos for money, you'd better stick around and get familiar with the people you'll be working with.

THE PRODUCER DEALS WITH THE
BUSINESS OF THE PRODUCTION

The producer on a video production has the overall responsibility to get the video made. For an information video or an infomercial this may involve close to full-time activity. A local commercial may require less of the producer's time. An interactive multimedia project may take months or years and can become practically a career in itself.

The producer is the person who looks after business: he or she deals with the client or sponsor, negotiates the bid, signs the contract, collects the money, hires the crew, pays the bills, and handles administrative details from preproduction through to delivery of the finished product. Most times the producer is responsible to the client for the finished product while the director has creative control of the production. But the role of the producer in the creative process can vary. Some producers will be intimately involved with the director, crew, and editor at every stage of production; others will leave the creative realization of the production to the people they have hired.

Producers often are hyphenates—producer-writer or producer-director—directly involved in both the business details of the production and the creative process of bringing it to the screen. A producer-director has a lot to do—sometimes too much. I was making a sponsored documentary for a mental health organization in Philadelphia, wearing both hats of producer and director. The client's representative, who had no experience with film and video, had been convinced that a lot of strong material would come out of a series of "town meetings" the organization had sponsored across Pennsylvania, and had insisted that about a third of our shooting budget go to recording one of these. When the town meeting we were shooting on location turned out to be pretty much of a bomb—as I had predicted—the client panicked and called me back to Philadelphia for a meeting. Because as producer-director I couldn't be both places at once, I had to cancel a day's shooting at a state mental hospital. That meant we had to pay the crew for doing nothing and lost a day's shooting out of the budget. If we had had a separate producer on this project, the producer could have gone back and held the client's hand while I kept shooting in a productive location.

A good producer can do dozens of things to make the production run smoothly. These may range from making sure the production budget is adequate and providing excellent living and eating arrangements on location to keeping the client out of the way of the creative team so they have room to do their work. And that's the point: to deliver the best possible completed video to the client.

THE WRITER CREATES THE BLUEPRINT

Client-sponsored productions are always carefully written in advance—except when, for some really good reason, they simply cannot be. The writer for the video may be employed by the client, may be a copywriter at an advertising or public relations agency, or may be a freelancer. Or the scriptwriter may be employed by the production company that will make the video—either as a scriptwriter or as a writer-producer or writer-director.

The writer conducts content research, organizes the material, and creates a blueprint for the production. The writer is not only responsible for telling the client's story completely, accurately, and effectively, but must do it within the budget and within the capability of the production company. And that means the writer needs to be an experienced scriptwriter who truly understands how videomakers tell a story with pictures.

Inexperienced Scriptwriters

A writer without video experience, a print writer, for example, will invariably overwrite the words and underwrite the pictures. Having to work with a writer who does not understand video and film is number one among the pet peeves of producers and directors I interviewed for *Video Scriptwriting*.

"I sometimes have to work with a scriptwriter the client has hired because he loves his work in print," Tony Bond (of Take One, Inc., Las Vegas) said. "The writer doesn't understand video and produces a script that is totally inappropriate."

. . . And producers and directors working on commercial videos for clients absolutely don't want to deal with the writer's ego. When they ask for rewrites, they want rewrites, not an argument. "Writers can get too attached to their own words," (producer-director Tim) Bradley said. "I just went through this with an ad agency where the writer was one of the owners of the agency, and he was far too attached to what he had written." (pp. 233–34)

My own pet peeve is people who call themselves writers who do not understand how their language works. Grammar, diction, and the connotation and denotation of words are the technical tools a writer works with. A writer who hasn't mastered them is like a carpenter trying to build a house with lumber and nails, but no tool kit.

Pick a Writer Who Writes What You Need

It's important to realize that there are many different ways to write about the same topic, and different writers will have their own specialties. The three writers described in chapter seven who produced scripts for the United Way of Greater Minneapolis certainly demonstrated this. The purpose was the same, but the three approaches were quite different. For this reason alone, writers should be selected based on their body of work.

If you are choosing a writer, ask to see scripts he or she has written, not finished videos. Too many hands are involved with a video after the script is written for it to be a fair gauge of the writer's ability. I've seen bad directors ruin good scripts and I know an outstanding director of commercials whose reputation was based partly on turning a mediocre script into an award-winning production. If possible, try to see a first draft script. That's the only one that is completely the writer's own work.

THE DIRECTOR *REALIZES* THE VIDEO

In French films, the director's credit is given as *realization by*, which has always seemed to me to be a much clearer statement of the director's task than the authoritarian term *directed by* that we use in English. That's what the good director of an information video actually does: realize the vision which may have started as a vague itch with the client, has been fleshed out into a comprehensive plan by the scriptwriter—often in collaboration with the client, the producer, and the director—and must be turned into visual reality through the combined efforts of the cast and crew.

If the producer is the one who gets the project made—in the sense of starting and finishing—the director is the person who gets it recorded on video and organized for showing to the target audience. Since a video—even a short commercial—is usually shot out of sequence, the only continuity, other than the script itself, may be the vision of the finished product carried in the director's head.

The director is the person in creative control of the video—the creative decision maker. He or she decides when, where, and what to shoot and, in consultation with the camera operator or director of photography, how to shoot it. The director of a sponsored video will normally stay with the production from preproduction planning through the completion of postproduction. He or she will select the narrator or spokesperson, will supervise recording of narration and music, and will work with the editor in organizing the elements of the video for presentation to an audience.

CAMERA AND SOUND

A producer with no experience can often get a decent video made just by hiring the right people to do the rest of the job. Even an inexperienced director can often come up with an acceptable program. After all, directors have to learn somewhere. But the people who record the image and sound have to be professionals who know what they are doing.

Shooting on video—even though there may be a monitor available on which to check the shot—does not make this sort of professional expertise any less important. Video is not Polaroid movies and never was.

Director of Photography

The director of photography has responsibility for the overall look of a production. In consultation with the director, he or she establishes the lighting, frames the shot, selects the lenses and stock to be used, and instructs the camera operator. On a large production, the director of photography does not actually operate the camera. On a small crew video, the functions of director of photography and camera operator will probably be handled by the same person.

Camera Operator

The camera operator is a professional who records the images. He or she must have a strong technical knowledge of the camera and recording equipment in use and must know how the lighting in use—whatever the source—will affect the images that are recorded. In any hot shooting situation, the camera operator may function as codirector, making crucial decisions about what to shoot and how to shoot it.

Sound Recordist

The sound recordist is the person who records audio during production and also records wild track or natural sound, when needed. Recording excellent sound for a video is a technical skill which requires both professional knowledge and experience. The sound person has to be able to record voices in a noisy situation so that they are well separated from the background noise. He or she must know where the camera is pointed at all times and must be sure to record sound that goes with the picture. In certain situations, the sound recordist may be receiving audio from several microphone sources, and must be able to record each source cleanly or to mix the sources so that the important sound at any time is clear. Just as the director of photography or camera operator will select the lenses and stock appropriate to the video, the sound recordist will choose microphones, recorders, and even tape to suit the production.

THE CREATIVE EDITOR ORGANIZES IT FOR THE AUDIENCE

The creative editor is the final member of the creative team putting together the video the client wants made—the one who turns it from raw material into a shiny new finished product. I think the best directors often start as editors, because one of the most important contributions the editor brings to the production is the sense of how the elements go together and what it takes to make a finished program.

From the outside, video editing looks like a fairly mechanical, computer-driven operation. But in the hands of a truly creative editor it becomes something very similar to sculpture. The editor uses the raw footage from the shoot to give shape to the meaning of the video.

The creative editor may work independently, viewing and selecting footage and creating the production. The editor works from the approved script with the footage that has been shot, giving the production pace, rhythm, and style. The editor may also bring in other source materials such as stock footage, graphics, special visual effects, sound effects, and music.

The creative editor also may work in collaboration with or under the control of the director. In this case the director makes the final creative decisions about the way the video goes together, often sitting next to the editor as the video is built shot by shot.

If anything goes wrong during production, video people will say, partly as a joke, and sometimes as a prayer, "That's okay, we'll fix it in post." It is the creative editor, the person in charge of postproduction, who has to make the fix. And the amazing thing is that they often do.

TALENT: THE PEOPLE ON CAMERA

The most common use of talent in an information video is as a narrator or spokesperson. The talent represents the client to the audience. If the audience believes and trusts the spokesperson, they will probably believe the client's message.

We were casting an information video for the state department of labor. One of the people who came to the audition was a woman who had been a news anchor on a local TV station and had quit to pursue other activities. Although her agent had sent her to read for the part of an occupational safety and health inspector, we asked if she would be willing to be the spokesperson for the video. She agreed and we gained a spokes with immediate credibility with our target audience.

In another situation, I was involved with a sales project for an old and experienced company that was marketing into a new area where it wasn't known. We decided to use a well-known actor in the company's sales video because the use of a major—and *expensive!*— figure as its spokesperson would say to the viewer, "Although this company is new to your business it's a major player. Just look who's doing the talking for it."

The actors in an information video represent either the client or, in some cases, the client's customers. When talent is used appropriately, the audience can't imagine anyone else in the role. But when the talent used is not right, the production can suffer immeasurably, and this reflects on the client.

In a sales video I wrote for a resort, the concept had three different couples getting together on the last day of their vacations to chat about their experience. This sort of thing would be deadly if it wasn't credible. But if the characters played their parts believably, the audience would eavesdrop on something quite interesting. The production was turned over to a staff director for casting. The video went into production and then into post.

And then I got a call from the producer who told me there was a problem. The client had loved the script, but was not at all happy with two of the characters as they appeared in the video. Would I come over and take a look and see what could be done?

Of course.

I saw immediately that the problem was that one couple hadn't been cast as I had written them.

> STEVE and GINNY DeANGELO are in their forties—
> middle Americans from Minnesota, where he is
> middle management and she teaches school. He
> wears Sears slacks and a plain color sport shirt. She
> wears shorts and a top.

I had seen the DeAngelos as the salt of the earth. Nice people who have saved up for a vacation, brought the kids, and were enjoying themselves. Steve was an accountant or an engineer, a pipe smoker who liked facts and became the source of factual information about the resort. Ginny was a teacher and a nice person, having the time of her life in a new environment about which she didn't know very much.

The director, unfortunately, saw them as comic figures. He cast a heavyset, loud-talking actor as Steve, and instead of dressing him in subdued slacks and a knit shirt, he put him in noisy Bermuda shorts and the sort of loud shirt worn only by tourists. Instead of playing Ginny as ingenuous, he turned her into an airhead. The client was not amused. These couples had to represent customers of the resort. The people viewing the video were supposed to identify with one of the three couples. But no one was going to identify with the De-Angelos. They weren't likable.

Eventually I rewrote the script to use a straight narration over pretty pictures. The client accepted it. The video won a Telly Award. But we all knew that the wrong actors, directed the wrong way, had taken away something we thought we were going to like much better.

PRODUCTION STORY—CASTING THE WRONG SPOKESPERSON

When I was serving time as the media producer for a not very good ad agency we cast a spokesperson for a series of commercials for a chain of gas stations. I auditioned all the likely prospects on video, picked the one I liked, and the one I could live with, and then showed the entire audition tape to my boss at the agency and to the client.

Big mistake. They selected a young actor from my discard pile and said he was the one they wanted. I went over my notes, told them my reservations about the actor—among other things I thought his delivery was flat and he didn't follow directions well—and pushed for one of the others. But I was overruled.

And when we got on location, the designated spokes turned out to be even worse than I thought. He gave a performance like a depressive, going downhill from take to take. It should be hard to lose your energy in a 30-second spot, but he could do it. I quit directing from the monitor and would stand in front of him just out of camera range, grinning, jumping up and down, and engaging in embarrassing antics to try to keep a smile on his face and a little excitement in his voice.

Then there was the day we were shooting a spot, I called a break, and the talent forgot to turn off his wireless microphone while he went to make a phone call. My client listened with interest as the spokesperson's voice came over the monitor telling the person he was talking to what a lousy director I was, what a lousy shoot this was, and what a lousy client the gas stations were.

For the next commercials we had a new spokesperson, a smiling young woman I selected with no interference from above. The camera loved her.

And she could get it right in one take.

PART III

MAKING INFORMATION VIDEOS

HOW INFORMATION
VIDEOS ARE USED

Now let's take a look at the various kinds of information videos you might be hired to make and how they are used to carry a client's message to an audience.

SALES AND MARKETING

More than fifty years of experience with TV commercials have shown that video sells. Sales and marketing videos are an excellent way to demonstrate new products and services to potential customers. Businesses send out videos showing new cars and trucks, major appliances, investment programs, and almost any big-ticket commodity. A sales video is a powerful gate-crasher, gaining attention for the salesperson who will follow it. And it makes a prestige leave-behind item.

Demonstration and Benefit

A sales and marketing video demonstrates a product or service, stresses its benefits to the user, and explains how the viewer can get it. Because sales and marketing videos can have a direct impact on a company's sales income, they often have better budgets than most other information videos.

PUBLIC INFORMATION

Public information videos are made by clients to get out the good news about what they are doing and, occasionally, to counteract whatever bad news about them may be going around.

Positive Attitude
The purpose of a public information video usually is to create or maintain in the target audience a positive attitude toward the sponsoring institution. It may be used to explain a specific project or activity or just to get a feel-good response in general. The 3M video, "Imagine," described in chapter five, for instance, shows a lot of 3M products, but always in the context of 3M solving problems for the company's clients.

Government Information
Government agencies like to tell the taxpayers about the good things they are doing with tax dollars. For instance, the Missouri Department of Conservation made "Legacy of Life" to inform viewers "of the many ways the department manages their fish, forest, and wildlife resources" and to "promote a good feeling among residents for the department's work." It uses spectacular wildlife pictures and a good mix of conversational narration and documentary sound bites to tell the story of state wildlife conservation. When I saw this video I thought that if I were a resident of that state, I'd be proud. That's creating a positive image.

Dealing with Negatives
When you're responding to negative information, deal with it head on. A Hawaii developer with a solid reputation for quality construction built a condominium that was having termite problems. Termites are a fact of life in Hawaii, and the developer had scrupulously followed all of the existing government regulations pertaining to termite prevention. The company had even made repairs and modifications long beyond the expiration of the buyers' warranty period.

The condominium homeowners association, however, thought they had a case against the developer and took a hard line. Rather than negotiate, they decided to sue. Having taken that step, the association was unwilling to let the developer tell its side of the story at a homeowners' meeting. The developer decided to create a video that could be mailed to every one of the 375 homeowners in the project to explain exactly what the situation was. And did.

Video Annual Reports

Some corporations are now issuing a video version of their annual report so that those who don't want to read the shiny, four-color printed version can watch the video instead. Annual reports are also being posted as multimedia productions, including video, on the organization's Web site.

FUND-RAISING

Like everyone else, nonprofit organizations have found that a video showing the good work they do can be more effective than a brochure that merely tells about it. A well-made video makes a great presentation at meetings of service clubs and community organizations, overcoming the problem of the after-dinner speaker who is a dedicated worker for the organization, but not necessarily a spellbinding talker. Just show the video and answer questions.

Nonprofit Sales and Marketing

Fund-raising videos combine public information with sales and marketing in the highly competitive arena of charitable good works. The purpose is to inform the target audience of the benefits they receive— either directly or indirectly—from the sponsoring organization and to get them to pledge or send money.

Benefit in a fund-raising video is often expressed in terms of general benefits to society, rather than direct benefits to the viewer. It is not good for society to have people starving or sleeping in parking garages or abused by their parents or spouses. Therefore, the video may imply, if the viewer will help end these problems, the world will be a better, cleaner, safer, happier place in which to live.

Other fund-raising videos may stress direct benefits. Money donated to a community symphony or theater group will help make these arts available in the viewer's area. Money donated to medical research promises long-term benefits for the viewer and his or her family. Money donated to a worthwhile building project will eventually result in a building—easing overcrowding and offering modern facilities and greater convenience for those who will use it.

TRAINING

The use of motion media for training goes back at least as far as World War I, when the military faced the problem of quickly turning raw recruits—some of them illiterate—into soldiers. They used motion pictures. Today, it's almost impossible to find a movie projector in a corporate environment, but every training room has a VCR and monitor. Training videos are a fact of life.

Demonstration and Standardization

A training video usually shows an audience a new way—or a better way—to do something. It should demonstrate what needs to be done and why. To do this, it should be strongly based on visual evidence. An entire cottage industry has grown up to produce videos which explain visually how to use computer software. In less than an hour, the video can demonstrate what otherwise sometimes takes days of poring over the software manuals to understand. And, sometimes, the way software manuals have traditionally been written, no amount of study can make sense of the program. But a video which shows that if you want to accomplish this task, just do these things with your mouse and keyboard, can make a complex procedure easy to understand.

A training video may also be made to standardize training. A company with many locations would like to know that all of its employees are receiving the same good level of training. In the past, you had a master trainer train the trainers who would go out to the various sites and train employees. And, as in the game of "whisper" we played in grade school—where one person whispers a phrase to the next person, who whispers it to the next person, and so on—powerful changes would creep into the message as it moved down the line. Having the basic information committed to video ensures that everyone starts out with the same message.

Watching an Occupational Safety and Health Inspection

One of the best uses of a training video is to provide an overview to something new. The Hawaii Department of Labor commissioned a training video to show businesspeople what happens during an occupational safety and health inspection and to let them know that they can request a compliance review, which is like an OSHA inspection but with no penalties attached. After viewing the twenty-minute video, business owners and managers have a good idea of what actually goes on during such an inspection and the sorts of things the inspectors would be looking for. Armed with this overview they could go back to the bureaucratic and legalistic language of the written law and better understand what they need to do to be in compliance.

The video is also used to train new safety and health inspectors. As with employers, it gives them an overview of the entire procedure.

"The Guest"

An ITVA Golden Reel winner is a marvelous video called "The Guest." It was made by Media Partners Corporation in Seattle for sale to company training departments to remind employees that "the secret to great customer service is to treat customers as you would a guest in your home." This video is practically a clinic on how to do a spokesperson video, combining humor and dramatic vignettes to demonstrate some basic principles about getting and keeping customers. The video is anchored in a little restaurant run by Shirley, who knows everything about making a customer feel like a guest. As the spokesperson says:

> I love this place. I wish I could buy my shirts here. I wish they took deposits. I wish Shirley sold life insurance. I don't think I'm nuts. I know I'm not alone. I think I'm just like everybody else. We all want to shop or eat or do business where we feel comfortable, where we feel like a welcome guest.

That's the plot and that's the theme. And the viewer gets a refresher course in how to keep customers in a competitive marketplace.

INTERNAL COMMUNICATION

Obviously, training videos are a specialized form of internal communication. But most internal communication is just a way of talking among ourselves. It's much like public information except it's designed to be kept in the family. Organizations create videos for internal communication as a way to keep their members informed about what the organization is doing and as a way to tell their members or employees about useful information, such as a change in organizational policy or benefits.

"Excursion II"

Pioneer Hi-Bred International, a key player in agribusiness, commissioned the video "Excursion II" to convince its sales force that "agriculture will change drastically in the future [and] . . . the sales force needs to begin preparing today for their future role . . ." The video shows farmers in the near future—and their Pioneer representatives—facing problems with crops and farm animals and quickly finding solutions using computers, high-tech instrumentation, and sophisticated knowledge of new scientific developments. The video begins by acknowledging that it's hard to predict the future and admits that the changes in agriculture may not be exactly as shown, but that change is inevitable, and Pioneer plans to be on the cutting edge of whatever changes may occur.

"Welcome to CAP"

Every employer needs a benefits video, and "Welcome to CAP," made by CME Video and Film, Minneapolis, is one of the best. In less than seven minutes it covers eligibility and enrollment in a company's 401(k) capital accumulation plan—the "CAP" which the video welcomes the viewer to. And does it with charm and humor. The humor is of the inclusive sort, that seems to say we're all in this together. Using the metaphor of a computer screen, with a cursor clicking on a heading to introduce each new topic, this video uses a strong visual presentation to give a comprehensive overview of a complex subject.

Organizational News

Many companies have supplemented—or replaced—the company newsletter with a video news program as a form of internal communication. These may be shown daily, weekly, monthly, or quarterly, either on closed-circuit television or on videocassettes sent out to various employee sites throughout the organization. They usually follow a video magazine format with an on-camera spokesperson or news anchor introducing several stories of three to five minutes in length. These inform the viewers of new developments in the organization, new products or services, and important employee information, such as essential safety information or changes in benefits.

Organizational news videos have traditionally been created by in-house production units. But with the trend toward outsourcing media production, more and more of these programs will be made by independent videomakers.

Videoconferencing

The economics of videoconferencing are compelling. Consider the cost of bringing key people from different geographic locations together for a face-to-face meeting. Not just the cost of plane tickets, motel rooms, rental cars, and meals—which can be substantial—but the real cost to productivity of perhaps a day or more lost to travel time for several people who, if they are important enough to travel to the meeting, are valuable enough that they have serious work they should be doing. Compared to that, videoconferencing, even at a rate of several hundred dollars an hour for conference room and line costs, makes good economic sense. And, as with all other technology, the cost can be expected to drop as use of the technology rises.

Obviously, production of a videoconference requires no less thought and preparation than a face-to-face meeting in a conference room. In addition, planning the use of video is an important consideration. Perhaps some of the plane ticket and motel money being saved can go into the production of a documentary or information video to kick off the conference. Provision must also be made for showing slides, graphics, and documents and for displaying computer information.

Reporting Upward on Video

In chapter six I discussed a video that was a report to top management on how a new employee time tracking system had worked in the pilot project. This is internal communication directed upward, and is another example of the way video is replacing the written report or meeting presentation. A decade ago, no one would have considered the expense justified to make a video just to report on a project to the executive committee or board of directors. Today they're doing it.

So communication upward on video is likely to be a growing area for video production. Especially if it can be justified by a secondary audience such as company employees or the general public. The video for the secondary audience need not be exactly the same as the one made for top management. With digital editing, making the changes is simple and relatively inexpensive.

CONVENTION PRESENTATIONS

Two blocks from me is the Las Vegas Convention Center which hosts some of the largest conventions and trade shows in the world. These include NAB—the convention of the National Association of Broadcasters—that brings more than a hundred thousand people to the city in April, and COMDEX, the giant computer show in the fall that draws more than two hundred thousand people. The trade shows for these events extend for acres and include close to fifteen hundred exhibitors for NAB and far more than that for COMDEX, which uses every available bit of display space in the convention center and in a half-dozen major hotels.

In that kind of competitive atmosphere, a convention presentation has to stop traffic and pull people into the booth to watch the presentation or talk to the salespeople. It has to be colorful, exciting, and *visual*, because the noise level on a convention floor is such that people passing by may not be able to understand the words a narrator says.

Showing a Laptop

The key to a convention video is to be short, punchy, entertaining, and informative. "HiNote and HiNote Ultra," made for Digital

Equipment Corporation by Multivision Inc. of Needham, Massachusetts, is an outstanding example of this. Its stated purpose was, "to compete with the vast array of audiovisual distractions at large trade shows [and] . . . entice potential customers to obtain more information on the product line." It demonstrates completely the attributes and capabilities of two laptop computers in two and a half minutes using visual imagery backed by exciting music. Only two words are spoken in the video. These are by a parrot, and don't have to be heard. All necessary verbal information is displayed in graphics. It works.

Working with a Presenter

I've done several convention booth presentations that used a live presenter in conjunction with video displayed on a video wall. These play to an audience that has come into the booth and taken a seat to view the performance, either because they were attracted in by a short video such as the one above or because they just wanted a chance to sit down.

To sell computer-assisted design software, for example, we combined visual evidence on video with an on-stage presenter. She extolled the benefits of the system while the audience watched video of real-life applications showing everything from designing and manufacturing actual cars and airplanes to designing the facilities for the Atlanta Olympic Games and then modeling them in three dimensions to see how everything would work long before they were built. In several scenes the presenter seemed to be talking with or interviewing people in the video who were telling how they had applied the software to their businesses. A neat trick, since all of the video was stock footage that had been supplied to us by IBM before the script was written.

Combining video with a presenter can be as prosaic as show-and-tell, where pictures appear as the presenter talks, or it can be a real creative opportunity. The presenter breaks your program out of the video frame and brings it into the audience, while a wall full of video gives viewers something more to look at than just a person talking. In one of these convention shows, for example, we used a comedian posing as a convention janitor to disrupt the presentation and get into a dialogue with the audience and with the on-screen video image of a programmer who said she had gotten sucked into the computer network and couldn't get out. In fifteen minutes it explained a lot about network applications in a way that was fun for everyone.

And that's the point. Convention presentations operate in a highly competitive environment and have to inform and sell an audience that has far too much to see and far too little time to see it in.

DOCUMENTARIES

Videomakers are finding new opportunities in the rapidly expanding use of the documentary form in broadcast and cable television, in corporate communication, and even in theatrical release. Documentaries can range from those shot in a hot situation, happening *right now* with the outcome in doubt, to fully scripted reenactments or re-creations shot with the same preparation and attention to detail as a feature film or network television program.

Historical events and the biographies of important or interesting people have always been a major area of documentary. Today, television and the education market make these prime areas for videomakers. History and biography are after-the-fact reports on past events. The problem for the documentarian always is to find a way to make such documentaries visually interesting.

The ability to go anywhere with lightweight recording equipment has made it possible to follow people around and observe on film or videotape whatever they do. In the early days of direct cinema there were a lot of films made about ordinary people living out their ordinary lives. And this is very much with us today. *Hoop Dreams* follows the lives of two young basketball players for nearly eight years. *Crumb* looks at three strange brothers from a very weird family. Reality-based documentaries often look at unique events with the end in doubt. These can range from documentaries of sports events such as Bud Greenspan's quadrennial Olympic films to process documentaries such as *Unzipped*, which covers a year in the professional life of designer Isaac Mizrahi.

The market for video documentaries has grown wonderfully in recent years.

- Many cable channels virtually live on documentaries.
- Companies want documentation on video of their projects, processes, and programs.
- Some of my friends make a good living documenting the speakers and events at conferences and conventions, handing out a VHS copy to participants on the last day.
- Marathon races and other sporting events routinely offer a documentary video to participants.
- Corporations approaching a major anniversary in corporate life—fifty, seventy-five, a hundred years, or more—like to see their histories on video.

In making a video documentary, your job is to find, record, and organize visual evidence to make a powerful, dramatic statement on the screen. It takes planning, the ability to recognize what you're after when it happens, and careful organization and editing so that what you show the audience is true to what happened when you were recording.

VIDEOS FOR CONSUMER SALE

Take a look in the drugstore or discount store and you'll see racks of videos for sale, many of them occupying space formerly reserved for books and magazines. Yes, many of these are feature films released on video. But an increasing number are not. Exercise videos, travel videos, home maintenance videos and the like are coming into their own, replacing or at least supplementing how-to books and magazines. It is a measure of the way times have changed that the reviewer for the prestigious *Library Journal*, writing about my book on documentary, stated:

> He is meticulous, even including a chapter on informed consent called "Ethics in Making a Documentary," and a most helpful index that provides information on professional associations. Still, despite his use of sound bites and personal anecdotes, one senses that he should have produced a series of videos on the subject instead of writing it all down for its specialized audience of film

students, film professionals, and large companies that make informational films.

This is a *librarian* writing about a *book*!
Consumer videos are here to stay.

OVERLAPPING CATEGORIES

Obviously there can be a lot of overlap among categories. A convention presentation is probably also sales and marketing. A public information video may also be used for internal communication. A documentary may be used in many different ways—for internal communication, external communication, sales and marketing, training, whatever.

Multimedia producers talk about *re-sourcing* video, which means taking video produced for another purpose and using it for a Web site or a multimedia CD.

Many documentaries now find a secondary sale as retail videos after they have appeared in theaters or on television. One theory is that the broadcast agreement pays all or most of the production costs while retail video sale brings in the profit.

What this all adds up to is that information videos, in all their different forms, will continue to be a growing market for videomakers for the foreseeable future.

PRODUCTION STORY—A SALES VIDEO FOR JAPANESE DOCTORS

One of the strangest—and most interesting—information videos I've made was done for a company created to offer continuing medical education courses in Hawaii for doctors from Japan. The package included several days at a golf resort on the island of Oahu, a distinguished international faculty, and all the delights of a Hawaii vacation. This was one of those projects that came up at the last minute. The proposed faculty was gathering at the resort in forty-eight hours, and I barely had time to put together a budget and contract, deposit the advance, schedule a crew, and make a shot list.

We recorded coverage of the planning sessions, field trips to hospitals and golf courses, beauty shots of the resort, and statements from each of the faculty members. Half the statements were in English, the other half were in Japanese. The client had provided me with an interpreter—his wife—who asked my questions to the Japanese doctors who then spoke in Japanese for as long as they considered necessary. Since I didn't know what they were saying, and was not getting a simultaneous translation, all I could do was look interested, nod my head encouragingly, and time the sound bite on my stopwatch. At the end of each statement, I'd ask what we got and my "interpreter" would tell me, "It's good." Then I'd check my stopwatch and usually say, "All right, we're going to record it again, and ask them this time if they can make their answer shorter." By day's end I had several tapes full of interviews, in which I had no idea what had been said.

A week or two later I got a transcript of the Japanese tapes and began creating an editing script. The challenge was to write a narration in English that would be translated into Japanese and recorded by a Japanese narrator. I had statements from the Japanese doctors that read like this:

> DR. NISHIYAMA
> (in Japanese)
> Doctors prepared themselves before to treat
> their patient's illnesses, but recently the
> patients have begun to ask why they are sick,
> or what it is in their lifestyle that is causing
> their illness, and the doctor must be able to
> respond. The answers are not in the books,
> and it is very important to the doctor to be able
> to answer the patients' questions.

So I decided that a very simple English narration, written to sound as if it had been translated from Japanese, would be the way to go. Here's an example:

> NARRATOR
> Each seminar will have five faculty members
> chosen from Japan and the United States—all
> experts in their fields. And it will be limited
> to just twenty-five participating physicians.

> Thus each participant should have the
> opportunity to work closely with a professor.
> This is a far different approach from most
> medical seminars.

It worked. We sent the script off to Tokyo for approval and received back a version written in Japanese. We found a narrator in Honolulu who spoke with a Tokyo accent, recorded the voice-over, edited the video into the final version, and shipped it to the client, who was now in Tokyo. Back came a fax saying everyone loved it.

Just for fun, I kept that fifteen-minute video with its Japanese sound track and graphics at the end of my sample reel for years, listing my credit as producer, director, and *writer*.

. . . .

12

HOW INFORMATION
VIDEOS ARE MADE

When I was editing a high-tech business journal, we put out our first business computer issue sometime in 1988. I'd had my stone-age IBM PC for several years at that time, but that year more desks still had typewriters on them than workstations, and *networking* meant getting to know people who could help you in business. In that issue we bravely predicted, "By the year 2000, 75 percent of businesses will be using computers." A year later, in our second computer issue, we had to admit that we'd been a bit too conservative. "In a little over a year," we wrote, "the Selectrics have come off the desks to be replaced by monitors and keyboards. We're still a decade away from 2000 and we must be close to, if we haven't already passed, the 75 percent mark in business computing." Technological change, when it comes, often comes in a rush.

And that's one reason why I don't intend to write about specific equipment and technology in a book that my publisher, my editor, my agent, and I all hope will be around for several years. The generational half-life for video equipment by my reckoning is about eighteen months. So any equipment I might write about here would be on its way to obsolescence before you could read about it.

Another reason is that I assume you either know how to record decent video images or will hire someone who does to record them for you. Getting a good, reproducible image recorded is what I call zero level knowledge. Without it, you can't make even a bad information video. But knowing it won't guarantee a good one.

A third reason is that the equipment doesn't make the video, people do. I once ran an audiovisual unit for a teacher training project. The project often put on conferences for teachers, and my people would take Polaroid snapshots of each day's activities and display them on a bulletin board. The teachers always said how much they liked those photos. And, invariably, they'd ask, "What kind of cameras do you use?" Actually, they were the simplest, thirty-dollar, wide-angle-lens, no-frills cameras that Polaroid made. As if that mattered. Because it wasn't the cameras that made the pictures work. It was a couple of good shooters finding people doing interesting stuff and photographing them in a way that made that clear.

THE GOAL OF PRODUCTION

In the production phase of making an information video, your goal is to produce a stack of videotapes containing everything you need for editing. That's it.

You want to get all the footage and sound you need as quickly and economically as possible, while maintaining the highest level of quality you can manage. That means recording good, highly visual images—and shooting enough of them so that you have covered the subject and will have good choices in editing. And it means that you keep shooting until you have what you need. It does no good to save a little time or tape on location only to get into the editing room and wish you'd shot the scene again from a different angle or done one more take on the speech that was acceptable but not really great.

Shoot at the Highest Level You Can Afford

Always shoot at the highest level the budget will tolerate to give your production every chance for greatness. It is an axiom that what you've recorded deteriorates a little with each generation from camera original to copies in release. And, yes, digital editing eliminates some of the editing generations by cloning from one generation to the next. But you're still going to go from original to edited master to a release copy. And the way to give the release copy—the one the audience will see—the highest quality look is to start with a high quality original.

By the time you read this, many productions will be all digital from camera original to release copies on CD-ROM, computer disk, or some other medium. But many videomakers will still be recording analog video and releasing on analog VHS for years to come. And no one pretends that a VHS dub has the same look as high quality camera original.

If you can afford it, bring extra lights and hire a lighting director. Lighting sets the look of the video. It may be acceptable to shoot documentaries and weddings in available light and live with the video you get. But a sponsored information video should look professionally done. And nothing takes the sheen off a production like poor lighting. Clients may not know all the nuances of production lighting, but they watch television and go to the movies. They'll know whether or not the video they've paid for measures up.

Select the best video production medium that you can afford—and that your crew knows how to use—so that you will always start with the best possible pictures. Be sure the camera, recorder, and videotape are compatible with the off-line and on-line systems available to you for postproduction. Otherwise you may find you have high-end production original that will have to be dubbed to a lower quality system for editing. You'll have paid for the more expensive production tools and tape and for the dub, and will have no appreciable increase in quality to show for it.

What about Film or HDTV?

Is there any reason to consider shooting the production on film? Will you need to release copies in more than one video format, such as NTSC and PAL? Film can provide a high quality original that goes easily to other standards with minimal loss. And if there is any thought that this production will be projected in theaters, film may be the best choice, since you can make release prints on film for projection. Film can also get around technical problems that interfere with good video. I once had to shoot a video in a restaurant located near several radio transmission towers. The radio frequency (RF) interference was fierce, making it impossible to record a clean video picture. So we shot on film, transferred the footage to video, and treated it as a video production from then on.

Digital High Definition Television (HDTV) has arrived and is available as a production medium. It, too, can be used to provide an extremely high quality original for transfer to either NTSC or PAL with virtually no loss of quality. HDTV projection systems are easily the equal of 16mm film projection and rival 35mm for bandwidth and resolution. And a tape-to-film transfer from HDTV should look about like a print from good film original.

PRODUCTION CONSIDERATIONS

Keep It Visual

Always try to record powerful visual evidence. When you're scouting, look for the pictures that tell the story and then record them when you shoot. Try to record the unusual and unexpected. If I'm in production and it starts to rain, I shoot. Since most production happens only in good weather under clear skies, a scene in the rain gives a unique look to the video.

Be sure that whatever you shoot yields good imagery. Even if you are shooting an interview, don't just settle for the easy-to-do desk shot. Try to bring more dimension to your pictures. Can you record a hotel executive standing in the hotel's ornate lobby? An industrialist on a catwalk overlooking a manufacturing floor? A teacher on the playground during recess with kids playing in the background?

Shoot Enough

Be sure you get enough footage. When I see the same shot repeated two or three times in a video, especially as a cutaway, I know the videomaker didn't shoot enough during production. Often it's not sufficient just to shoot whatever the script calls for. Try different angles. Use a low camera or a high one. Get reaction shots—and not just the canned one of the spokesperson listening and nodding. Shoot the kids playing in the sandbox, the dog lying on the rug, the goldfish swimming furiously. You may never use any of it. Or you may be oh-so-glad you shot the extra stuff.

Shoot enough takes. Don't settle for an "acceptable" take; keep shooting until you get what you need. I tell cast and crew, "Okay, we've got one we can use. So the pressure's off. Now let's go for great."

And I may shoot several more takes. What I've learned is that the take that looks good on the monitor in the field may not be the one you'll elect to use when you get in the editing room. I'm not one to shoot takes promiscuously—although I've done thirty or forty takes on two or three occasions when something just wouldn't go right—but I expect to do at least three as we explore the possibilities of the scene and perhaps as many as six or seven until we get something really good.

Shoot for Editing

When I was teaching documentary film, I wouldn't let my students touch a camera until they had learned how to edit. Having editing always in mind changes the way you look at the scene through the viewfinder or on the monitor. It means being sure you have "handles" at the head and tail of each shot so there's room to get in and get out. It means covering the scene with reaction shots, cutaways, and atmosphere shots that suggest the ambiance of the location. It means going outside and shooting an establishing shot of the building, even though what you came for was an interview with a doctor in a laboratory.

Use a Style Appropriate to the Audience

You may like shaky-cam and tilted shots because you feel they bring a vitality and freshness to video, but if you're doing a sales piece on investments for older folks, don't use them. Most seniors don't like that style, and the few who may like it won't complain if you use a more conservative approach.

In my house, where analysis of what appears on TV is a blood sport, we play a game called, "Not for Us." One of us looks at a video on television and says something like, "That makes no sense. Why would they do it that way?"

And the other answers, "Either the production was out of control, or they're *not talking to us*."

LIGHTING

It's one thing to understand that it takes a certain minimum amount of illumination to record a videotape—and with today's video cameras that actually can be not much light at all—and quite another to ac-

cept the fact that *a video is made with light.* I would guess that between the two concepts lie about five years of experience at working
with the tools and trying to get the image on the screen to look like
the image in your head.

Lighting Quality

The amount of light available either does or does not permit an image
to be recorded on video. If there's not enough light for an exposure—
no image. The quality of the light—balance, highlight and shadow
areas, position of light sources, lighting contrast ratio, color tempera-
ture, and so on—determines the look of the image. The better the
lighting, the better the final copies of your video will look to the
audience.

Effective use of lighting can make your images more dramatic,
more colorful, richer, and more luxurious. Throwing a colored
shadow on a wall with a set light and a kukaloris—a cutout placed in
front of the light to cause a shadow pattern—can turn a boring blank
space into an interesting background.

Good lighting can make product shots gleam beautifully and can
take years off the visual age of your spokesperson.

Bring Enough Lights

I have shot documentaries with no more than a four-light Lowell
Tota-Kit and I've shot commercials with access to a full grip truck,
and while the shooting situation determines the type and amount of
lighting one can use, I'll always opt to have extra lighting and grip
equipment available in case I need it.

Just being able to clip a flag in front of a light to move a shadow or
remove an unwanted highlight can save a tremendous amount of time
that otherwise would have to go into relighting. Having one more
light than you thought you'd need sometimes makes the difference
between a conventional scene and one that jumps off the screen with
excitement. So be sure you bring enough lighting and grip equipment
to do the job.

And then a little extra—just in case.

SOUND

Good pictures are the sine qua non of video production, but bad sound makes bad video. Be sure that you have provided for good, professional sound recording as part of your production package.

A Couple of Don'ts

It should go without saying that it's almost impossible to record good production sound solely by using a shotgun microphone mounted on the camera. Even TV news, which has never put a premium on quality, uses the camera mike only for ambiance or as a last resort in an emergency to capture sound that otherwise would be lost. The closer you can get the microphone to the person speaking, the cleaner and clearer the sound will be. A camera mike just doesn't let you move in close enough.

Don't record sound on automatic gain control. It may work all right as long as people are talking. But each time there's silence, the AGC boosts the record volume trying to find something to record. And you get a kind of whooshy, windy sound in every pause. Sounds terrible and can take forever to edit out of the track.

Keep the Sound Clean and Well Separated

You need a sound recordist. Someone has to wear earphones and listen to the sounds being recorded to know what is happening on the sound track and to keep an eye on the recording level to raise or lower the record volume as necessary to maintain clean sound.

In my documentary days I was a staunch believer in the use of a shotgun microphone which the sound recordist held and pointed toward the person speaking. But once I started making information videos and commercials I became a convert to lavaliere microphones, preferably with a wireless transmitter. Today, if possible, I hang a mike on each person speaking so that we get clean sound from everyone. If the recording technology will permit, I'll feed each mike onto a separate audio track to give even greater control and separation in editing and mixing. That way, when several people speak at once, you can pick out the one you want to listen to and mix the other voices in at a low level as background sound.

If you can't use lavalieres, use a boom or fish pole to get the recording microphone as close to the speaker as you can while keeping it out of the picture.

CAMERA WORK

In my early days in production I had to shoot my own stuff. But as I improved as a director, I decided I just wasn't a good enough camera operator to work for me. Since then I've worked with good camera operators, great camera operators, and a couple of pretty bad ones, and what I've learned is that it takes real skill to get consistently good pictures.

Single or Multiple Camera?

How will your video be shot? Most information videos are shot *film style* with a single camera and then edited into final form. This requires a new setup for each new shot.

In some cases you may decide to use multiple cameras. For the installation video for the home security system described in chapter three, I used two cameras so that one could always be on the speaker while the other shot close-ups of the components he was showing or reaction shots of the audience. We fed each camera into a separate VCR with a separate monitor, and then edited the two hours of tape to an hour show.

Be sure that the cameras are balanced alike and matched to present a similar picture. Don't necessarily trust the monitors as they can be off in color or balance. Try switching monitors from one camera to another to see if the picture appears the same.

In a multicamera shoot you may decide to use switched video, calling shots on the fly to produce a program in the form known as "live on tape." If you're going to do that, also feed each camera into its own isolated recorder so that you retain all your options for editing.

Continuity

Assuming your video is a film-style shoot and not a multiple camera, single event like the installation demonstration, the scenes will probably be shot out of order. And that means someone has to be responsible for seeing that what happens in one shot will match whatever happens in the next. There's nothing worse than getting into the editing room and finding out that your golfer walked toward the green with his putter in his left hand, but arrived there in close-up holding the putter in his right.

Actually you can probably get away with that. Even though it's *wrong*, most viewers either won't notice or won't care. But they will notice if a man is on the right and a woman on the left in one shot but their positions are reversed in the next. Or if your character is wearing a colorful hat in one shot and not in the next. And they'll notice if the white or black balance is off from one shot to the next or the color of the scenes just doesn't match.

Camera Support

A shooter running around with a video camera on his shoulder, the Hollywood image of a videomaker, may be okay for broadcast news — after all, Hollywood always shows war correspondents shooting sound interviews in the field with a handheld Bell & Howell *silent* camera — but the unsupported camera has almost no place in shooting an information video. Handheld shooting may sometimes be necessary for covering action and moving quickly from event to event. An audience will accept a little camera wiggle and bump when the scene reeks of spontaneity. But they don't expect to see stationary objects such as buildings, signs, bookcases, furniture, and so on bouncing around on the screen when these things don't bounce around in real life.

Almost all scenes in an information video will be shot with some form of camera support, usually a tripod. That doesn't mean that everything must be at eye level shot for the convenience of the camera operator. Some shots will use a high camera, some a low one. In addition to a standard tripod, it can be nice to have a set of baby legs or a high hat along for low-angle shooting with tripod stability.

A dolly allows smooth camera motion while supporting the camera, and yields a look that is different from merely zooming in or out. To move the camera smoothly in the vertical plane you can use a crane or a jib arm. Either will provide support while offering generous freedom of motion.

To give a steady handheld look there are also options such as the

Steadicam and a new generation of lens stabilizers that can be quite effective.

Camera mounts—often combined with other stabilization devices—provide steady support for cameras mounted on automobiles, boats, planes, motorcycles, and helicopters.

And when all else fails, you can put a small camera on the shoulder or under the arm of a large camera operator and hope for the best. But handheld should always be the last resort, never the first option.

DIRECTING

If the goal of production is to produce a stack of videotapes with everything that you'll need for editing, the purpose of directing is to be sure that the images on those tapes are the best possible and will edit smoothly together. In order to realize the program blueprinted in the script, the video director uses the monitor screen as a palette, creating a set of unique combinations of elements which go together like the paint on an artist's canvas to make a complete picture.

Foreground and Background

While the action of the video normally takes place in the foreground, close to the camera, the director must not neglect the background. Select an interesting setting for the shot. And then, if needed, people it with one or more extras doing something to breathe life into the scene. Otherwise you end up with half a scene, poor verisimilitude, and inadequate visual evidence.

Here's a case in point, a training video about providing better service to customers made for a bank with a humorous detective as its spokesperson in a parody of an early TV private eye show. Early on it shows a scene with the detective and a customer service representative in the main bank during business hours. The scene includes several wide shots of the bank interior. There are no customers in the background. The director was concentrating so hard on the two actors in the foreground that the background was forgotten. Instead of looking like a bank that's doing its best to provide excellent service for its customers, it's shown as a bank that's doing no business at all.

For a health education video I needed a shot of a person having blood drawn in a hospital laboratory. The chair where the person sat was against an uninteresting blank wall. But by moving the chair a foot or so to camera left, the scene would include another part of the lab where there was a receiving counter and some telephones. As I was setting up the shot, a woman who had been hidden by a wall walked into view talking on the phone. It was a nice piece of business, and I incorporated it into the scene. I asked her to stand so that she was hidden by the wall and when she heard me say "Action," she was to count two seconds and step into view. That was all. But it added immensely to the total look of the scene.

Working with People Who Are Not Actors

Some information videos have to be made with volunteers who are not actors. And the prime rule in directing such people is to respect their amateur status and not ask them to act. Just ask them to do whatever they do and videotape it so it looks good.

Don't ask people who are not actors to speak written lines. If you need a sound bite from the new products manager, get it in an interview situation. Ask a question such as, "What would you like to tell people about this new product?" And then keep shooting and asking open-ended questions until you get what you need.

Try to keep the people talking even if they make mistakes. It's a way for them to figure out what they want to say and actually rehearse the statement without realizing it. In editing a video from footage shot by someone else, I came across an interview with my client's marketing director. The video director wanted a two-sentence statement. Each time the marketing director made a mistake of any sort, the director stopped and did another take. It took thirty or forty takes before the marketing director worked out what he wanted to say and how to say it. If the director had encouraged him to make a complete statement each time, regardless of mistakes, he'd have gotten a good one in far fewer takes.

In *Making Documentary Films and Reality Videos* I have a list of mistakes directors often make in working with people who are not actors. I originally listed these as seven deadly sins in working with people who are not actors. But, with the exception of the first one, they're really ways you can get in trouble regardless of whether you're working with volunteer amateurs or professional actors.

One: Treating Amateurs as Actors

The essence of amateur volunteers is that they are not actors. So don't ask them to memorize long speeches, to emote, or, in short, to act. Set up a situation in which they can behave naturally. If they must speak lines, keep the lines short and shoot them in short takes.

Two: Failure to Explain What You're Doing and How Long It Will Take

All producers have a tendency to underestimate the amount of time it will take to shoot a scene and then to shave it a little more when asking for volunteers to be in the production. Even when you are working with paid actors, common courtesy demands a realistic explanation of the task and the time it will take.

Three: Failure to Discuss Wardrobe and Makeup

We're gradually getting past the day of the TV-blue shirt, but checks and patterned fabrics still cause moiré patterns on video, and some colors will bleed in VHS dubs. Makeup is a matter of individual taste, but it should be discussed. Dark beards and transparent skin still cause problems that might be alleviated with a shave and some makeup.

Four: Putting Pressure on the Person

A friend of mine, a physician, was asked to make a statement in a film about patient treatment. Just before the scene was shot, the director said, "We're almost out of film, so we have to do this right." Of course the doctor fluffed a line, and the director blew up. But being low on film was the director's problem, and he had no right to put the pressure, or the blame, on my friend.

Similarly, failure to explain that retakes have to be made for technical reasons may make people wonder if they've done something wrong.

Five: Stopping the Process to Get Them to Do It "Right"

Anything that calls attention to people who are not actors is another way of putting pressure on them for a performance. If they fluff a line, assure them that it's all right, you'll pick it up in the close-up. If they stumble when they enter the room, tell them not to worry, you want to shoot it again from a different angle.

Most professionals will stop when they go up on a line and immediately get ready to shoot another take. In fact, sometimes when they don't like a reading, they'll deliberately fluff a line so you won't use that take. But even with professionals, it's best to keep the pressure off and maintain an attitude of "We're getting closer, and you can do it."

Calling attention to errors just tends to magnify them, until it is the error that the person remembers, not the way to do it right.

Six: Letting the Crew Take Over

When the crew starts to give directions to the people you are recording, you're in trouble. By all means discuss the scene thoroughly with your crew and ask them to bring up any potential technical problems. Make sure the crew understands that when something goes wrong, they are to talk to you, and you'll decide what to say to the talent—regardless of whether you are using a professional or an amateur. It may be that you've been working with your on-camera person, very carefully, building toward something you know you've almost got. That's not the time to burden him or her with a technical something-or-other from your camera operator or sound recordist.

There can be only one director on any shoot. Keep it that way.

Seven: Concentrating on Your Needs Instead of Concentrating on How to Get What You Want from the Person You're Directing

Even a professional actor won't give you what you want just because you want it. That's what directing is all about. With a person who is not an actor it's even more important to make no demands and to find a way to get the person to do what you want—naturally and unselfconsciously.

Calling the Shots

The primary purpose of almost every shot in an information video is to show something to the audience. If it isn't important for the audience to see whatever's in the shot, then it's visual wallpaper, filler stuffed in to provide something on the screen while the message is conveyed through the sound track. And when you find yourself shooting filler, it's time to rethink what you're doing.

Beauty Shots. A beauty shot is meant to show whatever is in the scene to its best advantage. If you're doing a video for a housing developer, you want to show the model homes—exterior and interior—at their most attractive. If it's a golf course, you want to show it as a lush, green environment with lovely flowers, shrubs, and trees. For a restaurant or packaged-food company you may want beauty shots of the ingredients—a perfect red tomato, a cheese with a single thin slice curling away, crusty brown home-baked bread—you get the idea. For the perfect tomato you may have to buy a box of tomatoes and go through it to find two or three *heroes*, the best of the best.

Product Shots. A product shot may be a form of beauty shot. My teacher and friend Sol Worth spent several days setting up and lighting a bottle of Joy perfume for the advertising still that has long since become a classic. But a product shot may also be a demonstration—a new car driving though a beautiful countryside, a side-cutting can opener leaving no sharp edges, a stud or studette working out on a piece of exercise equipment.

Establishing Shots. If it's important for the audience to know where in the world they are at the start of a scene, a short establishing shot will tell them. It may be the exterior of a building, a "love boat" at sea, the HOLLYWOOD sign up in the hills, the Eiffel Tower, a plane taking off or landing—whatever. It lasts a second or two and establishes the geographic or psychological landscape in which the scene takes place.

Atmosphere Shots. Where an establishing shot defines the location of the scene, an atmosphere shot shows its ambiance. The book-lined study suggests a scholar. The crucifix on the wall tells us about the beliefs and may suggest the social status of a family. Antique furniture describes one sort of lifestyle while stark modern chrome and glass furnishings imply another.

Reaction Shots. The tendency when someone is speaking or doing something is to keep the camera on them throughout the speech or action. But video is as much a medium of reaction as one of action. How others respond to what is being said or done is the visual evidence of its importance and impact. Be sure to shoot reactions: the listener nodding in agreement, a big smile, a little kid making a face, a couple of guys doing a high five, the audience standing and applauding the speaker. Reaction shots can be a source of visual humor if the reaction shown is unexpected.

Cutaways. Cutaways are the suture binding up surgery on a scene. They are used to cover an edit from a person talking to the same person earlier or later in the speech. Without a cutaway you have a jump cut where the person's face suddenly jumps to a different position on the screen at the point of the edit. Or a dissolve from the speaker in position at the end of the outgoing speech to the person in another position following the edit. Such a dissolve is always an admission that the videomaker forgot to shoot cutaways. The simplest and best motivated cutaway is a reaction shot. Cut from the speaker to a listener and then back to the speaker. Other cutaways can be any motivated shot available within the scene, such as an atmosphere shot or product shot that complements whatever the speaker is saying.

Dumb Shots and Empty Shots. Every shot in a well-made video should show the audience something they want or need to see. If it doesn't, it's either a dumb shot or an empty shot. A dumb shot is a close-up of the smiling face of a dancer or ice skater in the middle of a routine. They don't dance or skate with their teeth. In cooking shows we often see a tilt down the chef's long white hat, across his face and torso to look into a bowl where he's mixing ingredients. Dumb shot. It's a long cutaway that keeps us from seeing what the chef is doing. No information.

Empty shots are filler: sky and clouds, a turning camera looking straight up into the branches of a tree, an unmotivated tilt up or down the staircase in a historic home, the turning wheels of a truck, car, or train—used once, this may be an establishing shot, but if it's repeated it's filler—meaningless shots of cows in a field, ducks on a pond, or flowers in a vase, or a slow pan across the pictures on a wall or sitting on a piano, where we neither know nor care about the people in the pictures.

Pans, Tilts, and Zooms. Moving camera shots are a ready tool in every videomaker's kit. Sometimes too ready. The director often reaches for a moving camera shot because nothing is moving within the frame. But the slow zoom in or out from a speaker's face may announce to the audience that (1) we're not convinced the speaker alone is interesting enough just to show, and (2) we don't have any better idea for the shot than to move the camera.

Pans and tilts are a slow way to show something too wide or too long to fit comfortably within the frame. It's best to shoot several seconds of the start of the pan or tilt with the camera still, then do the move, coming to rest and shooting several seconds at the end with the camera still. Quite often it's more interesting to cut from the still shot at the start to the still shot at the end, leaving the move out altogether.

PRODUCTION STORY—THE LADY WITH THE WHITE GLOVES

The best shot I ever made in my brief career as a camera operator was a reaction shot. I was shooting a confrontation between student activists and the members of a suburban church for the documentary *The Trouble with Adults Is . . . .* In the scene an earnest young man tries to talk with a well-dressed, middle-aged woman who is leaving church. She answers his initial questions politely. He mistakes this for interest and goes into a monologue about his perception of suburban attitudes. After about thirty seconds, the woman starts to put on her white gloves. I move in for a close-up of her smoothing them down each finger one by one. The reaction shot shows far more elegantly than words that even though he was still talking, she had stopped listening.

13

FINISHING OFF: INFORMATION VIDEO POSTPRODUCTION

Because it's not what you shoot but what you show that counts, postproduction is the heart of the process of creating an information video. Post is where you shape and organize what was envisioned in the script and recorded on tape into a professional program to be shown to an audience.

"WE'LL FIX IT IN POST"

The statement "We'll fix it in post" used to be a joke among video editors because producers would bring in horrendous footage and expect miracles. But as editing tools and toys have become more sophisticated, miracles in post have become almost routine.

It's important to shoot the best possible footage you can. But sometimes a little back room magic can help.

Get a Little Closer
I had a complex dolly shot in a restaurant at the Aladdin Hotel and Casino that ended with a waiter placing a huge whole lobster in front of a guest. We shot a lot of takes and finally ended up with one that I thought showed the ambiance of the restaurant and the attractive food served there. When we showed the cut to the client, however, the food and beverage manager complained that we weren't showing his

beautiful lobster close enough. Back to post, where we did a digital push to a close shot of the lobster filling the screen. Client satisfied.

Overcoming Bad Camera Work

In a video for a hospital's urgent care facility that had been shot by a beginning camera operator who worked part-time for a small-town cable company, there were serious problems with composition and lighting. The client contacted us to see if we could save the project without reshooting. All I saw was the footage, so I don't know what the camera operator had in mind. Nor do I have any idea if the camera had the wrong viewfinder or the shooter just didn't know what to do.

Most shots were framed too wide. Ideal composition would have been at least 50 percent closer. Everything was shot in auto iris, so that when the doctor walked past an open window, the scene went way too dark in order to accommodate the bright backlight. We went through the footage and decided that the best thing to do was to adjust the composition by framing each scene the way it should have been shot. This meant getting closer, and since the original was shot on three-quarter-inch video, it didn't have the resolution for a digital close-up.

The solution we used was to create a black background for the entire video and then open up windows in the background within which we showed the needed shots, properly composed. This actually allowed us to make the video visually richer than the original, because we could open more than one window at a time, giving the effect of multiple events happening throughout the hospital. With digital editing, the images shot on three-quarter-inch video held up as we layered on a second and third window, rather than deteriorating as they would have in rerecording several analog generations.

The Wrong Sign

In that same urgent care video, we had added a shot of a road sign with the name of the hospital on it. There was another sign on the same signpost but it meant nothing to us. Unfortunately, it named another medical entity belonging to the hospital, which had moved or no longer existed. The client loved the shot, but that sign had to go. And it did. The sign had white letters on an orange background. In post we mixed up a digital palette with a matching orange and painted out the letters on the sign.

Other Magic

When you have a problem in the footage, talk it over with a state-of-the-art digital postproduction house and ask for suggestions. Today, if you have a clear idea of what you want and a big enough checkbook, you can make almost anything happen in post.

LOOK AND LOG

Before you go to post, you've got to go over the footage. Yes, you've kept a camera log while you were shooting, and you've marked the takes you think you want to use. But you still need to step back from the hot situation of shooting and look at what you've shot as if it had been done by someone else. Make a VHS dub with a windowprint time code and then log what you've got, tape by tape. For each shot your log should include:

- starting time code
- scene and take numbers from the script or other identification such as the subject of the shot
- brief description of the shot
- your comments, where appropriate

I log everything into a database in my computer so that I can then reorganize the data to print out either a shot-by-shot log for each reel or a tentative editing script of the takes that have been marked good. When you're in post with the clock running you don't want to be saying, "I wonder what happened to that shot of . . . ?" You want to know where it is. The better your logs, the better your chance of finding what you want quickly.

Today there are programs that will let you run the video through your computer and catch the time code and a still of the shot on the fly.

Logging Footage from the Client

If the client will be supplying any or all of the footage to be used, you've got to go over it carefully. Clients think in terms of content. So when they say they've got shots of the opening of the new building or of the product in use, they may simply be telling you that they know a video crew took pictures of it. They may have no idea of what it looks like, and probably have no idea if it can be edited with whatever new footage you plan to shoot or will go with stock footage from other sources that you plan to use.

A client who was a management consultant wanted a sales video—quickly and on the cheap—so shooting was limited. Among the footage he offered were amateur camcorder shots of a seminar he ran on a cruise ship—backlit, his face in shadow, poor resolution, camera always in motion—and footage of the opening of a new hotel by one of his clients, shot outside at night with available light, by a camera operator who would tilt up to the sky to chase fireworks each time they went off. The client had no realization that nothing there could be used in a professional video. Indeed, he probably never looked at the footage.

You have to view and log client footage before you shoot additional footage to go into the video. First, you want to know if the client's footage can even be used. And then you need to know what you'll need to shoot to go with it.

OFF-LINE EDITING

Off-line editing gives the creative editor the opportunity to play and experiment to find the best possible way to present the client's story. The distinction between off-line and on-line editing may soon disappear as more and more production companies and post houses install broadcast-quality digital nonlinear editing.

Originally an off-line was done as a rough cut in an inexpensive editing room, where sophisticated manipulations were few to none—cuts only, no character generator, and no computer graphics, Paintbox, or whatever. But the off-line cost might be about a third of the hourly rate for an on-line suite, giving you a chance to work out the way you wanted the video to go together at an affordable rate. When you had it the way you liked, you showed it to the client, who usually asked for a few changes. And then you took the production to the on-line room where you made a first-quality edited master with all the bells and whistles.

Nonlinear Editing

The first generation of nonlinear systems generally didn't have the memory capacity to output broadcast-quality video. They, too, became off-line systems. In this case, all the camera tapes—or all the takes you planned to work with—were digitized from the original footage to the nonlinear system's hard drive. Once that was done you could call up any shot just by typing its time code into the computer. Nonlinear, for the first time, gave video editing the "what if" capability that film editors have always had. With a few computer keystrokes you could add or remove a shot anywhere in the assembled video just as a film editor splices in a change. In analog editing, making a change has always meant rerecording all the video after the change or working in modules which means more generational deterioration.

Nonlinear editing is fast and flexible. It gives the editor and director the chance to play with the footage. To ask: what happens if we make this shot shorter or longer or put it over here instead of there? Because all the footage you're using is stored on a big hard drive, every shot is accessible in a second or two. No reeling through miles of tape to find the shot you want. As a result, if you know exactly what you want, editing can go much faster in nonlinear than in analog. Or in the same length of time as it would take to do an analog off-line, you can explore many more creative possibilities in nonlinear editing.

Systems are becoming available that allow the videomaker to shoot directly onto a computer disk which can then easily be loaded into the nonlinear system for editing. It's possible tape may become a thing of the past—but don't count on it. They've been saying the same thing about film for my entire professional life. Digital video, however, whether recorded on disk or on videotape, is the wave of the present.

When you do a nonlinear off-line, all of your editing decisions are saved to an edit decision list, called an EDL. The EDL can be moved on disk to the computer controlling a digital on-line editing system where it will automatically reconstruct the video as you did it in the off-line. All you have to do is load the next roll of tape into playback when the computer calls for it.

When an off-line edit is completed it is shown to the client for approval to go to on-line. The approval is based on the content of the off-line video. You have to explain to the client that graphics, effects, and additional sound will all be added in the on-line.

Editing Style

Because of my grounding in documentaries, I'm partial to an editing style that lets the audience see the visual evidence being presented. So I like steady camera work and logical cuts—telling the story with pictures. Most important is to use an editing style that is appropriate to the audience. Show what the audience wants to see in the way they want to see it.

When I was doing golf shows, I learned that golfers want to see how the player on camera swings the golf club and care much less about what happens with the ball. Young viewers are believed to have a short attention span and must be constantly jazzed with special effects, music, and bizarre camera angles, although I've found that young viewers have no problem staying interested in a well-made narrative. Older viewers like videos that look like movies—linear, narrative, well composed, and well realized—that move logically from scene to scene.

Obviously different generations favor different music, and the way you score a video can gain audience acceptance or turn off the audience so much that they can't even watch.

AUDIO POST

If the information video uses a narrator to carry the audio message to the audience, his or her voice has to be recorded in an audio studio. This may be done at an audio house or at a video post house with audio facilities.

The narration may be recorded in the blind, working from the script alone without reference to the picture. This has been the traditional way to do it. The narration is then edited into the video at the appropriate points. Today, however, it's almost as easy—although slightly more expensive—to have the narrator read to picture. A monitor is provided in the announce booth, and the narrator can watch the scene while reading the words from the script. When both audio and video are recorded digitally, it's easy to play a scene over and over until the narration comes out the way you want it. And a narrator reading to picture often brings extra excitement and animation to the reading.

Looping Dialogue

The ability to read to picture and quickly reset the scene digitally makes it easy to loop dialogue for a video. Known as automatic dialogue replacement (ADR) or electronic line replacement (ELR), this is the postproduction technique whereby the actors replace dialogue that wasn't recorded well or has too much background noise. The actors can see themselves on the screen and hear what they said in the original take until they have the timing and inflection down, and then can read their lines again matched to picture.

Music

Once you've worked with a good composer, you'll never want to score a video any other way. Unfortunately, most videos for clients don't have budgets that will permit composed music.

Stock music libraries can provide everything from the musical wallpaper that has been the staple of industrial films to contemporary sounds similar to current popular music and recordings of virtually all classical music. Stock music is relatively inexpensive and easy to use. You pay the audio studio for the time it takes to find and record the music and a licensing fee for the right to use it one time in your video.

What about popular songs from well-known recording artists? These are protected by the copyright on the sheet music and the copyright on the recording as well as by contractual agreements with the artist and the musician's union. So you can't just pull a CD off your player at home and score an information video with it.

But all is not lost. You sometimes can acquire the rights to a specific recording or piece of music. You should be aware, however, that this can be a time-consuming and expensive process. If you have any thought of using popular music, tell your client that you don't know if the rights are available, but if they are they will probably be expensive. Then start early to work on getting the rights. There are companies in Los Angeles and New York that specialize in clearing rights. Otherwise contact the American Society of Composers, Authors, and Publishers (ASCAP) or Broadcast Music Inc. (BMI) in New York (see appendix one). They are the two associations that collect royalties for recorded music.

Sound Sweetening

One of the big advances in video sound has been the use of sound sweetening. Most videotape has room for only two audio tracks on it; a few can handle four. So it has been difficult to give a video the kind of audio richness and complexity that has always been available to filmmakers. A film goes to a sound mix where all of the sounds the filmmaker might want are laid onto a composite audio track. Sound sweetening performs the same function for video.

The edited video—either off-line or on-line—is taken to a digital audio studio where the existing sound on tape is augmented by music, narration, and sound effects and mixed to provide optimum sound quality. The resulting mixed track, usually recorded on digital audio tape, called DAT, with a time code to match the video, can be laid back onto the on-line master in all its glory. Build money for sound sweetening into the budget. It's worth it.

GRAPHICS, TITLES, AND DIGITAL VIDEO EFFECTS

You can do almost anything you can think of to a video image in post. Paintbox has permitted the creation of highly sophisticated and animated graphics as well as the enhancement of video images. Morphing—where one image changes its shape to become something else—has become commonplace. It's relatively easy to rotoscope a video image today—cleaning out all of the background around a person or object so that the remaining image can be moved onto a new background. And digital video effects, called DVE, permit the image to be flipped, shrunk, enlarged, or moved anywhere on the screen while being manipulated in other ways.

Beware: Video Effects Can Be the Car Chases of Editing

Video effects have opened a new world of possibilities for the videomaker. For not a lot of money the image can be manipulated and enhanced in countless ways. The problem is that the sheer availability of video effects allows them to be used promiscuously to shovel in a little erzatz excitement. Hollywood directors tie together a thin script with car chases and explosive special effects to create a production that, like a magic meal, resembles food but contains no nourishment. And some videomakers reach for DVE when they feel the video they're editing lacks intrinsic interest.

Unmotivated effects send a message to your audience that your video lacks a good idea. So beware.

ON-LINE EDITING

The final stage in post is the video on-line. Here, everything that is a part of the video is recorded onto the edited master videotape. The on-line computer will take your off-line edit decision list and record everything that was in the off-line edit onto the edited master. To this you add dissolves and effects, if they weren't built into the off-line, graphics and titles as needed, and final sweetened sound.

One of the virtues of digital editing is that it permits you to add layer upon layer upon layer of images without generational deterioration. Because the images are cloned digitally rather than rerecorded in analog, you are still essentially at first-generation video no matter how many layers you've added.

Film-Look Video
Some post houses now offer what is called a film look in video. It purports to give you a finished video that has the rich look of original shot on film. If this interests you, check it out.

APPROVAL COPY

Unless your client sits with you through the editing process, you'll need to take a copy, usually a VHS dub, of both the off-line and on-line edit to the client for approval. An approval copy should have a time code window along with the superimposed words APPROVAL COPY. This serves two purposes. First, it gives the client a ready reference in time code for any changes. And it prevents the sort of thing that happened with the client mentioned in chapter three, who decided the cost of professionally made release dubs was too high, so he went to his neighborhood video store and had dubs made from the approval copy.

DISTRIBUTION

Your contract with the client probably calls for delivery of an edited master. Distribution copies will normally be the client's responsibility. For most information videos, the number of copies is too small to make it worthwhile to handle making the dubs. But it's your call. You may want to encourage the client to run everything that has to do with the video through you. Therefore you'll handle getting the dubs made even though the mark-up on the job won't cover the cost of your time. Or you may be in the dubbing business as well, in which case making distribution copies is a little profit center for you.

PRODUCTION STORY—WIDE-ANGLE BLUES

For a convention video, we received a number of videotapes with an amateur look that had been shot, I think, by an in-house unit. The client also sent me a beautifully shot, professionally produced video on new approaches to office furniture. The in-house stuff had been shot at a wide-angle setting to include as much as possible horizontally. But this left it with a lot of ugly, empty nothing at the top and bottom of the frame. Cutting it in with the professional video would be like sticking a couple of your Uncle Louie's camcorder shots of his vacation in Atlanta into *Gone With the Wind*. It might get your idea across, but it wouldn't be a pretty sight.

We tried blocking off the top and bottom of the screen, creating a sort of video letter-box effect, and that wide-angle footage began to look less like a mistake and more like wide-screen cinematography. We found that the professional footage, although obviously much better composed than the in-house stuff, could tolerate a similar trim. We let some titles bleed into the black margins at the top and bottom of the screen, and suddenly we had a video with the look of a high-definition television program.

And the client was ecstatic.

Making
Commercials

. . . .

14

ANALYZING COMMERCIALS

For a long time I wouldn't make commercials, not because I had anything against them, quite the opposite. I've always considered making good commercials to be a special skill, practiced by people who love to sell. I just thought they took a kind of talent and dedication that I wasn't sure I possessed. Then a bump in my career path landed me in a small ad agency. I discovered that many people who knew far less about communicating with film and video than I did— and who cared not at all about their clients, but only about their clients' ability to pay—were making spots and making money.

That ended my hands-off attitude. Over the last couple of decades I've made a lot of spots. And nothing pleases me more than to get a call from a client saying, "That spot you made for me is really working." Because there are two bottom lines in making videos for money. One is the money we make. If a project doesn't turn a profit, then it wasn't a money project. The other is client satisfaction. As I said in chapter one, our clients are paying for our best professional skill—and we owe them nothing less.

HIGH COST PER MINUTE

On a cost-per-minute basis, commercials are the most expensive productions known to man. I thought they might run second to a Hollywood special effects movie. But I ran the numbers and even the most expensive of those rarely runs as much as a million dollars a minute, whereas it is not unknown for a national commercial to cost a million dollars or more for thirty seconds.

At the level of local video production the budgets are much lower, of course. They may range from a few hundred dollars for a retail spot, shot in the studio at a TV station in less than an hour, to five figures for a location spot with sophisticated postproduction. Adding a celebrity spokesperson—and these are becoming more common in local spots—can add many thousands of dollars more to the budget. So you can make good money making commercials.

PURPOSE

The purpose of a commercial is to create a favorable impression in the target audience toward the client's products or services. This may include an immediate urge to action or a long-term association of the client's name with some occasional need.

A commercial is always about a benefit to the viewer, either directly or indirectly. National ads promise prettier hair, better nutrition, financial security, higher quality at lower cost, or the experience of driving a wonderful car.

Local retail spots will often be what are known as "price and item" ads. They tell the viewer you can buy these items you want at these low prices at this store. Any spot with the word *sale* in it offers low price as a benefit.

Real estate advertising tends to stress the benefits of location, quality construction, and amenities. I just wrote a spot for a real estate development stuck on a lonely piece of desert in southwest Las Vegas. The agency suggested that the spot stress the benefits of "country living with city convenience."

CONCEPT

The concept for a commercial will usually come from the client or the client's advertising agency. The ad agency will probably write the script, but if the agency lacks a writer experienced with video, it may ask the video production company to script the spot. I know of a production company that made a lot of money doing high-end local commercials for ad agencies that wrote only the audio portion of the script. A director at the production company would create the visual concept.

Doing Creative Work "On Spec"

Clients and small ad agencies will sometimes ask videomakers to do a script "on spec" with the tacit understanding that if they like the concept, they'll give the contract for production to the videomaker. I am opposed to doing creative work speculatively. For one thing, clients who ask for work on spec are usually not the kind of clients one wants to cultivate. Obviously, they tend to be people who want to get something for nothing. For another, once your creative ideas are out of the box, there's no way to stuff them back in. The client has gotten you to work for him without paying for it. This is sometimes a way for ad agencies to come up with creative ideas to impress their clients, and you get no guarantee that you'll get the work.

I recognize that if you're a newcomer to the field, you may feel you need to do some spec work to gain experience, prove your ability, and build up your sample file. Mostly, you'll just be exploited. When I relocated into a new market I had a producer suggest that I write commercials for him on spec and if he sold them to a client he'd pay me very well. When I declined, he said, "I don't see how you're ever going to make any money in this market if you won't." I didn't see how I'd ever make any money giving my services away. A year later he'd closed his big office and moved his operation into his house, which may tell you how effective his spec work marketing strategy turned out to be.

If you really feel you need a speculative project to learn on, find a nonprofit organization you like and volunteer to do something for them. You'll feel good about it, and you may even be able to take a tax write-off.

Is the Concept Shootable?

When the commercial concept comes fully scripted from the agency, the videomaker really has just two things to do. The first is to review the script to make sure it is shootable.

Can it be done in the time available? I once had a client send me the script for a 30-second spot that timed out to four and a half minutes.

Does it make visual sense? Is the script organized to make a visual argument? Clients and even agency copywriters can get hung up on the audio side and neglect to tell their story with pictures.

Is it complete? Have all the essential elements been included? Does it show benefit? Does it tell how to get the benefit (name and address of the store, 800 number, etc.)? Does it have a call to action?

What's the Budget?

The videomaker's other responsibility is to cost out the production and come back with a budget or bid. It's always good to get some idea of how much the client hopes to spend. Then if you find budget-busting elements in the script—such as helicopter shots, celebrity talent, copyrighted music, or costly special effects—you may be able to suggest a less expensive alternative.

If the client's expectations are unrealistic, be careful. I just did a bid for a spot that will involve shooting on location in two shopping malls. The agency said that the client "hopes to do this fairly inexpensively." I had to point out that the concept involves two locations on opposite sides of town, which means setting up and breaking down twice. And that trying to record dialogue in a noisy location could take a long time. We put together a bid that we could live with if we got the job, even though we expected that it was significantly higher than the client's expectations. The only thing worse than losing a bid is getting the job and losing money.

WHAT A COMMERCIAL CAN AND CANNOT DO

A good commercial should make the target audience want to *try* the product or service, but it won't overcome a shoddy product or one that fails to deliver the benefit it promises. A good commercial will put a bad product out of business in a hurry, because it will get a lot of people to try it, after which they—and everyone they talk with—will know that the product is no good.

As pointed out in chapter four, your job as the videomaker is to deliver the target audience to the sales situation. After that it's up to the client to make the sale.

Target Audience

A commercial is designed for the target audience most likely to be interested in buying the client's product or service. The reason Cadillac commercials are found in televised coverage of golf tournaments is that General Motors believes that's where they'll find potential Cadillac buyers. That's also the reason Cadillac never sponsored *Beavis and Butt-head*. Someone else worked that side of the street.

McDonald's tried to sell adult sandwiches to grown-ups without a clear idea of target audience and ended up alienating both the adults they were targeting and the kids and their families who are the solid backbone of their business. It may also have been that their marketing concept was all wrong. Maybe a fast-food place with a playground in front should consider any adult business they get pure serendipity. Or maybe like Coca-Cola with the "new Coke" fiasco, they forgot that their most loyal customers are those who grew up with their product and like it just the way it is. What I do know is that the McDonald's adult menu spots were smarmy, trying to suck up to adults by making fun of kids. In essence, they were designed for a childish mentality, not for real grown-ups. Missed the target audience; missed the sale.

Every Frame a Perfect Picture

A 30-second commercial is nine hundred frames of video, and every frame must be perfect. This is one reason making commercials is the most expensive form of video production. Unintentionally jiggly camera work or out-of-focus shots will interfere with the direct connection between the client's message and the viewer's buying impulse. You wouldn't use an audio take in which the narrator stumbles over a line of copy, and you shouldn't use a video take in which the camera operator bobbles the shot.

STYLE

The best style for a commercial is the one that works:

- It attracts the target audience and carries the message.
- It makes people on the way to the kitchen or bathroom during the commercial break pause to watch the spot.
- It leaves an indelible impression on the viewer of the benefit being offered, the name of the product or service, and where or how to get it.

Straight Sell

There's an attitude prevalent among people new to advertising—and some who have been around long enough to know better—that a straight sell is a hard sell is a bad sell. That's ridiculous. *Most* advertising is straight sell. Its message is "to get this benefit; buy this product now."

- Those thirtysomething women on TV earnestly explaining the value of feminine hygiene products are doing straight sell advertising.
- The ads for your local department store, furniture store, appliance store, drugstore, or supermarket are almost all straight sell. They say: we have this product at this price and you can buy it now at our store.
- How about the old guy selling Medicare supplement insurance? The used car dealer pushing second-chance financing? The aging actors selling lawn care products or dog food? All straight sell.

The reason straight sell works is that people want to know about products and services that fill a need in their lives. Just as all the unsolicited advertising in your mailbox *that you're not interested in* is called junk mail, the straight sell commercials that try to convince you to buy something you don't want are considered bad hard sell. All other straight sell commercials are just *information*.

Fantasy

New car commercials are often fantasies. They won't show a spouse complaining about your driving, kids whining in the backseat, or a dog slobbering all over the upholstery. Instead, they'll show the new car alone on a country road, away from traffic and stoplights, moving swiftly and skillfully through gorgeous scenery. Hey, if buying this car can change your life that much, it doesn't matter what it costs.

Perfume and cologne ads are almost always based on sexual fantasies. Jeans ads have gone that way, also. Greeting card commercials will often sell the fantasy of a happy family to whom every special day is a loving memory. Diet plans sell the fantasy of a thinner, more attractive, sexier you.

Humor

Spots that make you laugh get your attention and, if they are well done, help you to remember the product. They cut through the clutter of a commercial break, standing out amid the straight sell commercials. And once they've established a humorous theme for the product, they may even cause you to look forward to the next commercial as a form of entertainment.

In advertising, it doesn't get much better than that.

A spot from Germany that made the international CLIO awards shows a new car arriving at an airport. A couple gets out and the man, in a hurry, hands the keys to the woman. She has obviously not driven the car before and asks, "Where are the headlights?"

"Left of the steering wheel," he says. "The little lever."

"And the reverse gear?"

He's already hurrying into the terminal, but turns to say, "Top left."

She runs after him and asks, "And the gas tank?"

He stops dead, pauses to think, tries to remember, says nothing as the silence stretches out. It's clear he has no idea. As he stands looking confused, a narrator says simply, "Up to eight hundred miles without refueling. The Audi A6 TDI." Information that makes you smile.

Realism

The documentary approach to advertising adds heavy credibility to the sponsor's message. The more the viewers are convinced that they are watching something that really happened, the more likely they are to try the product. Volvo ran a campaign which showed a number of real people, called them by name, and said in narration that each of them was convinced that a car—their Volvo—saved their life.

New product demonstrations are often done as realistic approaches, often with some reference to a hidden camera. We see people trying a new detergent or tasting a new dessert, supposedly unaware that they are being videotaped as they react to their first use of the product. Or, as one of my professors at The Annenberg School of Communications pointed out years ago, the folks we see in the spots could all be actors, and, yes, the camera may be hidden, but that doesn't mean that they don't know it's there. They may be well aware of the camera, even though it is actually hidden from view.

Dramatization

I like good dramatizations; hate bad ones. Good ones show me people I wouldn't mind living next to, doing something believable, in which a sponsor's product plays a part. There's an ad for Tylenol that shows a woman talking with her father while he washes the car. He asks her if the stress on her job is still causing headaches. She says it does, now and then, but she takes Tylenol to handle it.

He says, "I still think you should quit that job and come to work for me."

She answers, "Oh, sure. No stress there."

This spot works because we believe in those people. The dialogue is realistic, and the situation fits with our knowledge of human behavior.

Bad dramatizations are just the opposite. The situation doesn't ring true. And the dialogue sounds like it was written by the president of the sponsoring company, not by a scriptwriter who knows how to put believable words in an actor's mouth. Ask yourself, "Would I want to have dinner with these people?" If the answer is no, it's probably a bad dramatization.

Just the Name

Budweiser has created a body of advertising that simply shows an interesting scene leading up to the Budweiser logo and slogan in the last five seconds. One spot shows a highway in the desert. A chicken crosses the road—tentatively at first, then with more assurance. She reaches the other side while the theme from *2001* plays triumphantly. Cut to two guys sitting on a porch watching, then back to the chicken as she looks up at a large Budweiser sign and seems to cluck the word, "Bud."

The two guys on the porch look at each other, and one says, "Well, guess that answers that question."

Twenty-five seconds of spot to get your attention. Five seconds to sell the product.

Nike has done the same thing with spots showing an extreme—sometimes impossible—sports effort leading up to the Nike check and the slogan, "Just do it!"

This kind of spot is only effective when the advertiser has a good reputation to start with and an immense budget for air time, so that the spots are being seen over and over again by the target audience.

Look and Learn

The way to learn to make good spots is to watch spots. Lots of them. The bad with the good. When a spot catches your interest, ask yourself why. Try to see it again. Try to tape it so you can study it. I tape the spots during special events such as the Super Bowl, because I know I'll see what the sponsors consider their best work.

But when a spot turns you off, don't turn away. You can learn the most from a spot that fails. Watch it. Tape it. Analyze it. See if you can pinpoint what makes it not work for you. If you're not in the target audience, then check with someone who is. It sometimes happens that I see a woman's spot, and just as I'm about to say, "Phew, that's bad," my partner, who has been a female all her life, will say something like, "That's nice. I like that." And I have to re-evaluate.

ELEMENTS AND STRUCTURE

The elements of a successful commercial are easy to list, harder to do. In thirty or sixty seconds, the spot must:

- get the audience's attention
- demonstrate a product and/or present a benefit

- tell how and where to get the product or service
- ask for the sale or ask the audience to take the next step

Beginning, Middle, and Ending

Every well-made commercial has a classic beginning, middle, and ending structure. The beginning catches your attention and introduces the topic. The middle demonstrates the product or presents or implies the benefit. And the ending gives the good news—how you can take advantage of this wonderful thing.

There is a spot for Baked Lay's Potato Chips that opens with Miss Piggy in a nightclub being offered her choice of two bags of chips. She chooses both. It catches our attention because we know that if Miss Piggy is there, something funny has to be coming.

In the middle a handsome man in evening clothes arrives, and he and Miss Piggy lock gazes as we hear someone singing "Some Enchanted Evening." The handsome man dances lovingly with Miss Piggy, kissing and nibbling at her. He says, "Oh, Miss Piggy, I nuzzle your neck. I nibble your hand. I eat your chips." Miss Piggy says, "Hunh-uh," and backhands him out of the room.

The ending shows the two bags of chips and Miss Piggy eating more chips. The narrator says, "The low-fat new flavors of Baked Lays Potato Chips. You'll really want to hog 'em." A complete romantic comedy in thirty seconds.

Solving a Problem

Commercials often open by showing a problem of some sort. The middle shows how the client's product or service can solve this problem for the viewer. The ending reinforces the name of the product and tells the viewer how and where to get it. Good spots use a real problem and real solution.

Some spots try to set up a straw man and knock him down. IBM has a spot that asks, "What does it take to run an airline? In order to get everything done, you have to meet with everyone." And the spot shows a crowd of different people who have something to do with airline operation from mechanics to chefs to flight attendants. Then it shows two men and one laptop at a conference table, while the narrator says, "Let IBM do it for you." Okay, we all know that a lot of information can be moved quickly by computer. But almost anyone in a management position also knows that trying to meet with *everyone* is the worst possible way to run an airline. If you can't delegate, you become a bottleneck. And it doesn't matter whether you are trying to meet face-to-face or on a computer network.

If the problem you pose isn't believable, how credible can your solution be?

ACTING IN COMMERCIALS

If you are making a local spot that requires actors, you are usually limited to the talent available in your locale for the amount of money your budget will tolerate. Since the actors will carry the sponsor's message to the audience, it is crucial that they be able to play the part believably. A good actor can often triumph over badly written dialogue, although they can give you so much more if they have decent words to work with. But bad acting will always ruin a spot, no matter how well-written the script.

In a 30-second spot you have no time to develop character. The audience must understand the player's part in the scheme of things instantly, because if they are wondering who this person is and what he or she is doing, they're not getting the message. And the players must be able to work together effectively. So hold auditions. And try different combinations of people until you get what you need.

VISUAL PRESENTATION

Remember that the best commercials are strong visual statements. Even if you are using a spokesperson who tells the sponsor's message to the viewers, put your spokes in a situation that is interesting to look at and then shoot in a way that makes the person look interesting. There is nothing duller than a man or woman walking slowly toward the camera, talking sincerely, and moving their hands up and down for emphasis. Anything you can do to improve on that will improve your spot.

PRODUCTION STORY—THE UNION MAIDS

A production company I worked with had been hired by the local hotel workers' union to do several commercials to arouse public support for the union before they went into contract negotiations with several major Waikiki hotels. Among other things, the client feared the hotels wanted to cut back on the benefits they had been providing to retired workers, and they asked the videomakers to do a preemptive strike. The theme of the campaign was, "All Hawaii's hotel workers are asking for is fairness and dignity."

The last thing anyone wanted to do was to put the union president on camera complaining about the hotel owners. Who'd pay attention to that? The producer wanted spots with a strong emotional appeal. The videomakers created a spot that shows a group of grandmas sitting around a picnic table in a lovely Honolulu park, passing around a get-well card for each person to sign. They're a nice bunch of ladies. When you see them, you've got to like them. We hear the voice of one of the women.

                    WOMAN
                 (off camera)
          We all worked together in the hotels, and
          we're retired now. Today, we're sending a
          card to Esther. She's in the hospital. . . .
          But she'll be okay. She has medical
          benefits through our union.

The card comes to one of the women as the camera pushes in slowly to a close-up of her face. She looks concerned.

                    WOMAN
                 (off camera)
          But now they say the big hotels want to
          reduce medical benefits for their workers.
          And they want to take away the benefits
          we retired workers have always had. Is

> that fair? To take away something we've
> planned our lives around?

The union logo comes up as the announcer states the theme.

> ANNOUNCER
> All Hawaii's hotel workers are asking for
> is fairness and dignity.

And the woman speaks for the last time . . .

> WOMAN
> (off camera)
> Don't take it away.

This was one of three spots that ran during the contract negotiations. What makes this spot work is, first of all, it's visual. We see the people we're talking about dealing with the kind of situation we're talking about—a woman like them, who is in the hospital. The clearly implied message is that a change in health care status for retired workers would take away the dignity these grandmothers have worked for all their lives. It just wouldn't be fair. Who could sympathize with a large hotel corporation that would take away a grandmother's health benefits?

The result of the campaign was that the union didn't have to go on strike. And the grannies didn't lose their health insurance.

15

FACTORS AFFECTING SALES SUCCESS

When I had my first job in advertising, there was a lot of talk about a brewer who had dumped his ad agency. The agency had created a television campaign using humorous cartoon characters, and it seemed to accomplish all one could ask of a commercial. Viewers enjoyed and remembered the spots and had a positive attitude toward the company's beer. But sales didn't go up, and eventually the agency was fired.

The way the story went, the problem was not the agency's at all. Marketing studies showed that customers were asking for the beer at their beer distributor or supermarket—and not finding it. It turned out that the brewer had undertaken a national advertising campaign without first setting up effective nationwide distribution. The commercials were working. But sales failed to go up because the beer wasn't in the stores for people to buy. A year later, when the brewer had solved the distribution problems, it brought back the award-winning and highly effective cartoon campaign. And this time sales went up.

MOTIVATE THE AUDIENCE

Sales success obviously depends on how well a commercial motivates the audience to do whatever is wanted—to buy the product, make the phone call, vote for the candidate, or send money to save the rain forest. If a commercial doesn't motivate the audience, it's useless.

Worse than useless, in fact, because a bad commercial could be turning off potential customers who otherwise might try the product if they simply ran into it at a point of purchase.

How well the spot motivates the target audience is, therefore, a production consideration. You must design and produce commercials that make people want to buy—and doing that rests on a combination of creative concept and professional execution.

Bad Concept

If the concept comes from the client or the client's ad agency, and in your opinion it is no good, what are you going to do?

I think it is reasonable to raise some questions about a concept you think won't work. You might ask if the spot is pitched at the right age level, or if the spot should have more benefit in it or a stronger call to action. But if the client and agency are adamant, you either have to walk away from the job or make the best spot you can from the script you've been given.

FACTORS BEYOND YOUR CONTROL

Let's say you make a spot that's so good the postproduction crew gives you a standing ovation when you finish editing. Everyone who sees it is interested in the product. There are still a number of factors beyond your control that affect the sales success of the client's product or service.

Price

Sales can never be great for a product that costs too much. Price has to equal perceived value or the public won't buy. And you won't be setting the price.

How much is too much? The price is too high when people say, "Yeah, I like it. But I'm not going to pay that much for it."

The Spot Buy

No matter how good a spot you make, it can't be effective unless it's seen by the target audience. And that depends on the size of the spot buy and the location of the commercials.

Is the buy large enough to reach a significant percentage of the target audience, not just once but several times? It is asking a lot of a commercial to expect it to make a deep and lasting impression the first time it runs. It may be a great spot, but it isn't going to reach the people who have gotten up to go to the bathroom or the kitchen, the ones who have clicked to another channel during the commercials to see what's going on, or those who have started a conversation while they wait for the program to return. What normally happens is that the viewer gradually becomes aware of a commercial, and usually needs to be exposed to it several times in order to get the full message.

Have the spots been placed in programming which the target audience watches? In buying spots on local TV and cable stations, the advertiser can either select positions within specific programs or within a block of time. It's less expensive to buy in a time period than in a single show, and the broader the time period the lower the cost. But unless the advertiser has reasonable assurance that the commercials will run in programming that attracts the target audience, the lower cost may be false economy. Unless the videomaker also is functioning as the client's ad agency, the spot buy is in someone else's hands.

Campaign Support

Is your commercial out there standing alone, expected to do the whole job itself like a Texas Ranger at a riot, or is it part of a coordinated campaign? Will there be supporting ads in newspapers? Will your TV spot be backed by radio commercials? Is there a direct mail or coupon campaign?

Do the other elements of the campaign reinforce the message of the TV spot? I've seen advertisers create a TV spot that is wholly different from the message of the newspaper ads and the concepts for their radio commercials. Instead of a coordinated multiple medium campaign, they're running three separate campaigns, each in a different medium. And that's much less effective.

Point of Purchase

As part of a coordinated campaign, has the client commissioned point of purchase advertising? This can be anything from a stick-on label that reads "AS SEEN ON TV" to a stand-up full-sized figure of the spokes-person in the commercial holding a sign that says, "HERE IT IS!"

Is the product getting decent shelf space? Has the client arranged for special displays of the product? The more that is done to call attention to the product and remind the prospective customer of the sales message at the point of purchase, the better sales will be.

Competition

What's the competition like? Is there a better product available? Is there an equivalent product at a better price? Is your product able to beat the competition on quality or price, or on some other benefit such as service?

PRODUCTION STORY—CREATIVE INTANGIBLES

There are a host of little things that can bring a routine spot to life. Christopher Toyne, a producer-director who is a lot of fun to work with, showed me the value of whooshes in a sound track some years back. These are soft whooshing sounds accompanying graphics as they fly onto the screen, calling attention to them and giving them more substance. I've also accomplished the same thing with a single tone from a triangle. It just adds that little bit extra.

But I'm convinced that the best creative intangibles are human factors that add an extra measure of believability to the message of the spot. I once did a series of commercials over a couple of years for a hospital. Each spot dramatized some aspect of the hospital's service to the community. One was on the hospital's family-based obstetric ser-vices, which encouraged fathers to be in the birthing room for the delivery of their child—a relatively new idea at the time.

The spot shows a well-dressed man hurrying through the hospital, washing up and putting on a scrub suit, just as if he were a doctor. He enters the delivery area and joins a woman there who is obviously getting ready to deliver. The woman turns to him and smiles, and it is only then that the narration lets the audience know that this is a father, not a doctor. We shot several close-ups of the man, and in one he winked at his "wife."

I put twenty frames of that wink—two-thirds of a second—into the final spot, and it made all the difference in the world. Suddenly, what had been a sort of realistic reenactment of one of the benefits of using the hospital's obstetric department changed and became the story of two people having a baby. Yes, it was well cast. Yes, we had the complete cooperation of the hospital staff so that we had a realistic look throughout. I'm even willing to grant that I wrote a good spot and directed it with care.

But it was that loving twenty-frame wink that the actor did spontaneously—I never thought of it—that lifted the scene out of a routine institutional commercial and brought the spot to life.

16

PRODUCTION AND POSTPRODUCTION OF A COMMERCIAL

Commercial production is the most meticulous, frame-by-frame recording and editing known to man. In shooting a commercial, you're going to keep in mind all of the principals of production detailed in chapter twelve plus an unrelenting determination to get the best possible video for each scene in the script. In editing a spot you'll select from the various elements of postproduction technology described in chapter thirteen to create the richest and best organized short video you can make. The aim is to deliver to your client a little gem of a commercial, nine hundred perfect frames of video—eighteen hundred if you're making a 60-second spot—that unerringly deliver the sponsor's message to the viewer.

GET IT RIGHT IN PRODUCTION

The first critical element of commercial production is to shoot it correctly. You never want to have to say, "We'll save it in post." And that means making sure that each shot is properly lit and the sound is clean and clear, being certain that the action works and the words are spoken exactly as written, and ensuring that the scene times to the proper length—neither too short nor too long.

In an information video the videomaker often has many options and a great deal of flexibility, so that if a scene doesn't go exactly as hoped, it may be possible to substitute something else. Possibly the scene may even be eliminated. A commercial, on the other hand, is the most carefully planned and documented of all media productions. Each scene is written, timed, storyboarded, approved by the client, blocked for action and camera, and then shot over and over again. It is not unusual in commercial production for the same three- or four-second shot to be repeated twenty, thirty, even fifty times until the director is satisfied that what has been recorded is what is needed. By way of comparison, consider that a scene shot for a feature film rarely has more than a handful of retakes.

Rehearsal on Camera

One reason for retakes is that modestly budgeted local commercials almost never allow time for rehearsal prior to principal photography. One hopes the actors will arrive at the set with their lines memorized. After all, a 30-second spot has only about fifty or sixty words in it. That's not a lot for the actor to learn the night before. One can hope. But it is not uncommon for actors actually to learn the lines during the camera rehearsal and the first few takes.

I promise you'll make a better spot if you can build money into the budget to pay the actors and director for a rehearsal prior to production. That way you work out any problems in private and may actually save some of the cost of crew and equipment time on location.

Timing Is Crucial

In a commercial, if each scene runs a fraction of a second long, you could end up with a 31- or 32-second spot that no TV station in the country would play. Often the scriptwriter, especially if fairly inexperienced, will underestimate the time a scene will take or the length of time required to read the narration. So you need to have a clear sense of the maximum running time for each shot. And you need to time each take with an accurate stopwatch so that you know precisely how long it runs.

Technical Excellence Is an Absolute Necessity

A commercial must go into postproduction with excellent picture and sound. Therefore every frame must be pristine—or must be capable of being made so. Everything counts:

- lighting
- camera work
- composition
- color
- sound quality
- acting
- continuity

In addition, the sponsor's product must look appealing, and if it's some kind of foodstuff, it has to look good enough to eat. Two hundred hamburgers might be cooked for a fast-food commercial in order to get one perfect hero to show on camera.

CUT THROUGH THE CLUTTER

Commercials always exist in a tumultuous, competitive environment of too many products competing for the viewer's attention. And today's viewers feel no sense of obligation to the sponsor providing the movie, sitcom, or ball game they're watching. In the early days of television the sponsor's commercial message was showcased as a special part of the program. Today, especially in local television, stations try to cram as many spots into a commercial break as they can. Which means that most of the time your spot is trapped in a crowd.

Some advertisers make their commercials loud to try to attract attention. Some repeat the message over and over. Some go silent and put the message in images and graphics in the hope that this will stand out among all the shouting. Some go black and white for the same reason.

In short, anything that you can do in shooting and posting the spot that will help to cut through the clutter and make the client's message stand out, is worth doing. In planning the production of your spot, try to find ways to make it jump out of the crowd. You may be shooting a simple dialogue between a husband and wife, but if you can set them in an unusual and interesting location that is also appropriate to the message, you may give your spot that extra something that makes it memorable.

MAKE IT RICH IN POST

Postproduction of a commercial is much more than just selection and assembly of the best shots from production. It is a process of enrichment and refinement to produce the best short video possible. A commercial is the most pampered of all video productions. And your goal as the videomaker is to send copies to air that are crisp, clean, colorful, and burnished to a high gloss in editing.

Pictures First
Remember that audiences will recognize and react to what they see much faster than to what they hear. And in a commercial, time is limited. Edit the commercial to make a strong visual statement to the audience. The more clearly you demonstrate the product or service visually, the easier it will be for the audience to get the sponsor's message. So your first job in editing is to be sure that the visual message is clear.

Image Modification
In the digital postproduction facilities available today, almost any modification to the image that you can think of can be accomplished—as long as you have the money to pay for it. The best of these are graphic manipulations that help to tell the story and to stimulate audience interest. The poorest are unmotivated effects that seem to have been included just because the postproduction facility had the ability to make them.

Avoid Tricky Transitions
Be careful about the use of video effects, especially in transitions from one scene to the next. All other things being equal, the best presentation is still a strong visual sequence in which each scene cuts cleanly to the next one. Even changing from a cut to a dissolve changes the meaning of the transition. It also makes each scene a little harder to grasp, because a dissolve overlaps one scene with another, and meaning becomes fuzzy in the overlap. In a commercial, where it is not uncommon to have a scene that lasts less than a second, a fuzzy overlap may not leave enough clear image to be recognizable. And

when the transitions become even more complex and time consuming, the area of fuzziness becomes larger, making the commercial harder to understand.

On the other hand, if a push or wipe or other transition helps to clarify the change from one scene to the next, by all means use it. But take a look at the best commercials, the ones that win the top awards and are showcased in high-priced programming. You'll find that the narrative line is very clean. Videomakers with big budgets don't spend the money on "car chase" visual effects. They use it to make sure everyone understands the message.

Character Generator and Graphics

You may hang a lot of information in a commercial in little signs and graphics. At the elementary level these are created with a character generator during the on-line edit. If your spot features price as a benefit, you'll probably include a graphic that shows the price. If it's a sale price, you may be required by law to put up a graphic that tells when the sale ends. If the price includes a monthly payment, you probably have to show a disclaimer that tells how the monthly payment is arrived at. And so on.

You need to be thinking about how and where you are going to place these graphic elements in your spot while you are shooting, so you have room to fit them in when you get to post.

AUDIO POSTPRODUCTION

Keeping the spot visual doesn't mean to neglect the audio track. There's a school of commercial making that holds that since everyone is on their way to the bathroom or the kitchen when a commercial comes on, the sponsor's message needs to be in the audio track so that the audience will hear it even if they don't see it.

The head of a small agency told me a story about people *listening* to TV commercials. The agency did a series of TV spots for a storage locker company. Each spot showed black-and-white silhouettes of people acting out the need for more storage space. The spots all had a strong soundtrack to go with the visuals. The agency had instituted a tracking system to find out how people coming in to rent a storage locker had heard about this company. "There was a blank on the application form that asked, 'How did you hear about us?' " the agency manager said. "About 20 percent said they had heard the company's commercials on radio. That was interesting, because we weren't doing any radio advertising for that client.

"When we looked at the whole advertising plan, we found the answer. We had been buying a package of daytime spots aimed primarily at talk shows and soap operas. The package also scheduled a few spots in late afternoon children's cartoon shows. They were so inexpensive that we just let them run. And these, we finally deduced, were our radio spots. Mom was using the cartoons as a baby-sitter while getting dinner ready. She wasn't watching TV, but she was listening to it. And when our ministorage spots came on, she heard them. To her, they were radio commercials."

Music Selection

Music libraries abound with 30- and 60-second cuts that you can license as background music for your spot. The trick is to find music that exactly fits the mood of your commercial and that hasn't already been used by someone else. One solution, of course, is to work with a composer who will score your spot with original music. This is effective, but expensive. Another is to work with a music director at a sound studio who keeps up on what music is in use by what sponsors. It may also be possible to arrange for a limited exclusive use of a piece of stock music.

And there are companies that will create a jingle for your client and provide you with a variety of 30- and 60-second music beds for use in television and radio commercials. Sometimes the same tune may be used for different sponsors in different cities with the lyrics of the jingle changed to suit the sponsor. But each sponsor has exclusive use of the jingle in its market.

Recording Narration before Editing

Because timing is so critical in a commercial, many videomakers record the narration before going into editing. They can then adjust picture to fit narration—or move narration to fit picture—as needed.

If the spot has wall-to-wall narration, the narration absolutely has to be recorded first, so that the picture can be edited to fit the words.

Sweetening

Usually the last step in postproduction is to sweeten the sound, mixing voice and narration and adding sound effects as necessary. In today's digital editing suite you are limited only by your own imagination. Be sure that you have good separation between voice and music. That is, when the narrator is speaking, the music level is held well below the level of the voice so that the words are clearly audible.

As with the use of visual effects, adding sound effects just because they are available will probably just clutter the spot with audio.

APPROVAL AND DISTRIBUTION

I try to have my client with me during the on-line edit or I arrange to have the client meet me at the postproduction facility just before the on-line session ends to view and approve the spot. The reasons for this are:

- It's expensive to make changes after the on-line session has ended; much less costly to make them during the session. If the client is with you during post, his or her presence alone gives tacit approval to what you are doing.
- The client almost always wants to get the spot on the air as soon as it is made. You don't want to have to go through a lengthy approval process if you can avoid it. Approval by the client during the on-line session means that you can go ahead and get dubs out to the stations.

Bear in mind that there are some clients you simply don't want to have with you during post. They don't understand what's happening. They get nervous that "everything seems to be taking so long." They may try to take over and give instructions to the editor. Or they have no tolerance for experimentation, for trying something in editing that if it works could be great and if it doesn't is instantly forgotten about.

They'll see this kind of play as evidence that you don't know what you're doing.

For this kind of client, the best thing to do is a fairly complete off-line with as much of the final graphics and sound included as possible. You then take this to the client and show it for approval to go to on-line. And build in a contingency fee for additional on-line time in case the client changes his or her mind.

Station Dubs

The last step is to have the post house make copies to send to all the TV and cable stations that will be airing the spot. Be sure that each spot you make has a job number and a title, and that these are clearly shown in the countdown graphic on the videotape before the spot and on each videocassette and box. If you're working with an ad agency, the job number and title of the spot will probably come from the agency. If it doesn't, use your own.

The number and title are used by the TV station's traffic department to schedule spots for broadcast. You want to be sure the right one goes on the air. If you're doing a sale spot, for example, you may make the same basic spot with three different endings. One says the sale starts Friday. The second says the sale is on now. And the third says the sale ends today. Each of these versions should have a different job number and title, so that the correct version runs at the correct time.

Allow Time for Distribution

A video spot is technically ready to air the moment the dub is made. But that doesn't mean it can go directly from the post house to the station and play tonight. You have to allow sufficient time from the end of on-line editing for:

- *Dubs to be made.* Many post houses do these overnight at a reduced rate. Yes, you can have dubs made during the on-line, and you'll pay on-line prices for the privilege.
- *Delivery.* Someone has to pick up the spot at the post house, the ad agency, or your production office and take it to the station. Be

sure you understand who is going to be responsible for this and how much time to allow.

- *Station review.* You not only have to have approval from your client, but also most stations want to review the spot to be sure it doesn't violate any of the many regulations about advertising they have to live with, and that it is technically made to broadcast-quality standards.
- *Station technical activities.* The station airing the spot may make a further dub from the tape you send out to a tape cartridge or hard drive so that it can be scheduled and played automatically. This, too, takes time.

Be sure you give your client at least one really good VHS copy of the spot. A personal VHS copy is the best way to schmooze a client. If I'm working with an ad agency, I'll make a minimum of three VHS copies: One for the sponsor, one for the agency, and one for my files. More if there are several people involved.

Incidentally, these VHS dubs will come from the post house bearing a printed label with the post house's name and address, unless you instruct otherwise. Six months from now, when the client needs a new spot, you don't want them calling the post house; you want them to call you. So make your own labels and be sure they are on the box and the tape when it goes to the client.

PRODUCTION STORY—THE 150-TAKE SPOT
THAT ELECTED A GOVERNOR

A commercial has to be right or it's not worth airing. When John Waihee, then lieutenant governor of Hawaii, decided to run for governor, the ad agency handling his campaign and its production company decided to do a series of documentary-style commercials to introduce him to the voters. They tapped me to write and direct the spots. In the primary, Waihee was up against Congressman Cec Heftel, who was generally considered by most political analysts to be far and away the front-runner. As the primary campaign progressed, we moved away from the documentary spots we had started with to straight message commercials. The final spot was to air in the last couple of days before the primary election, which was held on a Saturday.

This was the message:

> JOHN WAIHEE
> Saturday is election day. And here's what
> matters. What matters is that I have the
> most experience in state government and
> have tackled the tough issues as lieutenant
> governor. What matters is that when you
> need help, you can count on me to open the
> door and say, "Let's talk about it. Let's do
> something about it." What matters is that I
> love Hawaii the way you do. As governor, I
> want to keep the things that are good—and
> fix the things that are not. And I can do it.

We shot this commercial in the lieutenant governor's conference room with Waihee speaking to a group made up of his staff and campaign workers, from behind a podium and backed by the state seal. Working with John Waihee always involved a lot of takes because he was not a naturally gifted speaker. He is a very personable man and very likable in a one-on-one situation. But in those days he had a tendency to get stiff and formal in any public presentation. We shot this same 30-second spot over and over again as I worked with him to polish each part of the speech. We shot for an hour, took a break, looked at what we had, and came back to it again. We shot for another hour and finally decided we had gotten the best takes we were going to get. The problem was that all we had was a politician at a podium making promises.

That's what the spot looked like, and that's how it was going to seem to voters viewing it. Astute politician that he is, Waihee said, "We can't use this. Let's do it again tomorrow, but somewhere else. Not stuck behind that podium." We settled on the capitol steps, and went at it again the next afternoon with Waihee walking toward the camera as he said the lines, ending in a close-up speaking directly into the camera.

The first forty takes were unusable because of sound problems with the wireless mike. Why did we keep shooting with a technical problem? Because the technician on the crew kept assuring us that the problem didn't exist. Finally he actually got it fixed and we settled down to business. And did take after take after take trying for one in which John Waihee's warm, friendly personality and confidence would shine through.

Understand, this was a one-take spot, starting with Waihee in a long shot on the capitol steps and ending with him in close-up at the camera. The walking looked good. But when he stopped in front of the camera and came to the payoff line, "And I can do it," he just sounded like he was bragging. By now our takes for the day were numbering in the sixties, and we still didn't have a great take to go to air.

We stopped again, looked at what we had, and made a change in the ending. We put the camera on a dolly, and adjusted the timing so that Waihee arrived in front of the camera as he was saying, ". . . you can count on me to open the door and say, 'Let's talk about it. Let's do something about it.' What matters is that I love Hawaii the way you do." He turned and walked to camera right with the camera following on the dolly as he said, "As governor I want to keep the things that are good, and fix the things that are not." Then he started to walk away, but turned back to the camera and spoke the final line, "And I can do it."

It took about a dozen more takes to work out the timing and delivery and to teach the lieutenant governor how to throw away the final line instead of punching it—saying it softly with conviction. Then we recorded two perfect spots in a row, checked the tape and wrapped the shoot.

It had taken two days, but we finally had what we wanted. The spot went out to the TV stations scheduled to air as the exclusive campaign message for the last couple of days before the voters went to the polls. When we showed the finished spot to campaign workers, the delivery of the final line got a standing ovation. People kept saying, "That's so like John."

But the real test came with the primary election on Saturday. Waihee's opponent was expected to have a strong following in Honolulu and on the island of Oahu. We assumed that Waihee would do better on the neighbor islands—Kauai, Maui, Molokai, and the Big Island. Because the votes were counted in Honolulu, we would get Oahu results first and neighbor island results a couple of hours later. So we were prepared for the opponent to start off with a lead. We hoped that Waihee would stay close in the early results and then pull ahead as the neighbor island returns came in.

My partner and I were just arriving at the election night party for the Waihee campaign when the first returns were announced. We heard a great shout come up from the crowd at the party and figured that Waihee must have stayed fairly close to Heftel in these early returns. We rushed in and asked the first person we knew what the shout was about. "John's ahead by two thousand votes!" she said. And as the evening progressed, his lead got larger and larger. He went on to win the general election and serve two terms as governor.

Did that spot make a difference? Sure it did. Would he have won without it? Possibly. Who knows? There are so many factors in any election that trying to pin a win or a loss on just one of them is an exercise in finger-pointing rather than political analysis. What I know is that by persisting through what must have been at least a hundred and fifty takes over two days, we ended up with a commercial that showed our candidate to his best advantage.

And he won by a landslide.

MAKING
INFOMERCIALS

17

INFOMERCIALS: SELLING DREAMS
TO DREAMERS

In one of his books, Marshall McLuhan characterizes advertising as "good news"—information people can use—as opposed to the news in newspapers and other media, which is so often "bad news" and not very useful to the average family. An infomercial is all good news. It's a long demonstration of benefit in a setting similar to a TV program.

In their early days, infomercials tried to pretend to be some kind of entertainment or information program and only incidentally a half-hour commercial for a product or service. They did it often enough that infomercial producers are now required to put a disclaimer at the opening of the show that says:

The following program is a paid advertisement sponsored by

_____.

Current thinking holds that an infomercial should not masquerade as regular programming but should seem to be precisely what it is: good news about a product or service for those who are interested in that product or service. It does your client no good to attract and hold viewers who are not interested in buying what the client is selling. When viewers feel they've been tricked into watching an infomercial, they are likely to become annoyed at the sponsor and the product.

Mark Williams, who has produced scores of infomercials, says an infomercial is the electronic version of the old door-to-door salesman. "It's a thirty-minute demonstration of a product or service that has apparent value for the consumer." You wouldn't let a door-to-door salesman in the house if you weren't interested in what he was selling, and you won't watch an infomercial if you don't care about what is being demonstrated.

INFOMERCIALS SEEK BUYERS, NOT VIEWERS

Aside from the fact that an infomercial is thirty to sixty times longer than a commercial, the major difference between a commercial and an infomercial is the way in which each attracts its audience and the purpose for which each has been made.

A commercial sits within regular television programming and plays to whomever may be watching that programming. The audience does not tune in to watch the commercials—it is there to watch a situation comedy or news show or sporting event. And while viewers may consider commercial breaks to be the price they have to pay to receive the program, they feel no obligation to watch the commercials, and will leave the room or go surfing with the remote control while the commercials are running.

An infomercial is a show in itself, rarely advertised, and today usually shown in the TV listings simply as "paid programming." Regular TV shows want to attract as many viewers as possible in order to deliver those viewers to the sponsors of the commercials. Infomercials, on the other hand, want to attract buyers, not viewers. Their goal is to convert everyone who keeps watching into a buyer before the infomercial goes off the air.

Grabbing the Random Viewer

Virtually all viewers of an infomercial will be watching simply by chance. Either they were watching the show prior to the infomercial and have remained on the channel, or they will surf in while the infomercial is on. In either case the infomercial has a very limited time to attract and hold their interest. This may range from a few seconds in which to trap a hyperactive remote pusher to up to nine minutes, which is the average length of an infomercial segment. In order to grab the potential buyers from among the viewers passing by, an infomercial must be constructed so that:

- Something interesting to potential buyers is happening all the time.
- The content makes clear that this is a program about something that can be ordered right now.
- All content is aimed at the target audience.

If your delight in life is to go fishing for bass, and you surf into a program in which you see people like yourself catching the big ones, you're likely to hang around to see how they do it. But if you click onto a program showing a group of women talking with a famous model or actress about a makeup program, and you're either not a woman or you don't care about makeup, you'll surf on. And that's how it should be. A sponsor might sell the occasional makeup kit to a guy looking for a bass lure who decides to order the makeup as a gift for someone, but the sponsor will sell far more to women who want to look better, younger, smoother, sexier, and prettier.

Forcing an Immediate Buying Decision

The goal of every infomercial is to motivate the viewer to make a buying decision while the program is on the air. Once the show ends, the buying impulse dissipates as other programs and products compete for the viewer's interest. The producer must be absolutely clear about the exact audience behavior the commercial should produce, and then must build everything in the program toward getting that behavior.

Usually, the purpose is to deliver the viewer to a telephone, to call the 800 number and buy the product or order the free information. To accomplish this, a well-made infomercial will be constructed with a series of carefully produced elements designed to move the viewer psychologically and physically to the phone.

ELEMENTS OF AN INFOMERCIAL

Everything in an infomercial from opening to close is designed to attract and hold potential buyers and to urge them to a buying decision.

Opening: What's in It for Me?
Most infomercials will open like a TV program—a talk show, a documentary, a cooking show, an exercise or workout show, or something else. Infomercial producers vary in their opinions about how important the opening is, since so much of the audience must be captured on the fly during the program. But there will be some residual audience from the previous program, and surfers are likely to be most active at the start of a half hour, so there are good reasons to design a strong opening.

The opening should separate the buyers from the viewers by answering the question, what's in it for me? An infomercial is always about benefit to the buyer. If the viewer looks at the opening and sees no benefit, he or she will—and should—move on. The opening may introduce a celebrity host, whose presence, it is hoped, will lend credibility to the presentation. And the opening will always make a promise to the viewers that if they have any interest at all in this kind of product or service and will keep watching, they'll learn about something that can bring a real benefit to their lives:

- Keep watching and you'll learn how you can catch the biggest bass in the lake, every time.
- In a few minutes we're going to meet a man who, five years ago, was on welfare and living in his brother-in-law's garage, and who now has a net worth of several million dollars.
- We're going to show you the latest breakthrough in cosmetic science.
- You'll learn how to take off unwanted pounds and keep them off, easily and sensibly.

Demonstration

The first thing buyers want to know is that the product actually works. An infomercial is all demonstration. That's why so many infomercials deal with gadgets—exercise gadgets, cooking gadgets, automotive gadgets, sports gadgets, and so on—because you can watch a gadget do its job. If you can't (or don't) demonstrate the benefit, you probably won't sell the product in an infomercial.

When the infomercial is for a service, such as a system for making more money, the demonstration often takes the form of showing the benefits of learning and using the system. It's not going to get bogged down in showing the viewer how to analyze and make profitable real estate deals. Instead, it will show how people who have learned how to do this now have the use of large amounts of money they never before dreamed possible. They drive expensive cars, have expensive homes, own expensive boats and other toys, travel around the world on expensive vacations, and send their children to expensive schools.

The demonstration often presents a problem or need and then shows how the sponsor's product or service can solve the problem or meet the need. The demonstration sells the dream. It says to the buyer, all you have to do is pick up the phone and place an order, and you can do, have, or enjoy this.

Testimonials

The second thing buyers want to know is that ordinary people—people like themselves and not just the experts in an infomercial—can use this product or service. That's what testimonials do. They show people telling about how they have used the product or service and attesting that it did everything they were promised and maybe a little more.

A testimonial is just another demonstration of benefit. It helps to overcome the psychological risk in the buying decision. Many infomercials, especially those for abstract services, are almost all testimonials in which people who have used the product or service tell how it benefited them.

Testimonials continue to sell the dream. They say to the buyer, you can have the same success we did, just by picking up the phone and placing an order.

Calls to Action

An infomercial will have at least three complete segments, each consisting of a demonstration, testimonials, and a formal call to action. In most infomercials each call to action is designed as a two minute commercial. These formally present the offer, tell exactly what the buyer will get, provide some sort of guarantee, tell the cost and how to order, and urge the buyer to make the call right now.

Once the offer has been made in the first call to action, the 800 number can be put on the screen during demonstrations and testimonials in subsequent segments, and the host can urge people to make the call.

Varying the Emphasis in Each Segment

Each segment of demonstration, testimonials, and call to action should demonstrate the benefit of the product for the buyer. But each segment should emphasize a different aspect of the benefits, while recapping those already demonstrated. If you're showing an exercise machine, the first segment may emphasize feeling better and stronger, while maintaining or losing weight, and contributing to a longer, healthier life. The second segment might emphasize weight control while mentioning you'll feel better and be healthier. And the third would emphasize the health and longevity benefits while recapping the benefits of weight control and feeling better.

Closing

The closing follows the final call to action and gives a summary of the benefits. The 800 number remains on the screen throughout the closing. The spokesperson makes a final appeal to the buyers to pick up the phone and start enjoying the benefits they've been seeing.

COLLECTIVE INFOMERCIALS

While most infomercials are designed to sell a single product or service, another form of sponsored sales program has emerged in recent years devoted entirely to showing real estate. Realtors and developers present properties for sale or rent in a series of two- to four-minute sequences. Each sequence shows several model homes in a development of new homes, gives the price range, and tells the viewer whom to contact and how to come to the development to see the homes in person.

Sometimes a large real estate brokerage will sponsor a program of this sort and show only those homes that it has listed for sale.

A recent spin-off of this idea is a similar kind of program showing new or used cars for sale.

THE PEOPLE IN AN INFOMERCIAL

Who will appear in your infomercial? Presumably there will be some sort of on-camera spokesperson or host who anchors the show, introduces the segments, and urges the viewers to pick up the phone. If the infomercial will feature the inventor or owner of the product or service, usually there also will be a cohost, who handles the functions of announcer and spokesperson. The cohost can urge the viewers to pick up the phone and order the product, whereas this might seem a little pushy coming from the inventor.

Use of Celebrities

For a long time the popular wisdom was that an infomercial needed a celebrity spokesperson or cohost in order to attract and hold viewers. Now the thinking is that a celebrity is only good if he or she is appropriate to the product or service being offered. Of course, in some cases, a celebrity may have lent his or her name to the product—for instance Cathy Rigby with exercise equipment—or has become strongly associated with the marketing of the product or service, as Dionne Warwick is with the Psychic Friends Network, and therefore is expected to participate.

If a celebrity will be used, it is important to start the process of lining up the talent as early as possible. Most infomercial producers report that securing celebrity talent can be a long and costly process. As one producer said, "It is remarkable how much you may have to pay for somebody who was the third banana in a situation comedy, and who has not been on TV for nine years. It's shocking."

Testimonial People

The people in the testimonials must be real people who have actually used the product or service. And they must not be paid for giving the testimonial.

They must be the sort of people the buyer will either identify with or want to be like. They must be believable. They need to speak well enough to be credible, but they don't need to give a polished performance like a television professional.

It usually will be the sponsor's responsibility to find testimonial people for you. You probably should ask for at least twice as many as you will need, since not all of them will be good on camera.

Studio Audience

Some infomercials like to play before a studio audience. This can be valuable when you can get good reactions from the audience. And it will add to the verisimilitude when the infomercial is modeled after a talk show. You need the audience for a day and in order to have any control over them, you have to pay them.

CREDIBILITY

Because an infomercial urges the viewer to make a buying decision while the show is on the air, it must have strong credibility with the viewer. The viewer must believe that it is safe to order the product or service and that it will deliver the benefit that is promised. Everything in the infomercial must bolster its credibility—the people, the words that are said, the setting, and the way the product is presented.

An infomercial must have sincerity, demonstrate benefit, and tell enough about the product or service to overcome doubts and be believable without telling so much that it gives away the secrets the buyer must pay to learn.

Make Study Tapes

If you want to make infomercials, tape the infomercials that are on the air and study them. Analyze what seems to work for you and what doesn't. Pay special attention to how the infomercials demonstrate benefit, and how they maintain a high level of interest all the time.

Check out the people. Are they believable? If there's a celebrity, is he or she appropriate to the topic and does the celebrity lend credibility and help to urge a buying decision? What would the infomercial be like without the celebrity?

What about the script? Is it well written and believable and does it maintain pressure for a buying decision?

PRODUCTION STORY—WASTED EFFORT

Paradigm Communication Group in Cincinnati has done a number of infomercials dealing with diet and nutritional supplements for Tony Little. For one of these, according to Bob Leubber of Paradigm, they wanted to get across the idea that there were a lot of companies out there pushing diet supplements. To suggest that these were not always trustworthy products, they came up with the idea of using a carnival barker in loud clothes, in a carnival sideshow setting, handing out diet shakes.

They spent a lot of time and money creating the set, including renting a fully functioning merry-go-round for a couple of days and creating a realistic carnival midway with all the props and background to make it look like a carnival. "It took an incredible effort to build the set and make it work," Leubber said. "In the original two-minute version it was beautifully shot and it made the point.

"But during editing, the carnival scene kept being cut back to make room for more testimonials and demonstrations. We ended up with about thirty seconds of carnival. It probably wasn't worth all that effort."

18

PRODUCERS TALK
ABOUT MAKING
INFOMERCIALS

Because my own experience with infomercial production is limited, I went to some of the heroes of the business to find out what they had to say about the theory and practice of infomercial production. It was gratifying to find that much of their advice mirrored my own analysis from taping and watching infomercials and my own production experience.

SUCCESS REQUIRES A GOOD PRODUCT

Everyone I spoke with agreed that an infomercial will not sell if the product is not a good one. Successful infomercial producers are bombarded with requests from clients who see an infomercial as a practically risk-free way to make money. Dazzled by tales of spectacular sales results, these clients often believe that if they can just get a good infomercial on the air—made by one of the top producers—they're going to make a lot of money.

But it doesn't work that way. According to Stephen J. Smith, vice president of sales and marketing for Paradigm Communication Group in Cincinnati, "We used to figure that only one infomercial in eight would make money. Today it may be only one in twenty. The infomercials that have worked—aside from our doing a good job in writing and producing them—have all been for good products."

"It doesn't matter how good the rest of the programming is," said

Mark Williams, who owns Mark Williams Entertainment Organization in Las Vegas, "if the product is no good, it won't sell. What you have to do is position the product or service into the lives of the consumers watching the show, so they can see how it fits or how they will benefit. If the viewers can't position the product into their own lives, they're not going to buy it.

"You have to go looking for America's buttons.

"Everyone in America wants to be richer . . .

"Wants to be smarter . . .

"Wants to be thinner . . .

"Wants to be younger . . .

"Wants to look better . . .

"Wants to be loved . . .

"Wants to own things cheaper . . .

"And wants life to be easier."

"The most successful products have the most compelling promises," said Jack Kirby, head of Quantum Television, an international direct marketing company. "Make me rich, thin, and beautiful."

Sell Just One Product or Service

An effective infomercial needs to concentrate on one good product, according to Vince Clews, head of Vince Clews & Associates, located in Reistertown, Maryland. "When you do an infomercial, you are selling one product or one service. Tony Robbins, for example, has a whole bunch of tapes he markets. But if you are watching a Tony Robbins infomercial on doing better in your career, then the only tape they will try to sell you is the one on doing better in your career. Not any of the others." What they are after is a buying decision on a single product, because, as Vince said, "They know they'll get another shot at you with the telemarketer when you call the 800 number, and with the collateral material they send with the first tape."

And once you've bought anything at all, they have your name, address, and phone number, and they can make follow-up offers forever. That's why some infomercials actually offer a free tape or free materials. It's a way of building a prospect list for further sales.

THE WRITER

Assuming you start with a good product, then, according to Steve Smith, "The writer is the key to the project. The writer must become totally intimate with the product, until he or she knows it backward and forward. For example, in doing the Del Webb retirement communities we visited the communities and talked with people who live there. We found a number of things that were unique. After that, writing the script was much easier."

"No producer is going to get anywhere until a writer has done a script to format," said Vince Clews. "The writing is a science. I'm a writer, but I do not write the infomercials." His brother Carter Clews, who works with a company called Infomation, does, however, and successfully enough to have been named infomercial writer of the year.

Carter, who started out writing direct mail advertising, describes the technique using the acronym MISE, which stands for motivate, inform, sell, and encourage. "You generate some excitement to motivate the audience," he said. "Then inform them with technical details—the 'secret formula.' Sell them on how it works. And encourage them to pick up the phone and call right now."

He spends a long time on the script for an infomercial, and feels that by the time it goes into production he has considered virtually all of the possibilities for presenting the client's message. He has little patience with producers or talent or even clients who want to make last-minute changes in the script. "This thing was four weeks in the writing, and probably any idea they may have on the spur of the moment, I already had, and discarded it."

"An infomercial is highly formulaic," said Tim Hawthorne, chairman of Hawthorne Communications in Fairfield, Iowa, and author of *The Complete Guide to Infomercial Marketing*. "You must learn the formulas by watching a lot of infomercials and by studying the industry."

"You need to study the shows that work," Kirby said. "These will be the ones that air most frequently." In the world of infomercials, successful programs earn enough to make a profit and pay for more air time, while unsuccessful infomercials quickly disappear.

MEDIA BUY

The next critical factor in the success of an infomercial is the media buy. Usually there will be an initial test buy to see how well the infomercial does. And it is here that many clients do themselves in. Having spent substantial amounts of money on production and talent, they may skimp on the test buy.

"A lot of shows don't test well," Williams said, "because they don't market the test well. I'm going to suggest that you never test for less than twenty thousand dollars [in media time]. One network buy may give a good test. Low-budget tests in low-budget markets may not attract the right audience. You have to buy decent time and then see what happens."

Smith thinks a good test requires a twenty-five-thousand-dollar budget. "I have a client I think of as the norm. They buy the northeast United States and spend twenty-five thousand dollars over two weeks to see what response they get. Then they may come back to us for modification of the program, usually a change in the call to action."

Focus groups may help in determining the attractiveness of the product, but are no predictor of how an infomercial will pull, Williams said, "because people in a focus group are not like the typical buyer. The typical buyer is at home doing things when the infomercial comes on." The infomercial has to catch and hold the buyer's attention in ways that are impossible to test in a focus group.

Client Needs an Experienced Media Buyer

While the media buy is not usually the videomaker's responsibility, clients often will ask for suggestions. The client may not even have thought about the importance of the buy. "A lot of times a naive client might come to Paradigm and talk about production values," Smith said, "but they need the buy. Steer them to a good media buyer."

"Be very, very careful how you choose your media company," Williams added. "There are a lot of them out there who will tell you they know what they are doing, but they are quick-buck artists. Use a media buyer with a very high reputation. Ask for a list of seven to ten clients you can check with. And then call them. Don't just take one or two. Everybody has a couple of successes they can refer you to. What's their overall track record?"

WHAT ABOUT ENTERTAINMENT?

Carter Clews is emphatic that an infomercial should not pretend to be anything but a sales pitch. "It's a great mistake to say let's make an infomercial that looks like a talk show or an entertainment show or an outdoor show." He recalled one successful infomercial maker who decided to make an infomercial that would look like the *Tonight Show*. "He came out and did stand-up comedy. It was an absolute bomb. I don't think they sold any products. It was off the air pretty quick."

But Clews does try to make his infomercials entertaining enough that people will enjoy watching. And that they'll want to watch again. For a fishing infomercial for the Helicopter Lure he teamed up Roland Martin, whom he described as the "Mickey Mantle of bass fishing," with top country comedian Jerry Clower. The two of them kept the focus on demonstrating and selling the lure, but in a fun way. "We had people call up and ask if they could buy the infomercial."

For another fishing infomercial for the Jump'n Jig, he teamed Jerry Clower with Orlando Wilson, who had the longest-running fishing show on TV. "The chemistry was great. Orlando was very low key, while Jerry was pretty hard sell, but so affable it worked."

Hawthorne cautioned against over-entertaining, but emphasized that one creative goal is to keep the viewer watching. He stressed that "the more you tell, the more you sell. The longer you are in a relationship with the viewer, the greater your chances of closing the sale."

"You have to give the viewer a reason to watch," Kirby said. "Remember the medium. It's television. And there are three key words that apply to TV: *people watch programming.* You need to make your show compelling and entertaining." For an infomercial for the Power-Rider, he had a fitness guru ride onto the set on the back of an elephant to catch the viewers' attention. "Why an Elephant? It represented the tons of fat that people had already lost using PowerRider."

NEXT STOP, THE INTERNET

Vince Clews said that infomercial producers should be aware that the next stage of all this is Internet marketing. "We have created an Internet network of topical sites. The idea here is that you own the site and can pretty much do with it whatever you like to turn it into a revenue stream. Let's say a person is searching on the topic 'exercise.' They come to our site on 'exercise' and begin to explore it interactively. They'll come to a banner that says, 'For a free workout tape, click here.' At that point, we should try to get them to order a tape for an aerobic workout, because they've expressed an interest in that.

"If television and the telephone are great direct response media, the Internet is even easier. With one movement of your finger you can order the product. So if you are thinking infomercial now, you should be thinking along the lines of the Internet as well. And it's logical as a video producer to be doing that because that's what the Internet is all about." You can put all the video elements of an infomercial into an Internet site and have them waiting there for potential buyers who choose to come and see what you've got.

MARKET INTO OTHER MEDIA

Mark Williams cautioned against thinking of the infomercial as an end in itself. "Plan an upsell," he said. "When the people call in and say I want to buy that exercise machine, offer them a video to go with it. At the time the person is calling, they're excited about buying. That's when you can tell them we have a wonderful video that normally sells for $39.95, but we're offering it to buyers today at $19.95. Or if it's some other product, such as a diet supplement, offer to sell them more of it at a discount for ordering now."

Williams also suggested looking into retail and catalog sales to take advantage of the interest generated by the infomercial. Retail is a way to reach undecideds who need to be able to touch the product before they have the confidence to buy. You can put a sign on it that says, "As seen on TV."

You can offer the same product through catalog sales, again with an "As seen on TV" label.

Then you can also market it into Europe and Asia.

And with a successful infomercial run, it can be marketed through television shopping networks.

David Savage, vice president of agency services for American Telecast Corporation, West Chester, Pennsylvania, agreed, saying that the business had gotten more competitive and that rates have gone up. "People now have to depend on back-end sale," he said, "home shopping, credit card syndication, catalog, print, and retail in stores."

Both Savage and Hawthorne saw retail sales as a lucrative market that can be driven by infomercial success. Hawthorne quoted Ann Aronson, marketing manager for Target stores, speaking about consumer awareness through infomercials. "People come in knowing exactly what they want and how a certain machine works," she said. "The products really fly off the shelves."

Fortune 500 Infomercial Marketing

This double-barreled success has not escaped the marketing directors at large corporations, who, a few years ago, would never have thought of presenting their products in an infomercial. Today, companies such as Nissan, Black & Decker, AT&T, Kodak, General Motors, Magnavox, and many more are showcasing their products in the long form advertising of infomercials. They don't ask you to call an 800 number to buy a car, but they may urge you to call for a free video, which gives them another chance to inform you of the benefits of their product—and gets your name on a prospect list.

HINTS FROM THE EXPERTS

Market to the Audience That's Buying

Carter Clews talked about the Psychic Friends Network infomercials, which use Dionne Warwick as their host. These are heavily weighted to black women and they are effective in part because Dionne Warwick believes in psychic phenomena. "There is no attempt to disguise what it is," Carter said. "In fact, whenever they try to broaden beyond their market it fails. They shot an infomercial at the Mall of America

in Minnesota, mainly showing white women, that wasn't very successful."

Offer a Bonus
"When you come to the call to action, you must always have a bonus," Williams said. "This is something that has apparent value to the
buyer, that you offer free for ordering now."

Everything Has Been Tried
"By now," Vince Clews said, "infomercial producers have tried everything that works. If they aren't doing it now, it doesn't work. That's
why there are no infomercials designed as situation comedies. And
why they don't advertise the infomercial in *TV Guide*. It's been tried;
it didn't work."

Magical Transformation
"The most successful infomercial products have a unique selling
proposition that offers a magical transformation," Hawthorne said. "A
business opportunity program that has magically changed someone's
life. Or weight loss products, where we can show how fat you were
before and how thin you are after."

Sales Experience
"Talented producers are a starting point," Kirby said. "But you also
want someone who has sold something. Direct selling on TV is all
about orchestrating impulse. The viewer comes across the infomercial
by accident, and there must be something there to catch his attention
and cause him to act on the information."

NIMA INTERNATIONAL

NIMA once stood for National Infomercial Marketing Association,
but as the organization has expanded its efforts internationally, and
moved into such areas as television shopping, multimedia marketers,
on-line sales, and other forms of electronic retailing, it has gone far
beyond the infomercial. To avoid confusion, NIMA International pre-

fers to be referred to as "the association that represents the worldwide electronic retailing industry."

NIMA International is a powerful source of information for infomercial producers. It conducts conferences around the world on electronic retailing, offers periodical publications and best-sellers, and maintains a library of articles that have been written about electronic retailing.

Its marketing guidelines set the industry standard for ethical practices. These guidelines are reproduced in appendix two. Contact information is included in appendix one.

INFOMERCIAL MONITORING SERVICES

One way to keep track of what is happening in the ever-changing world of infomercials is through the weekly and monthly reports of one of the two main infomercial monitoring services—Infomercial Monitoring Service, Inc., in Broomall, Pennsylvania, which publishes the *IMS Report*, and Jordan Whitney, Inc., in Tustin, California, which publishes the *Greensheet Direct Response Television Monitoring Report*. Both provide rankings of the top infomercials on the air, along with descriptions of new infomercials, and other information.

Both services are sources of tapes showing current and past infomercials and maintain databases with historical information.

PRODUCTION STORY—BE CAREFUL WHAT YOU ASK FOR

Jack Kirby had a long-standing relationship with one of the largest car wax companies in America, and had done a number of infomercial ventures with them. "Then the company brought in a product that was too good to be true," he said, "so I didn't believe it would work. It was a car wax called Blue Coral that they said you could apply once and it would last for the life of your car.

"I didn't know what to do. I didn't want to offend a good client. But I didn't really want to try to sell this product. Finally I took the problem to my lawyer. He said, 'If both sides can't agree on the terms of the deal, then there is no deal, and both sides can just walk away. So ask for something we know they'll never agree to.'

"I thought about it, and I said, 'Tell them that in addition to our usual fee, I want a car. Tell them I want a Mercedes 500 SL convertible. Surely they'll never agree to that.'

"So he went into negotiation with the client. He showed them the production costs, and that was fine. He said we wanted our usual percentage of sale, and that was okay. Then he said, 'And Jack wants a car.'

"They said, 'What?'

"He said, 'As part of the deal, Jack wants you to buy him a Mercedes 500 SL convertible.'

"They said, 'There may be a problem with that.'

"So we figured the strategy had worked, until they called back and said, 'Okay, we'll give him the car.'

"All I could think of was: Be careful what you wish for, you may have to do it.

"Fortunately Blue Coral touchless car wax turned out to be a great product. It sold well and made us a lot of money.

"And I got a car, too."

INFOMERCIAL PRODUCTION AND POSTPRODUCTION

Infomercial production combines the length of an information video with the care of a commercial. Your infomercial will be roughly twenty-eight minutes and thirty seconds long, and every second of tape must look good and sell the client's product.

PRODUCTION VALUES

Fortunately, infomercials tend to have production budgets that are, if not lavish, at least more than adequate. You don't want to skimp on production values. You want to put the money up on the screen where the viewers can appreciate it.

The Set
A lot of infomercials are shot in a studio with sets that are especially constructed for them. If you're presenting the infomercial in a talk show setting, you almost have to construct a set, since talk show practical locations are few to none. If you are presenting a cooking product, you may be able to use an actual kitchen. But, again, it may be better to construct a set. Most actual kitchens aren't really big enough or laid out properly to do a show in. If you construct a set and bring in whatever you need, you have complete control of the look of the set along with the flexibility to move people, things, and cameras to wherever you want them.

Obviously if you are going to have a studio audience, you'll be shooting in a studio. Certainly if you have a celebrity host, you'll want to showcase him or her in an attractive setting. Again, that means paying careful attention to set selection or construction and set decoration. Put your host in a setting that's right for him or her and that's appropriate to the product or service you're selling.

Costume and Makeup

You want everyone in the program to look good. Ask your principals to bring several changes of clothes so that they can choose an outfit that will look good and won't clash with the others or with the set. Always ask for several different kinds of outfits. I learned this the hard way when I was doing golf shows. For one show my host pro showed up in yellow plus-fours—the knickers golfers used to wear but don't very often anymore—colorful argyle socks, and two-tone shoes. We were forty miles from his home and that was all he had to wear. He looked silly. And we had to shoot him that way or we'd lose several hours of crew time and daylight if he went home to change clothes.

Be sure you have a makeup artist available—more than one if you have a large number of people on the program. And be sure everyone gets made up, men as well as women. Some men have heavy beards that show up on camera, and your viewers may have a hard time accepting the statements of a person who looks like he hasn't shaved in two days.

If you are on a practical location, be sure you have provided dressing rooms or at least a private area where people can change. And bring some mirrors; not just little hand mirrors but a couple of good-sized ones so that people can see how they look.

Lighting

You're going to light an infomercial set the way you would light the set for a commercial. To me, that means a full grip truck of lighting instruments and grip equipment so that you'll have whatever you need. It doesn't necessarily mean using a lot of lights. You're likely to be on this set for a long time and you don't want to make it uncomfortably hot or bright.

And it means using a lighting director to design and set the lighting for the production. Good lighting with a natural look is hard to achieve. If you're not an expert at that, hire one.

Camera Work

Everything you shoot for an infomercial is shot to be edited. Even if you are doing multiple camera switched video in the style of "live on tape," you are still going to go into an editing room and do a final edit. So there is no reason for the camera work not to be smooth, in focus, well composed, and shot to demonstrate the product or service to the audience.

If you don't want to stop the flow of the program to correct something, make a note and shoot a pickup shot. Probably all product shots should be done separately as carefully staged and lit close-ups.

Lighting and camera work should be appropriate to the product or service and the people involved. If a TV star is displaying a line of fashion or beauty products virtually every scene must be a beauty shot. On the other hand, if a young man is selling a system for making money from classified ads, the look of the production can be a little more gritty and realistic.

Audio Recording

Audio for an infomercial must be clear and easy to understand. In a studio set you may decide to use a boom mike that you can move around as needed. If you have a limited number of people speaking at any time, then you may decide to mike them with lavalieres, either hardwired to an audio mixer or using radio transmitters.

The more people there are, the more careful you have to be to keep the background clean and the voices separated. If you have a lot of people speaking and can mike each one, then you might have each person's microphone feeding to a different track on a digital audiotape, synchronized to the videotape by time code.

Props and Products

Remember that an infomercial is one long demonstration of benefit. So be sure you show the benefit. Show the product doing its magic — whatever that is. Carter Clews told me about a fishing infomercial he wrote in which the director never shot any fish being caught. The host talked about catching fish. There were shots of the lure. But they never showed any fish. If you don't show the lure catching fish, you haven't demonstrated benefit. They had to reshoot.

Also remember that reaction shots demonstrate benefit. Let the product do its thing, and then be sure to get shots of people appreciating it.

STUDIO AUDIENCE

If you are doing an infomercial that requires a studio audience, then you have to find an audience that will be enthusiastic and will be able to stay through the entire shoot. The best thing to do is to put the money in the budget and hire extras. You can go to local talent agents and tell them what you need and how much you can pay. Or you can put an ad in the paper and do an open call.

You can pay the audience members the day rate for an extra in your area. Or, in some cases, the client will give the product to each member of the audience. If it's a good product, this can be good pay. Remember that if it's an all-day shoot you have to feed them at meal breaks. And you should have drinks and snacks available.

As always, be very clear to audience extras about how long the shoot will be. Plan to have someone warm them up before you begin shooting. And be sure to call regular breaks so that they can go to the bathroom and get refreshments. You have to keep the audience extras in a good mood, because you need a positive, high-energy performance from them when you show the product.

TESTIMONIALS

You may have your testimonial people on the set and shoot the testimonials as if they were interviews at a talk show. But you may also need to shoot them in the field, documentary style. Part of your production planning will be deciding where and how to record testimonials, always keeping in mind that a testimonial is just another way of demonstrating benefit.

The people used in the infomercial should be appropriate to the product or service. In general, people shown using a product should look the way potential buyers either see themselves or would like to see themselves. The audience should believe that the benefits of the product or service are not beyond them.

POSTPRODUCTION

The post for an infomercial should be exactly like editing an information video or a commercial. Virtually all of the time you'll be working from a script, although not all of the elements may be fully scripted.

Your spokesperson or host may be interviewing the developer or inventor of the product or service, and while the interview may have been scripted in advance, it's not unknown for people, especially if they are also the client, to depart from the script.

Testimonials may be done documentary style without a script.

Real world demonstrations, such as actually fishing with one of the miracle lures, will be shot as they happen, and must be dealt with as documentary footage.

Do an Editing Script

There is simply no reason to go into an editing room without a completed plan. Once all of the elements have been shot, view them, time them out, and log them. Then write an editing script that shows exactly where everything is going to go, how long it will run, and how you'll get from one scene to the next.

Do an Off-Line Edit

I'm a great believer in scripts, but I also know that what looks good on paper won't always play well on the monitor. So take your editing script and all of your picture elements and do an off-line edit. Make sure that things go together the way you want them to, and that you keep the energy level up and the sales pressure on.

Watch Out for Special Effects

I love a well-done video special effect, partly because it's so rare. I've already characterized special effects as the car chase scenes of video. A well-constructed infomercial should maintain high viewer interest through the content being presented. Any time you find yourself reaching for a special effect, ask yourself if this will help sell the product. If it will enhance the demonstration, go ahead. But if you're sticking it in because you're bored, then you've got content problems.

One infomercial producer told me, "Whenever I've run into budget trouble on a show it has usually been in post with special effects that ran more than I thought they would."

PRODUCTION STORY—COLOR ME CLIENT

My friend Mark Williams, who has done scores of infomercials, says he doesn't allow the clients to sit in on a postproduction session. "I bring them a completed show to review so that they are looking at a pristine gem in a perfect setting."

One reason for his no-clients policy may be an experience he had with a client in post. This was not long after Ted Turner began colorizing black-and-white movies.

"We were sitting there looking at the cut," Mark said, "and the client points at our female spokesperson and says, 'I don't like the color of her blouse. Why don't we change it to red?'

"I told him we couldn't do that.

" 'Why not?' he asks. 'Ted Turner does it all the time.' "

BUSINESS CONSIDERATIONS

. . . .

20

FINDING CLIENTS

It's not enough to be a terrific videomaker. If you're going to make videos for money, you have to develop a list of clients who will pay you to make videos for them. And once you've found a few good clients, you have to treat them with tender loving care so they'll keep coming back to you.

Finding clients requires a lot more than just putting an ad in the Yellow Pages and waiting for business to show up. Take a look at the Yellow Pages. See all those company names listed under *Video Production Services* and *Television Program Producers* and *Videotape Editing*? Those are the people who have gotten to the market ahead of you.

But don't let that discourage you. The point to this book is that marketing a product or service to potential customers, and then making the sale, requires a well-thought-out plan and some serious, hard work. My experience is that a videomaker needs to be *listed* in the Yellow Pages, so that prospects you've developed in other ways will know where to find your telephone number when they finally decide they want your services. But a listing in the Yellow Pages won't make the sale for you. You have to do that.

MAKING YOURSELF KNOWN
TO POTENTIAL CLIENTS

Finding clients means marketing yourself. You have to convince a critical mass of prospects that you're the person they should use to make their videos. Start by determining what you are selling: Are you a freelance camera operator or writer-producer looking for assignments? Or have you created a production company, opened an office, and either hired crew people or made arrangements with freelancers in order to be able to handle all of the aspects of production?

If you are a freelancer, your potential clients will include the major video production companies and corporate video departments in your area. You want them to know that you are available and to be aware of the professional services you can offer them. If you also package complete video productions by hiring a crew and renting whatever equipment and facilities you don't own, then you'll also be marketing to the same prospective clients as other video production companies.

This requires a little bit of tightrope walking, since sometimes you may find yourself in competition with a video production company that you also look to for freelance work. It's not that difficult if you maintain a good relationship with the video production company and never, ever try to steal its clients. That means that if you have met a potential client while working as a freelancer for a video production company, then for all time you must treat that client as belonging to that video production company. It's that simple. If the client should call you and say, "I'd like you to shoot something for me. What will it cost?" you have to refer the client back to the video production company. Then call the video company and tell them what you've done so that you'll get the work.

If you have created a video production company, then you are selling the services of your company and generally won't be marketing to other video production companies. The only exception is wedding videographers and those who have staked out low-budget production as their domain. It's worthwhile for these videomakers to make themselves known to the major production companies in the market. The reason is simple: a major video production company making high-budget commercials does not shoot weddings, does not *want* to shoot weddings, and would lose their credibility in the marketplace if they *shot* weddings. But they do get calls from people who want a wedding video or other low-budget production. If they know you're a good, reliable, professional videomaker specializing in that area they'll usually be glad to refer the business to you.

Be a Joiner

One good way to make yourself known to potential clients is to join the groups such clients belong to. The local chamber of commerce may be a good resource. One of the nice things about chambers of commerce is that they are all about business, and they provide a lot of opportunities for their members to market themselves to each other.

Investigate the advertising, public relations, business communicator, and professional organizations in your area. You'll find a list of these in appendix one. A call to their national headquarters will give you a local contact, and you should be able to attend one or two meetings before having to commit to membership. At the very least, membership in these organizations will give you the names of people at many of the agencies, companies, and government and nonprofit organizations to whom you hope to market your services. They may not be the people making buying decisions in your area—members of these organizations are often sales people who are there to market their organizations to others—but if they introduce you to the agency producer or head of the communication department, you'll be further along than if you were just making a cold call.

If you are a freelancer, you'll probably want to belong to the International Television Association chapter in your area. This will put you in touch with the video production companies and corporate videomakers who are members and who may have need of your services. Some ITVA chapters are very active and include most of the top videomakers in the area. Others may not. Check it out.

If you are interested in doing documentaries, you should definitely become a member of the International Documentary Association.

Networking Groups

Another way to make friends and find clients is to join one or more of the networking groups that may be operating in your area. Typically, these are groups of professional and sales people who meet once a week for a breakfast at which each member gets a chance to make a quick pitch for his or her product or service. To be worthwhile for a video production company, such a group has to include representatives of companies likely to commission an information video, commercial, or infomercial. Shop around. There should be lots of these groups in any metropolitan area.

Internet Marketing

Don't overlook the Internet. Skill in Internet marketing will be crucial for service companies in the years ahead. The Internet is changing so rapidly that it's hard to be specific about how to use it. We've already arrived at the point where a Web site is as important to any business as a listing in the Yellow Pages. It lets millions of prospects know who you are and what you do.

I put my e-mail address on my business card and letterhead so that prospects will know where to find me and my company. I've picked up clients just by being in the America Online directory and listing my residence city and the type of work I do. Other client relationships have started with an e-mail related to some problem and have gone on from there.

Sales Calls

Finding clients means getting your company's name in front of prospects who are likely to have work for you—and then keeping it there. That means part of every week must be spent on the phone trying to line up appointments with prospects and making sales calls on those prospects.

Who are your prospects?

- Advertising agencies who hire video production companies to make videos and commercials for them.
- Public relations agencies who commission information videos and public service announcements.
- Corporate communication, marketing, and human resource departments. Some corporations have their own video production departments, but in these days of downsizing and outsourcing

many companies find it cost effective to go outside for video production.

- Government agencies at all levels—local, state, and federal.
- Nonprofit organizations such as hospitals and educational institutions.
- Television stations and cable TV operators. These, presumably, have their own production facilities. But they may have to go outside for some services, such as extra crew people or for some writing and directing.
- Video production companies if you are selling your services as a freelancer.

MAKING CONTACT

Your objective is to get as many potential clients as possible to think of you or your company when they need video production.

Whom to Ask For

Your prospect—the person you want to talk with—may have one of several different titles. If you are a freelancer calling a production company, the person you need to talk with may be the head of production or might be called executive producer, producer, or even creative director. At a TV station your prospect may be the head of production, executive producer, or program director.

If you are calling an advertising agency or public relations firm, your prospect could be the agency producer or creative director or may have some other title. At a corporation or nonprofit organization there may be a communication director, marketing director, audiovisual director, or some other title that makes sense to the organization, but not necessarily to anyone outside calling in. I've found it never hurts to be frank with the person who answers the phone about why I'm calling and then to describe the functions of the person I want to speak with. If that elicits a name, I'm on my way. If not, I'll prompt with the various titles that might apply.

Be Clear about What You Want

This is what you are trying to accomplish with the phone call:

1. Get the name and title of the person at the organization most likely to contract for video production services.
2. Talk with this person if possible.
3. Make an appointment to meet the person and show your demonstration reel.

If your prospect is busy—and at least half the time he or she will be—you can call back later or send a letter introducing yourself and asking for an appointment. You can leave your name and phone number as a courtesy but don't expect the prospect to call you back. Some may. Most won't. The reason is that the person in this position almost always has more phone calls to return than time to return them.

What to Say

How you open the conversation may determine whether you get an appointment or get nowhere. If you are tentative, hesitant, or beat around the bush and waste your prospect's time, you'll mark yourself as an amateur and probably get a polite brush-off. So once you get on the phone with the prospect, you have to get to the point and accomplish what you called for.

- Introduce yourself and state your business. This is the most courteous thing you can do in a business call. Failure to do so will get you off to a bad start.
- Don't waste time with small talk; you don't know the prospect and he or she doesn't know you. When someone I don't know calls and asks, "How are you doing today?" I know it's a sales call.
- Tell the prospect you're a videomaker and you'd like to set up an appointment to show your work.
- Make sure the person you're talking with is the person who actually deals with videomakers or video production companies. If not, ask to speak to the appropriate person.

Even if you've got the right person, your prospect is going to be cautious at first. Prospects who really don't buy outside video production will probably say so and end the conversation quickly, either by asking you to send some materials for their files, or by saying, frankly, that they really can't use your services and meeting would be a waste of time for both of you. In either case, thank the prospect and send a follow-up letter.

If the prospects do buy outside video production services, then they should be interested in knowing more about you. They may ask, "What sort of things have you done?" They want to know what you've done professionally. At the moment, they don't care where you went to college or how many video and film courses you've taken. Everyone who calls them studied video or film somewhere. What will jump you out of that crowd is professional accomplishment. So talk briefly about the video work you have done that you can show the prospects. There will be time to talk about where you went to college and whom you studied with at the interview—if it seems relevant to bring it up at that time.

At this point, they may be willing to meet you. Make an appointment. If the prospect is too busy to see you right now, make an appointment for when you ought to call back to set an appointment to meet.

Send a Follow-Up Letter

Immediately after speaking with a prospect, send a follow-up letter. Include your business card. The letter should be very brief, because its primary purpose is to have the prospect start a file on you, in which will be your name and your company name, address, and phone number. Its secondary purpose is to reinforce your phone conversation. If you have set an appointment for an interview, mention that you look forward to seeing the prospect at the stated time and place. If the prospect has asked you to call back next week or next month to set an interview, say that you look forward to speaking with him or her again at that time. And if the prospect has said there's no point to meeting, just say thanks for taking time to talk with me, and if your situation changes in the future, I'll be glad to meet with you.

Be Persistent

Long ago, when I was doing documentaries in Philadelphia, I had a terrific cameraman, Jack Behr, who left for the West Coast and became a successful screenwriter. One day I got a call from a camera operator named Andy Dintenfass. He'd gotten my name from someone and wanted to come by and show me his reel. I told him frankly that I didn't have anything in production or scheduled, so it would just be a waste of time for both of us to try to meet right then, but I'd be glad to keep him in mind if anything came up. For more than a year, I got calls from Andy every couple of months—"just checking." Then I was asked to make a documentary on mental patients, and I needed a crew. I immediately thought of Andy, called him, looked at his reel—which was great—and hired him to shoot the documentary.

He got the job because he's an excellent cameraman. But he got the call because he had kept in touch with me even when I didn't need a camera operator. Persistence pays off.

BE BUSINESSLIKE

This is for those of you who are new to selling yourself or your production company. Your prospects are in business and serve clients who are in business. Because you've called to sell your services, the prospects assume you are in business also. Don't disappoint them.

Don't Be Late

Be a few minutes early for your appointment. Video production is a time-bound endeavor, and while promptness won't necessarily get you a job, being late will count against you. Bring along a book or magazine or something to work on. While the prospect expects you to be on time, he or she will be late to the meeting about half the time due to a call from a client, a shoot that's running long, or an emergency in the edit bay. It's the way the business works.

Dress for Business

Your prospect may show up for the meeting in jeans and a T-shirt, but you shouldn't. Wear whatever is appropriate for city office workers in your area. Video production is not a three-piece-suit business, but it will be comforting to your prospects to know that if they take you along to a client's office for a production meeting, you'll know how to dress appropriately.

Show Pristine Samples

If you are going to show samples of your work, make them the best possible quality. Don't show a grungy off-line; get a copy of the on-line. You may bring a VHS dub to leave behind, or to show if that's all the prospect can play back, but bring a production copy—Betacam, D-2, or whatever—just in case. It will show that you value your work and that you value the chance to show it to the prospect.

Keep the Focus on Benefit to the Prospect

In any job interview, you're expected to talk about yourself and your accomplishments. But remember to keep the focus on how what you have done or can do could help the prospect do his or her job better. All any salesperson has to sell is benefit to the prospect. Find out what this prospect needs and how you might help meet those needs.

Don't Expect a Critique

The prospect is not running a school or a consulting service for newbie videomakers. Do not expect the prospect to critique your work beyond saying either "I like it" or "No, it doesn't work for me." If you are showing your samples to prospects but not getting a very positive response, you may want to think about taking a production course or joining a group, such as ITVA, where you may get some helpful criticism.

Try for Additional Leads

There may be other people within the prospect's organization who also hire videomakers. You can tactfully ask if there is anyone else, there, whom you should meet. You should also ask if the prospect can suggest any other companies or organizations that might be interested in your services. A referral from a friend or colleague is always the best sort of introduction to a new prospect.

Send a Follow-Up Letter

After the interview, get off a timely follow-up letter to the prospect. Keep it short, cordial, and businesslike—one page, two or three paragraphs. Mention how pleased you were to meet the person and to visit his or her organization. Follow up on any suggestions or comments made during the meeting. State that you'll stay in touch, and that you hope you'll eventually have the opportunity to work together.

Call Again

Remember Andy and call back in a few weeks. If you've done some production work in the meantime, let the prospect know that. If you've followed up a lead the prospect gave you, thank him or her for it. If the prospect mentioned a project that might be coming in for which your services might be appropriate, ask how that is developing. Keep the call short and friendly. You just want to maintain contact and keep your name in the prospect's mind.

BIDS AND PROPOSALS

At last all of the work pays off and you get a shot at a production job. Typically, you'll be asked to make a bid or to submit a proposal. A request for a bid should come when the nature of the project is fairly well defined. A script—or at least a treatment—has been written from which you can determine how many people and how much equipment will be needed for how many days in order to come up with a price.

A request for a proposal generally starts a little earlier in the creative process and asks for a description of how you will handle concept and content as well as for the costs involved.

Reality Check

Those of us who have done this before have learned that the first step is to qualify a potential client in terms of the reality of the project and the nature of the bidding process. Is the project real, or is it just a neat idea that might, someday, be made? All too often someone gets an idea and says, "Wouldn't it be neat to make a video about _____? Let's see what it might cost." This is vaporware—pie in the sky, wishful thinking. As a project it doesn't exist and the odds are better than fifty-fifty that it never will exist.

Real projects, on the other hand, come with deadlines or delivery dates and budgets. Asking, "When do you need the video by? Where will it be used?" and "Has the budget been approved?" will help you to determine whether you're talking about a real video or vaporware.

Sole Source or Multiple Bidders? If you believe the project is real, then find out if you're being asked to submit a proposal as a potential sole source supplier or if you are bidding in an open competition. If it's a competition, how many other runners are in the race? If this client is talking with every video production company that has a bold-faced listing in the Yellow Pages, then it's a lottery, and you probably won't want to invest a whole lot of time and expense in making a bid or proposal. At the other extreme, if it's a sole source project, then it's yours to lose, and you want to do an excellent job on the bid and proposal so you *won't* lose it.

Creative on Spec? Does the prospective client want creative concept as part of the proposal or bid? Again, if you are sole source, you may be willing to do this, although in that case the client has already decided that you have the ability to do the job and should be willing to pay for creative work. If you are in a lottery, you shouldn't give away creative work. As I wrote in chapter fourteen, once your creative ideas are out of the box, there's no way to stuff them back in. The client has gotten you to do work without paying for it.

You either have to develop a sense of when it's worth it and when it isn't, or you have to make it a policy that you don't do creative concept without a contract and an advance.

Find Out All You Can about the Project

The more information you have about the client's needs and plans, the better will be the proposal or bid that you produce. If the project is clearly defined—even if not scripted—then you can probably put together a full proposal and a reasonable cost estimate.

If the project is not well defined, and the prospect is looking for the videomaker to develop the creative concept and produce the script, you may want to do the proposal in two stages:

1. Research and scriptwriting, for which you can attach a firm bid.
2. Production and postproduction with the bid for this to come on approval of the script.

Budget Is Critical

Part of the information you would like to have is some idea of the budget the prospect has in mind for the video project. You may not be able to get a fixed figure, but you should be able to probe for a ballpark figure or anticipated range. As discussed in chapter three, you neither want to propose an expensive production if the prospect hasn't budgeted for it, nor do you want to leave money on the table by underbidding if the client is prepared to pay for the best.

As you develop your cost estimate, you must be sure of your ability to make the video for the amount you bid. Can you shoot it with the crew and equipment estimated in the time allowed? Have you covered all the costs and allowed room for contingencies? You'll find a budgeting checklist in chapter twenty-two.

Have you ensured that cost estimates from subcontractors are complete and accurate? Get such estimates in writing and ask the subcontractor to state that these are all the charges there will be. I used to work with a post house that invariably gave me a reasonably low estimate when I was preparing the bid. But when I got the bill, there would be two or three things included that hadn't been itemized in the estimate. I can scream pretty loudly when I've been gored in the wallet, and usually I'd get an adjustment back to a figure close to the original estimate. But now I demand a written, itemized estimate in advance.

Remember that cost is not the only factor in securing a bid. The quality of the production, the experience and reputation of the videomaker, and the ability to deliver within a tight time frame may be equally important. Find out the prospect's priorities. Not all projects go to the low bidder.

Be Clear about the Money

Your proposal or bid should indicate how much you expect the prospect to pay for the project and exactly what you will deliver for that money. Normally the proposal will be for production through to an approved, edited master of the finished production.

State how and under what conditions the money is to be paid to you, for instance:

- one-fourth as a nonrefundable deposit on the signing of a letter of agreement for the project
- one-fourth on approval of the script
- one-fourth on completion of principal photography
- one-fourth on delivery of the edited master tape

Put a Time Limit on Your Bid

Every bid should have an expiration date. This is a sentence in the proposal or bid letter which says, "The prices quoted for this project will remain in effect for ___ days from the date of this letter." How many days is up to you. If you are low-balling the bid in order to stay busy in a slack time, then you want a fairly tight time limit—perhaps fifteen to thirty days. If you have quoted your standard rates, then you may be willing to go forty-five to sixty days.

I think sixty days is more than enough time for a prospect to make a decision and give a go-ahead. If, for some reason, the prospect takes longer than that, and then calls and says, "Let's go," you may be perfectly willing to honor the original bid. But you might be in the midst of another project by then and have to make some changes in order to do the job.

Make It Look Good

Put your proposal or bid in writing. Be sure that it is well written and looks professional. Your proposal represents you and is symbolic of your ability to do a quality job. If you send it out with typographical errors and notes written in the margins, the prospect is likely to ask, "If this company doesn't care enough to do a good job on a proposal to get business, why should I believe it will do a good job on my video after it has the business?"

If you want a reputation for quality, you have to do quality work all the time.

PRODUCTION STORY—BIDDER BEWARE

Not long after relocating to a new market, my partner and I had the opportunity to bid on writing, producing, and directing a fund-raising information video for the local public television station. We would provide creative concept and management and do production using the station's facilities and crew people. Because we were new to the market and thought this would be a good opportunity for us, and because we had no other work lined up at the moment, we came in with a fairly low bid for a ten-minute video.

Then everything stalled. I later found out this was a fairly common occurrence at that station. The job simply evaporated. Later we got another call from the station manager, asking if we could meet with him and a deputy superintendent of the local school district about a project for the school system. This was to be a half-hour video to recruit teachers from out of state. The meeting went very well. By that time the station manager had received a call from a friend of ours who ran a PBS station in another market, telling him what great folks we were. And we had impressed the deputy superintendent with our credentials in making educational films and videos. Eventually the station manager looked at us and asked, "You can do this for the same rate as the other one?"

Now, I understand *rate* to be some kind of a ratio, such as cost per minute—or in this case cost per ten minutes—not a fixed price. I did a fast mental calculation of three times what we had quoted for the ten-minute project, figured it was enough, and nodded my agreement. It looked like we had a deal. He turned to the deputy superintendent and said, "So it will cost you . . ." *and named the figure we had quoted for the ten-minute project!*

After the school district person had left, I set him straight that we were not offering to do three times as much work for the same price. He asked if we would look at the numbers and give him a firm bid. We did. But the project just drifted away.

In the meantime, we found other clients.

To this day, I have no idea if the station ever made either of the videos we had talked about.

21

DO YOU NEED
A CONTRACT?

You got the job!

What do you do now?

What you must do is spell out in a formal letter of agreement—or contract—the conditions that you set or implied in the proposal. A contract is the only way to protect yourself when a project starts to go bad. And quite often a written agreement will keep things from going wrong, because it spells out each party's responsibility.

Stored in my computer is a relatively simple, fill-in-the-blanks agreement that I use with clients. I'm not going to reproduce it, because I'm not here to give legal advice. Have your attorney draw up a form for you.

These are the things my letter of agreement includes:

Who the Parties Are

It states that this is a letter of agreement between my company and the client's company, tells where we are located, and says that this letter confirms our earlier verbal agreement.

What the Project Is

It next describes the work to be done, e.g. "CLIENT has asked PRODUCER to research, write, and produce a ten-minute information video on CLIENT's XYZ process." If any details about the project are pertinent, they can be included here.

Payment

The producer agrees to take on the project and the client agrees to pay the producer whatever the total amount is, plus normal expenses and applicable taxes. A schedule of progress payments is shown as set forth in the proposal or bid. I try to keep clients on a positive cash flow so that if anything goes wrong, I'm not stuck with a bunch of unpaid bills.

The contract states that time is an important part of the agreement, and that if any progress payment is not made by the time it is due, all work stops immediately and all delivery dates are canceled until renegotiated.

It also states that normal expenses include travel and living expenses when away from home, that such travel will not be taken without prior approval from the client, and that expenses shall be paid within fifteen days of submission of an itemized expense account.

It makes clear that this is an agreement between the producer and the client, that payment is due on receipt of invoice and is not dependent on the client being paid by a third party, that the client agrees not to "age" invoices or otherwise delay prompt, timely payment.

It sets forth a late fee for progress payments not made in a timely fashion and the client agrees to pay these. I include a clause that says that any discounts or concessions on price offered by the producer to the client are canceled if payment is not received within thirty days from the date of any invoice, and the full price shall be due immediately. And another clause in which the client agrees to pay any and all collection costs for collecting past due and/or unpaid fees.

The Work Process

In the next section, I spell out the process envisioned in the agreement. This includes each general task with a deadline for its completion. For instance:

- Acceptance and signing of the letter of agreement and payment of the first progress payment, to be completed no later than (date).
- Research and interviews about the XYZ process and writing a first draft treatment for the script to be completed by (date).

- Review of the first draft treatment by the client to be completed by (date).
- Writing the second draft treatment incorporating changes and revisions from the client to be completed by (date).
- Review of the second draft treatment by the client to be completed by (date).
- Writing the first draft script based on the approved treatment to be completed by (date).
- Review of the first draft script by the client to be completed by (date).
- Writing and delivery of the final draft script, incorporating changes and revisions from the client to be completed by (date).
- Principal photography based on the approved script to begin (date) and to be completed by (date).
- Off-line editing of the video, to be completed by (date).
- Review of the off-line edit by the client to be completed by (date).
- On-line editing and completion of the edited video master based on the approved off-line to be completed by (date).
- Delivery of the edited video master by (date).

This tells the client that we are going through all these stages in order to get the video made. It says that the client will have the opportunity to review and approve the work at each stage in the process. It not only puts a responsibility on the producer to deliver work on time, but it also puts a responsibility on the client to complete the review process expeditiously. Some of the dates also become progress payment milestones.

Insurance
Assuming that you carry production insurance and liability insurance, state in the contract that the production is insured from the commencement of principal photography until delivery of the completed program against loss or damage to the audio and video and edited masters or submasters, and say that the producer will provide liability insurance in the amount of $_____ during principal photography when filming and/or recording in public areas.

Designated Representative

In this section, the client assigns someone by name as its designated representative for the project and delegates complete review and approval authority to this representative. This is important, because you want to be sure that the person you're dealing with has authority to approve what you're doing. Without this, you're in the position of going through the entire production process and then having the person you've been dealing with say, "Well, now we'll send it upstairs and see what the boss thinks." What are you going to do if the boss doesn't like it?

Presumption of Acceptance

Sometimes a client cools off on a project after it has begun. You deliver the draft of a script or a completed off-line edit, and then hear nothing. When you call, the client says, "Oh, we've been busy with other things and haven't gotten to it yet." In order to avoid this kind of problem, I put a clause in the contract that says that the treatment, the script, the off-line, or the on-line shall be presumed to have been approved and accepted ten days after the date of its delivery, and any progress payment due upon such approval becomes payable, unless within the ten days client notifies the producer in writing that it has not been accepted, setting forth the reasons why it has not been accepted.

The agreement also states that regardless of notification, a script shall be presumed to be accepted if the client goes ahead and produces a video substantially in accordance with that script. In other words, the client can't reject the final draft script and refuse to make a progress payment because he doesn't like the wording of some of the narration, and then change the words himself and go ahead and produce the video, using a different videomaker. If the video that is made is essentially the video you described in your script, the client has accepted the script and owes you the progress payment.

The same conditions should be stated in terms of the edited video, although this is less critical since you will presumably control all the camera tapes and edited masters and submasters until final payment is made. But I never cease to be amazed by the things some clients will do to try to get around dealing fairly.

Changes in Concept or Content

I include that if the client requests changes in the treatment or script which are substantially different from the concept and/or content of the program as originally explained to the producer by the client during the research phase, the client agrees to pay the producer for such changes in addition to the fees already agreed to, at the hourly billing rate of so much per hour—whatever your hourly rate is or whatever is fair for this project.

And I add that if any changes or additions to the video are requested by the client after the commencement of principal photography, the client agrees to pay all additional costs resulting from such changes or additions.

Dissemination on VHS

I put in a disclaimer which tells the client that if the video is distributed on VHS tape, there will be some noticeable loss of quality from the original edited master videotape due to the limitations of VHS recording and reproduction.

Ownership

In the next paragraph, I say that once all the payments have been made, ownership of the work passes from the producer to the client. This reminds the client that he doesn't own what he hasn't paid for, and also makes it clear who owns the final product.

Production Credits

Some commercial videos have no credits at all other than the name of the sponsoring company. Others list the names of the people who made the video. The letter of agreement should state how your company's production credit and the credits of your creative and technical people will be handled on the video and on its packaging.

Additional Conditions

If there are any special conditions attached to the project, they would be listed here. For example, if you need access to certain people or projects in order to do your research, and the client has said, "No problem, I can get that," you may want to note in this section that getting you access to these things is the client's responsibility, not yours. Then when the client later says, "Here's their phone number, call and make an appointment," you can point out that that is not the deal.

Similarly if the client has offered to provide certain video clips or photographs, you list that here along with a statement that such materials shall be of professional quality and that they shall be provided at no cost to the producer.

If there is any question about rights to client-supplied materials, put in a condition that says that the client represents that it has the right to the use of this material and holds the producer harmless for any action which might arise from this use.

You may want to put in a cutoff date for the client to provide new material for inclusion in the video, or a statement that the information to be included is the information available at the start of the project. This is especially important if you are dealing with an information video about an ongoing process or for a new business. Things are constantly changing and the client's people will want to include the latest material. You have to have a point at which you can freeze the information you're dealing with so you can complete the video.

If talent is to be supplied by the client, especially critical talent such as an on-camera host or spokesperson, you as producer must either have a veto in case the talent just isn't any good, or a way to avoid both the responsibility for the finished product and for any additional cost, such as reshooting and hiring professional talent if the client's person doesn't work out.

Producer Copies

I have a paragraph in which the client agrees that the producer may keep a broadcast quality submaster of the finished program for promotional use, and gives the producer permission to enter or show the script and/or program in festivals, competitions, and the like, which give awards for creative or artistic merit.

Notices and Arbitration

Notices under the agreement, and changes and amendments to the agreement must be made in writing. And, because I don't want to spend a long time hassling over disputes at the end of the project, and I don't want to bear the cost of going to court, I include a paragraph that says disputes which cannot be settled within thirty days shall be submitted for binding arbitration to the local office of the American Arbitration Association.

Binding on Heirs and Assigns

Next is a statement which says that both the client and the producer agree that this agreement is binding on their respective personal and business heirs and assigns and shall be interpreted according to the law of (name of state).

Sole Agreement and Signatures

Finally, both sides state that this is the sole agreement between them, agree to be legally bound by the agreement and sign and date their signatures.

ACCELERATED SCHEDULE

"Hey, that's fine," you say, "all those milestones and progress payments. But sometimes a client comes in and says, 'Let's go' and we might have to do the whole job over a weekend. What then?"

Get a signed agreement and get as much money as you can before you start. Fifty or sixty percent in advance, with another big chunk before you go into post and the balance on delivery. That's all you can do. Again, I think that if a client is asking you to go out of your way for him or her, the client should be willing to do a little extra for you. Like cutting the company red tape to get you a check for a substantial advance before you start. You must have money in hand before you commit to shooting or editing.

MILESTONES

When you hit a milestone, such as approval of the script, get the client to sign off on it—in writing. Don't expect the client to pay you automatically. He or she will wait for your bill. So send an invoice. Right away.

BUT I WON'T BE YOUR LAWYER

I've included details from my letter of agreement because over the years I've learned some of the things that can go wrong in the producer-client relationship. These can become a checklist for your attorney in drawing up an agreement for you to use. If you write your own, you're on your own.

PRODUCTION STORY—NONPROFIT NONCHALANCE

I've done a lot of work with nonprofit organizations. For some people in such organizations, not all of them by any means, a symbol of their nonprofit status is a studied disregard for money. They consider payment due dates a capitalist malignancy and certainly not a matter of concern for high-minded types such as they. Paydays, of course, are different. Should their checks be late, they will *scream!*

I was hired to do a documentary for a nonprofit organization working in the mental health field. The contract was signed but it took a few days and several phone calls for the check for the advance to find its way to me. I finally had to say to the client something like, "You expect me to shoot an event in a few days and I won't be able to do it unless I receive money to buy supplies now."

My contract included the clause that said that if any progress payment is not made when due, all work on the project will cease immediately and all delivery dates will be renegotiated. As we came up to the next progress payment, I made sure that an invoice had gone to the client's representative and also made a couple of calls reminding him of the day the payment was due. He was an officious sort, a bully by implication, the kind of bureaucrat who radiates an aura of disapproval. This was not a happy project. In truth, I had only taken it on because I needed the money.

Of course the payment didn't arrive. As soon as the mail had been delivered and the payment was not there, I sent the client's representative a telegram, even though his office was just across town. This was back before faxes, when you could still send telegrams. It said:

PROGRESS PAYMENT DUE TODAY NOT RECEIVED. PER OUR AGREEMENT, ALL WORK ON THE DOCUMENTARY HAS STOPPED AND ALL DELIVERY DATES ARE CANCELED.

It didn't take long for the phone to ring, and there was my client, all injured innocence and disapproval. "Barry, what is this all about?" he asked.

"You owe me money and you haven't paid it," I said.

"But you didn't have to do this."

"Obviously I did."

"Well, this doesn't sit very well with us."

"Not getting paid doesn't sit very well with me. What are you going to do about it?"

"I'll have to call you back."

Again, it didn't take long. Probably less than an hour before he called to tell me that the check was cut and ready to be picked up.

I was willing to drive across town, even on a Friday afternoon, for that. And I did. And even if my blunt telegram didn't sit well with the client's designated representative, I noticed that all the rest of the progress payments came in a day or two ahead of time.

. . . .

KEEPING TRACK OF THE MONEY—
BUDGETS AND BILLING

If you are making videos for money, you have to earn more than you spend and then collect what you have earned. That's the name of the game and it's all about budgets and billing.

THE BUDGET

The budget for a video project is arrived at in one of three ways:

1. The client says, "I have this much money to make a video. What can you do for me?"
2. The client says, "I want to make a video production about _____. What will it cost?"
3. Negotiation between 1 and 2.

In the first situation the amount of money that the client is willing to spend controls everything. So the first question you have to answer is whether or not there's enough money available to make anything at all. If there is, then you have to determine what you can offer the client for that amount of money. If you've been doing this a while, you have a pretty good idea of what a script will cost, what your daily costs are for routine production, what the talent costs are, and what it should cost to edit and finish a video of a certain length. So you can come back to the client with a proposal that details the type of production you can offer for the amount of money the client wants to spend.

The second situation is a little trickier, because the sky is almost never the limit. The client may not mention a budget figure, but probably has one in mind. And the client may or may not have a clear idea of what sort of video is needed or wanted. If the client has given you a concept, you can cost it out with reasonable estimates of time and cost for all the elements, and come up with a number. If the client has not started with a concept, then you have to make some assumptions about the sort of video that is needed and provide a budget for that. In some cases you might prefer to give the client a budget range, showing a minimum and a maximum figure.

The third situation comes about when you've replied to number two with a budget estimate and the client says I don't have that much to spend. Then you negotiate. If you want this and this, it will cost this much, but if you really can only spend $_____, then all we can do is this.

Above- and Below-the-Line Costs

The budgets for feature films and for some other productions are divided into above-the-line and below-the-line costs. People accustomed to using this system of budgeting tend to think in these terms.

Above-the-line costs are generally contractual expenses that are negotiated on a run-of-the-production basis. These include the purchase of the script and property rights and the salaries of the producer, director, and cast.

Below-the-line costs are all those costs associated with the production that are calculated on the basis of use. These include salaries for the crew, cost of equipment and supplies, travel, editing, processing, and postproduction costs, and salaries not agreed upon as above-the-line costs before production starts.

PRODUCTION BUDGET CHECKLIST

When I was new to the business, I often wanted the job so badly that I forced my estimate to fit the money available and then occasionally discovered that I had left something out of the budget. As a result, I began to develop a budgeting checklist that included every cost I could think of in preproduction, production, and postproduction. That started as one page and grew over the years. What follows is a summary of that checklist, which I offer to you as a starting point to make a checklist of your own. Specific items will change as the technology changes and as your approach to making videos evolves. The most important thing is to have a reference point for creating a budget. There is so much to do, and there are so many different costs involved, that without some kind of checklist you can easily forget to include something that could cost a lot of money you didn't plan on spending.

Preproduction
- producer, director, producer's assistant/secretary (all run of the production)
- research
- script, scriptwriter, interviews, storyboards if needed
- production planning: casting, location coordinator, location research
- travel

Production
- crew and equipment if contracted as a package, or
- crew (individuals as needed): assistant director, director of photography, camera operator, camera assistant, sound recordist, sound assistant, electrician/gaffer, grip(s), production assistant(s), editor, makeup artist, property person, wardrobe person, driver(s), TelePrompTer operator, and others
- talent: host/spokesperson, featured actors/celebrity host, extras, animals
- camera and support equipment: camera(s), batteries and charger(s), tripod(s), dolly, Steadicam, crane, jib-arm, special mounts (car, helicopter), special rigs such as underwater housing, video recorder(s), video playback, monitor(s)
- sound equipment: recorder(s), microphone(s), wireless system, audio mixer, microphone boom or fish pole, cables and connectors

- lighting and grip equipment: grip truck, lighting instruments, grip stands, sandbags, shiny boards, cables, clamps, gels, dichroic filters, etc., background paper, large color correcting gels for windows, generator
- miscellaneous equipment: TelePrompTer, trailers, communication (walkie-talkies, cellular phones, headsets, etc.), portable toilets, etc.
- transportation: cars, vans, or trucks
- props and wardrobe
- location and studio costs: location fees, licenses as needed, studio rental, set construction, set decoration, storage and transportation
- processing: laboratory processing of film, VHS windowprint dubs for review, shipping
- travel: travel costs, rooms, per diem, shipping equipment and supplies
- supplies: film or videotape, audiotape, batteries for everything, gaffer's tape, camera tape, shipping tape, etc., replacement lamps
- meals and snacks
- contingencies: a percentage of the production budget set aside to handle unexpected and unbudgeted expense

Postproduction
- stock footage and stills
- review of footage: the director, along with the editor (if the director is not doing the editing) and possibly the producer, will want to review what has been shot to select the best takes, eliminate the unusable footage, and begin to organize the structure of the documentary; allow time for this
- editing facilities: the production company may have editing facilities available, or may rent a film editing room or editing system or a video off-line editing room or system by the week or month until postproduction is complete
- off-line editing (video): editor, assistant editor, off-line (rough cut) editing equipment, mastering tape and work tapes
- graphics and special effects
- music: composer, library music, music director, audiotape as required

- audio postproduction: record narration, voice talent, looping if required, record music, record sound effects, audio sweetening and effects, audio layback, audiotape and/or videotape as required
- on-line editing: on-line facility by the hour, mastering tape, work tape, protection master, dubs to VHS for review

Distribution
- prints for release as required: television broadcast standard, VHS video release copies including labels and boxes, shipping

General Overhead
- production company overhead: bookkeeper, office rent, telephone, utilities, furniture and equipment, supplies, licenses, and other expenses
- transportation
- legal: contracts, releases, rights, copyright
- insurance: office and equipment, errors and omissions, liability, production or negative insurance
- payroll company: tax, benefits, workers' compensation, etc., throughout the production

Budget Carefully and Completely
Be realistic in preparing the budget and be sure you've covered everything. The only thing worse than not getting the work is getting it at a price you can't afford to do it for.

OTHER BUDGET CONSIDERATIONS

Some budget items may not be easy to calculate in advance and may be left outside the budget as extra items. I usually handle travel costs this way, as a reimbursable expense rather than a fixed budget item. Sometimes talent fees are paid to the talent directly by the advertising agency or by the client and may be left out of the budget.

Insurance

You may need to budget the cost of liability insurance, which protects you in case of personal injury or property damage during the production, and production insurance, which protects you against loss or damage to the videotape you are recording on and may protect against delays in production for various reasons. Naturally, you'll also have insurance on your expensive equipment and vehicles.

Benefits

If you are using guild or union crew members, including writers and actors, they are entitled to health and pension benefits, which you need to budget for and must be sure to pay. One way to handle this is to use a payroll service accustomed to working with film and video production. They'll know exactly what has to be paid and how it must be paid.

BILLING

Most clients will pay your invoices on time and with no problem. But a tiny percentage of clients can cause very large headaches with your billing. I have never understood why a client, for whom I've done excellent work, would feel it necessary to try to beat me out of a few hundred dollars. But it happens. In some cases, it's just their nature. In others, it is symptomatic of a client with financial problems.

This is why I always set up production payments to provide a positive cash flow, starting with a nonrefundable advance to be paid when the agreement is signed. Then each payment milestone should bring in enough money to cover the next step in production. The agreement says that if any progress payment is not paid when due, all work will stop and all deadlines and delivery dates are subject to renegotiation.

Send invoices promptly, so that the client can't say, "I didn't get your bill." Discuss with the client when invoices must be received in order for progress payments to be made on time. Some companies have a thirty, forty-five, or sixty day billing cycle. If they can't cut a check faster than that, then ask them to put in all your invoices at once and hold the checks until you've completed the work leading up to the progress payment.

Be very wary of clients who have an inflexible payment policy. My experience is that this is often a ruse to delay or avoid payment. If the client starts to give you a long explanation about why the progress payment can't be made on time, I suggest telling them that you'll be glad to delay the production until the progress payment is made, as called for in your agreement. Otherwise you're at the client's mercy.

Hold on to the Master Until You've Been Paid

Once you have delivered the finished program to the client, you've given up all leverage for payment. I suggest presenting the client with a VHS dub of the program with a time code window and the words APPROVAL COPY superimposed above or below it. Hold onto the edited master and all distribution copies until you've received the final payment.

PRODUCTION STORY—OFFENSIVE LINE COLLECTION SERVICE

I had a client, an art director who decided to become an ad agency, who hired me to write some spots for him. He was one of these people who considered all of the money that came into his company to be his, and begrudged paying his subcontractors.

In this case, he said up front, "I can't pay you until I get paid by my client. Is that okay?" I was still learning about this sort of client, so I foolishly agreed. I wrote the spots. He praised them. He told me his client loved my work. And I sent him an invoice.

And waited.

And waited.

And began calling him for payment. Each time, he said that he had not been paid by his client. In the meantime the job was finished, the client had the use of it, months had passed, and I hadn't been paid.

Finally I contacted his client, who told me that he had billed her for my fee months before and that she had paid him.

Another phone call to the client in which small claims court was mentioned. He said, "Okay, I'll have a check for you tomorrow."

"What time?" I asked.

"Ten A.M. "

"Fine," said I. "Someone will pick it up."

I sent my son Scott, who was a high school senior and tight end on his football team. He took along a couple of offensive linemen.

When Scott walked into the client's office and said he was there to pick up the check, the client said it wasn't ready yet. Then two big 250-pound offensive tackles crowded in behind Scott, and the client quickly reached for his checkbook.

The collection fee was T-bone steaks all around. Maybe twice.

It was well worth it.

. . . .

USEFUL ORGANIZATIONS
AND ASSOCIATIONS

There are a number of national organizations—many with local chapters—which can be valuable to you as resources for information, networking, and marketing. Many have Internet Web sites you can contact for up-to-date information on the organization and its activities. Even if no Web site is shown here, I suggest you search the Internet for the organization as it may have come on-line after this book went to press.

You can contact the national headquarters of any of these organizations to find out if there is a local chapter near you.

RESOURCE ORGANIZATIONS

Academy of Television Arts & Sciences
The Academy was founded in 1946 and is devoted to the advancement of telecommunications arts and sciences and to fostering creative leadership in the television industry. In addition to recognizing outstanding programming and engineering achievements through the Emmy Awards, it sponsors activities for its membership, publishes *Emmy Magazine,* and through the Academy Foundation is responsible for the Archive of American Television, ATAS/UCLA Television Archives, ATAS Foundation Library at USC, College Television Awards, Internship Program, and the Faculty Seminar.

Contact:
Academy of Television Arts and Sciences
5220 Lankershim Boulevard
North Hollywood, CA 91601
Tel: (818) 754-2800
Fax: (818) 761-2827

National Academy of Television Arts and Science
111 West 57th Street, Suite 1020
New York, NY 10019
Tel: (212) 586-8424
Fax: (212) 246-8129

American Advertising Federation (AAF)

Headquartered in Washington, D.C., the American Advertising Federation serves more than fifty thousand affiliate members "by advancing the business of advertising as a vital part of the American economy and culture." Members join the AAF through one of its affiliated local advertising federations, and "have access to a national network that includes over 110 corporate members, 200 college chapters, and 215 local advertising federations all across the United States." Member benefits include a quarterly magazine, access to other AAF publications, and discounts on insurance, car rental, express delivery, and long distance service, among other things.

Contact:
American Advertising Federation
1101 Vermont Avenue, NW, Suite 500
Washington, DC 20005
Tel: (202) 898-0089
Fax: (202) 898-0159
E-mail: aaf@aaf.org
Web site: http://www.aaf.org

American Association of Advertising Agencies (AAAA)

The American Association of Advertising Agencies is the national trade association of the advertising agency business and acts as the industry's spokesperson with government, media, and the public sector. Membership is open only to agencies and not to individuals. AAAA member agencies operate 1,225 offices in the United States and more than eighteen hundred offices in 119 other countries. They place a large portion of all agency-produced national advertising. The association provides member agencies with a wide range of informational and educational services.

Contact:
American Association of Advertising Agencies
405 Lexington Avenue
New York, NY 10174-1801
Tel: (212) 682-2500
Web site: http://www.commercepark.com/AAAA

American Film Institute (AFI)

The American Film Institute is dedicated to the preservation and enhancement of filmmaking. Benefits of membership, in addition to helping to preserve America's film heritage, include: *American Film* membership newsletter, discounts to the AFI Los Angeles International Film Festival, discounts to AFI Theater in Washington, D.C., discounts on AFI seminars and workshops and other perks depending on the level of membership.

Contact:
American Film Institute
2021 North Western Avenue
Hollywood, CA 90027
Tel: (213) 856-7600
Fax: (213) 467-4578
Web site: http://www.afionline.org

American Society for Training and Development (ASTD)

Founded in 1944, ASTD is the world's premiere professional association in the field of workplace learning and performance. ASTD's membership includes more than sixty-five thousand individuals and organizations from every level of the field of workplace performance in more than one hundred countries. Its leadership and members work in multinational corporations, small and medium-sized businesses, government agencies, colleges, and universities. ASTD is the leading resource on workplace learning and performance issues, providing information, research, analysis, and practical information derived from the knowledge and experience of its members, its conferences and publications, and the coalitions and partnerships it has built through research and policy work.

Contact:
American Society for Training and Development
1640 King Street, Box 1143
Alexandria, VA 22313
Tel: (703) 683-8100
Fax: (703) 683-8103
Web site: http://www.astd.org

American Society of Composers, Authors, and Publishers (ASCAP)

ASCAP is a performing rights society which represents its members by licensing and distributing royalties for the nondramatic public performances of their copyrighted works. Contact ASCAP for rights to a published or recorded work.

Contact:
American Society of Composers, Authors, and Publishers
1 Lincoln Plaza
New York, NY 10023
Tel: (212) 621-6000
Fax: (212) 724-9064
E-mail: info@ascap.org
Web site: http://www.ascap.org

The Association for Women in Communications

The Association for Women in Communications is "a professional organization that champions the advancement of women across all communications disciplines by recognizing excellence, promoting leadership, and positioning its members at the forefront of the evolving communications era."

Contact:
The Association for Women in Communications
1244 Ritchie Highway, Suite 6
Arnold, MD 21012-1887
Tel: (410) 544-7442
Fax: (410) 544-4640
E-mail: womcom@aol.com
Web site: http://www.womcom.org

Association of Independent Commercial Producers (AICP)

For almost three decades, the Association of Independent Commercial Producers has focused exclusively on the needs and interests of commercial production companies in the United States. AICP has grown to represent some 80-85 percent of all domestic commercials whether produced for traditional broadcast channels or nontraditional use, public or private viewing. The AICP serves as a strong collective voice for this $4.5 billion industry. The mission of the AICP is: (1) to disseminate information on all phases of production for the edification of its membership; (2) to represent the production industry within the advertising community, business circles, labor unions, and government offices; (3) to develop industry standards and common business practices and procedures; (4) to facilitate dialogue on key issues with the industry's clients; (5) to educate the public and itself on elements of production and the programs of the AICP; and (6) to provide a neutral ground on which production company executives can meet to discuss industry issues and make decisions appropriate to the industry as a whole, as well as to its individual members.

Contact:
Association of Independent Commercial Producers, Inc.
11 East 22nd Street
New York, NY 10010
Tel: (212) 475-2600
Fax: (212) 475-3910
E-mail: AICP1@aol.com
Web site: http://www.aicp.com

Association of Independent Video and Filmmakers (AIVF)

The Association of Independent Video and Filmmakers is the national service organization for independent producers. It publishes *The Independent Film & Video Monthly*. AIVF states that it "preserves your independence while letting you know you're not alone. AIVF helps you save time and money as well. You'll find you can spend more of your time (and less of your money) on what you do best—getting your work made and seen. To succeed as an independent today, you need a wealth of resources, strong connections, and the best information available."

Contact:
Association of Independent Video and Filmmakers
304 Hudson Street, Sixth Floor
New York, NY 10013
Tel: (212) 807-1400
Fax: (212) 463-8519
E-mail: info@aivf.org
Web site: http://www.aivf.org

Broadcast Music, Inc. (BMI)
BMI is a U.S. performing rights organization that collects and distributes licensing fees for its more than 180,000 songwriters, composers, and music publishers. Contact writer-publisher relations for clearance of published or recorded works.

Contact:
Broadcast Music, Inc.
320 West 57th Street
New York, NY 10019
Tel: (212) 586-2000
Fax: (212) 245-8986
E-mail: NewYork@bmi.com
Web site: bmi.com

International Association of Business Communicators (IABC)
The International Association of Business Communicators links communicators in a global network that inspires, establishes, and supports the highest professional standards of quality and innovation in organizational communication. There are more than twelve thousand five hundred IABC members working in over forty-five countries throughout the world. The mission of IABC is to:

- Provide lifelong learning opportunities that give IABC members the tools and information they need to be the best in their chosen disciplines.
- Share among the membership the best global communication practices, ideas, and experiences that will enable development of highly ethical and effective performance standards for the profession.
- Shape the future of the profession through ground-breaking research.

- Lead the way in the use of advanced information technology in the profession.
- Unite the communication profession worldwide in one diverse, multifaceted organization under the banner of the International Association of Business Communicators.

Contact:
International Association of Business Communicators
1 Hallidie Plaza, #600
San Francisco, CA 94102
Tel: (415) 433-3400
Fax: (415) 362-8762
E-mail: service_centre@iabc.com
Web site: http://www.iabc.com

International Communications Industries Association (ICIA)

The International Communications Industries Association, Inc. is a not-for-profit organization that supports and advances the audiovisual/presentation industry. Representing dealers, manufacturers, and other professionals involved in communications, ICIA creates a showcase for audiovisual presentations technology through national and international expositions—INFOCOMM International in the United States and INFOCOMM Asia in Singapore—provides industry information through the *Communications Industries Report* and the annual *Directory of Video, Multimedia, and Audio-Visual Products*, and provides educational opportunities through its Institute for Professional Development and its distance learning program.

Contact:
International Communications Industries Association, Inc.
11242 Waples Mill Road, Suite 200
Fairfax, VA 22030
Tel: (800) 659-7469; (703) 273-7200
Fax: (703) 278-8082
E-mail: icia@icia.org
Web site: http://www.icia.org and http://www.infocomm.org

International Documentary Association (IDA)

This is what the IDA says about itself, taken from its *Membership Directory and Survival Guide*: "The International Documentary Association is a nonprofit organization founded in 1982 to support the efforts of nonfiction film and video makers around the world and to increase public appreciation and demand for documentary films and television programs. Our international membership includes producers, directors, writers, editors, camera operators, musicians, researchers, technicians, journalists, broadcast and cable programmers, academics, distributors, and members of the general public." Membership features include:

- one year subscription to *International Documentary*
- availability of IDA-sponsored health insurance
- listing and biography in *IDA Membership Directory*
- discounts to IDA awards, events, and screenings
- discounts on *IDA Membership Directory*
- discounts on advertising in IDA publications
- complimentary addition to IDA résumé file
- access to the International Documentary Foundation as a nonprofit fiscal sponsor for grant-supported projects

Contact:
International Documentary Association
1551 South Robertson Boulevard, Suite 201
Los Angeles, CA 90035-4257
Tel: (310) 284-8422
Fax: (310) 785-9334
E-mail: idf@netcom.com

International Teleproduction Society (ITS)

The International Teleproduction Society states it is "the recognized trade association servicing the worldwide professional community of businesses that provide creative and technical services in film, video, and sound, and is the largest and most influential professional organization representing the postproduction industry. Our mission is to advance the success of the teleproduction industry globally, facilitate exchange of information and knowledge within the industry, and enhance the success of our members." Members include executives from post facilities, manufacturers and suppliers as well as editors, engineers, colorists, animation teams, technical editors, graphic designers, audio designers and editors, audio mixers, on-line and off-line editors, and producers.

Contact:
International Teleproduction Society
2230 Gallows Road, Suite 310
Dunn Loring, VA 22027
Tel: (703) 641-8770
Fax: (703) 641-8776
E-mail: itspres@erols.com
Web site: http://www.itsnet.org

International Television Association (ITVA)

ITVA serves the needs of accomplished visual communicators who work in corporate, organizational, and independent settings. It has eight thousand members in over one hundred chapters throughout the United States. Its mission is to be the premiere organization devoted to providing accomplished visual communicators with professional and business development opportunities, to promote the growth, quality, and success of film, video and multimedia communications and related businesses, and to act as an advocate on significant industry issues. ITVA membership brings:

- career advancement through the many professional development opportunities provided at chapter meetings, local and regional workshops, and its national conference.
- networking through access to the expertise and knowledge of ITVA members around the block, around the country, or around the world.
- special services such as its conference and video festival enhance networking and professional development opportunities.
- discounts on association events, books, and group medical insurance.
- industry leadership through the association's membership in the Small Business Leadership Council in Washington.

Contact:
International Television Association
International Office
6311 North O'Connor Road, #230
Irving, TX 75039
Tel: (972) 869-1112
Fax: (888) 879-4882 (toll free)
E-mail: itvahq@worldnet.att.net
Web site: http://www.itva.org

National Academy of Cable Programming

The National Academy of Cable Programming was established in 1985 to credit and promote excellence in cable television programming. Its activities include:

- developing the annual national and regional CableACE competitions and ceremonies to recognize the best in cable television programming
- sponsoring, along with the cable program networks, local or regional premiere screenings of original cable programs
- organizing cable television industry meetings and panel discussions on timely industry issues

Contact:
National Academy of Cable Programming
1724 Massachusetts Avenue, NW
Washington, DC 20036
Tel: (202) 775-3611
Fax: (202) 775-3689

Public Relations Society of America (PRSA)

The Public Relations Society of America is the world's largest organization for public relations professionals. The society's more than seventeen thousand members represent business and industry, counseling firms, government, associations, hospitals, schools, professional services firms, and nonprofit organizations. Since it was chartered in 1947, PRSA has continued to provide a forum for addressing issues affecting the profession, and the resources for promoting the highest professional standards. It offers unequaled opportunities for improvement of skills and advancement of knowledge, as well as for exchange of information and experiences with other public relations professionals. The society's mission is to advance the practice of public relations by:

- uniting those engaged in the profession
- encouraging continuing education of practitioners
- playing an active role in all matters affecting the practice of public relations
- formulating the objectives and interpreting the functions of public relations, and those who practice it, to the public
- strengthening the relationships of public relations professionals with

employers and clients, with government at all levels, with educators, with media, and with the public
- encouraging high standards of conduct and public service

Contact:
Public Relations Society of America
33 Irving Place
New York, NY 10003-2376
Tel: (212) 995-2230
Fax: (212) 995-0757
E-mail: hdq@prsa.org
Web site: http://www.prsa.org

Society of Motion Picture and Television Engineers (SMPTE)
SMPTE sets technical standards for film and video, but its interests are broad enough to include anyone engaged in production activities. A clearly defined interest in any phase of motion picture or television imaging is the principal requirement for membership. Membership benefits include:

- the SMPTE Journal and News and Notes, the Society's newsletter
- the annual Progress Report and Directory of Members
- discounts on registration at all SMPTE conferences and on publications
- invitations to SMPTE sections and student chapter meetings
- free use of the employment service column in the SMPTE Journal
- savings on group life and medical insurance for eligible U.S. members

Contact:
Society of Motion Picture and Television Engineers
595 West Hartsdale Avenue
White Plains, NY 10607-1824
Tel: (914) 761-1100
Fax: (914) 761-3115
E-mail: smpte@smpte.org
Web site: http://www.smpte.org

University Film and Video Association (UFVA)
The University Film and Video Association provides opportunities to meet and share ideas with colleagues, receive evaluation of your creative work, monitor developments in the field, and receive announcements of interest to media practitioners, faculty, and students. Founded in 1947 as the Uni-

versity Film Producers Council, the University Film and Video Association has developed into an organization of almost a thousand professionals and institutions involved in the production and study of film, video, and newer media arts. Members include college and university faculty and students, archivists, librarians, educational institutions, businesses, manufacturers, and creators of films and videos that range from the avant-garde to commercial, industrial, and independent productions.

Contact:
UFVA Membership Office
USC School of Cinema-Television
University Park
Los Angeles, CA 90089-2211
Tel: (213) 740-2921
Fax: (213) 740-2920
E-mail: hfarmer@usc.edu
Web site: http://www.rtvf.nwu.edu/ufva/

GUILDS AND UNIONS

American Federation of Musicians
1501 Broadway, Suite 600
New York, NY 10036
Tel: (212) 869-1330
Fax: (212) 764-6134
E-mail: info@afm.org
Web site: http://www.afm.org

American Federation of TV and Radio Artists (AFTRA)
6922 Hollywood Boulevard, Eighth Floor
Hollywood, CA 90028
Tel: (213) 634-8100
Web site: http://www.aftra.org
or
American Federation of TV and Radio Artists (AFTRA)
260 Madison Avenue
New York, NY 10016
Tel: (212) 532-0800
Fax (212) 545-1238
Web site: http://www.aftra.org

Directors Guild of America
7920 Sunset Boulevard
Hollywood, CA 90046
Tel: (800) 421-4173 or (310) 289-2000
Web site http://www.dga.org

International Alliance of Theatrical Stage Employees (I.A.T.S.E.)
National Headquarters
1515 Broadway, Suite 601
New York, NY 10036-5741
Tel: (212) 730-1770
Fax: (212) 921-7699
Web Site: www.iatse.lm.com

Producers Guild of America
400 South Beverly Drive
Beverly Hills, CA 90212
Tel: (310) 557-0807
Fax: (310) 557-0436

Screen Actors Guild
5757 Wilshire Boulevard, First Floor
Los Angeles, CA 90036
Tel: (213) 954-1600
Fax: (213) 549-6603
Web site: http://www.sag.com
or
Screen Actors Guild
1515 Broadway, 44th Floor
New York, NY 10036
Tel: (212) 944-1030
Fax (212) 944-6774
Web site: http://www.sag.com

Writers Guild of America, west
7000 West Third Street
Los Angeles, CA 90048-4329
Tel: (213) 951-4000
Fax: (213) 782-4800
Web site: http://www.wga.org

Writers Guild of America, east
555 West 57th Street, Suite 1230
New York, NY 10019
Tel: (212) 767-7800
Fax (212) 582-1909
E-mail: info@wgaeast.org
Web site: http://www.wgaeast.org

INFOMERCIAL RESOURCES

Infomercial Monitoring Service, Inc.

Infomercial Monitoring Service monitors and documents more than ten thousand hours of programming every month. Its *IMS Report* grids provide the hard numbers on what programs aired, where, and when. It publishes weekly Top 25 and monthly Top 100 rankings that show the relative saturation achieved by paid programming, based on frequency and the IMS media index and also lists new short-form spots and a sampling of the most frequently seen spots of the week. All of this is made possible through a comprehensive database containing over three hundred fifty thousand airings detected from national cable television. Beyond numbers, IMS professionals provide detailed reviews of every new show or spot monitored. Publishes the *IMS Report.*

Contact:
Infomercial Monitoring Service, Inc.
Satellite 2—810 Parkway Boulevard
Broomall, PA 19008
Tel: (610) 328-6902
Fax: (610) 328-6791
Web site: www.imstv.com

Jordan Whitney, Inc.

Jordan Whitney, Inc. is a research, consulting, and publishing company that monitors, ranks, and critiques direct response television commercials—both infomercials and short-form spot advertisements—as they appear on cable networks and selected broadcast stations throughout the United States. Jordan Whitney publishes up-to-the-minute, detailed written reports, consults on direct response TV projects, and maintains a tape library of reference copies of infomercials and direct response spots. Publications include

Greensheet Direct Response Television Monitoring Report, Greensheet TV Merchandiser, Greensheet Annual Review.

Contact:
Jordan Whitney, Inc.
17300 17th Street, Suite J-111
Tustin, CA 92780
Tel: (714) 832-2432
Fax: (714) 832-3053

NIMA International

NIMA International, the association that represents the electronic retailing industry worldwide, has grown from its origins as the National Infomercial Marketing Association to include all electronic retailing, not just nationally, but internationally. If you are involved with infomercial production, you probably need to be a member of NIMA International. Benefits include a lobbying effort to protect the industry's interests, meetings and conferences, publications and research.

Contact:
NIMA International
1225 New York Avenue, NW, Suite 1200
Washington, DC 20005
Tel: (202) 289-NIMA
Web site: http://www.nima.org

INFOMERCIAL GUIDELINES

F*ollowing are the guidelines for infomercial production and distribution developed by NIMA International, the association that represents the electronic retailing industry worldwide, and reprinted with their permission.*

MARKETING GUIDELINES

It is the policy of NIMA International that all programs produced by its members contain truthful information and comply with all existing laws and regulations. NIMA supports the freedom of its members to exercise their First Amendment right by providing information to consumers. Because NIMA's policy is to foster public confidence in the accuracy and reliability of infomercial programming, it has adopted the following guidelines.

Sponsorship and Identification

Each video production should be preceded and concluded with a clear and prominent written or oral announcement that the program is a paid advertisement for {name of product}. A clear and prominent written or oral announcement should also be made prior to each ordering opportunity that the program the viewer is watching is a paid advertisement for {name of product}. In addition, each video production should include a clear and prominent written or oral announcement identifying the name of the party that sponsored, paid for, or furnished the program.

Program Production

The following guidelines shall be observed in the development and production of infomercials:

- No programs will be produced by NIMA members which are likely to mislead reasonable consumers with respect to the nature of the program, e.g., to lead viewers to believe that the program is a bona fide newscast or documentary or entertainment programming presented by a disinterested party solely for the purpose of providing entertainment or information.
- All statements made in the context of an infomercial program shall be truthful, whether or not they are specifically made with respect to the product or service being marketed.
- Infomercial producers shall not deceive the viewer through omitted or misleading information which is likely to affect the purchasing decision or the use of the product or service being marketed.
- Comparative advertising should inform buyers of the benefits of the advertiser's product, not run down a competitor's product. Comparisons should be made fairly and accurately rather than in a contemptuous manner that degrades the competitive product.
- No program shall be aired for which product is not available in sufficient quantities to meet reasonably anticipated demand. The marketer must have a reasonable basis to expect that he will be able to ship any ordered merchandise to the buyer within the times specified in the advertisement or within thirty (30) days after receipt of the order (if no shipping time is specified).
- No program-length commercial shall be produced primarily for an audience of children twelve years old and under.
- No programming shall contain statements, suggestions, or pictures which are considered indecent or offensive based on community standards.

Product/Claims Substantiation

- There must be a reasonable basis, consisting of competent and reliable evidence, for express or implied objective claims made in marketing the product or service.
- If the programming contains an express or implied representation either through the use of such language as "medically proven" or "here's proof" or the use of such visual aids as scientific charts or white-coated

technicians, that a claim's truth has been scientifically established, the advertiser must possess a sufficient level of evidence to convince the relevant scientific community of the claim's truthfulness. The amount of substantiation claimed in the programming, such as research or tests performed, must be present.

- Comparative advertising claims, whether about a competing product or the advertiser's own product, must be truthful and substantiated in the same manner as any other objective claim.

- Particular care should be taken to substantiate health, nutrition, or safety claims made in marketing products or services, such as foods, drugs, cosmetics, diet foods and plans, vitamins, and medical or cosmetic devices. All representations regarding the safety and efficacy of such products or services must be substantiated by competent and reliable scientific evidence.

- All demonstrations of the qualities of the product being marketed must actually take place as shown in the elapsed time as recorded or the details of the demonstrations must be disclosed, such as identifying it as a simulation and stating the actual elapsed time for the results. The demonstration must accurately depict what the product does.

- Comparative tests and demonstrations of competing product must take into account the purpose for which the products are intended, the manner in which they are normally used by the consumer, and individual label instructions.

Testimonials and Endorsements

- All testimonials from consumers shall be from voluntary, bona fide users of the product or service, where the program represents that the consumer is a user of the product or service, and shall reflect the honest opinions, findings, beliefs, or experiences of the consumer and be generally representative of the results to be expected by the average consumer. Alternatively, the advertiser may clearly and conspicuously disclaim that the experiences of the consumer offering the testimonial are representative of the results to be expected by the average consumer. Any claims made regarding the product or service by consumer testimonials must be substantiated in the same manner as if the advertiser had made the claims.

- All endorsements by "experts" shall be substantiated by the endorser's qualifications in the relevant area of expertise and shall be the actual result of the application of his expertise in the area in which he is qualified.

- Any "material connection" between the advertiser and the endorser must be disclosed, unless the endorser is a generally-recognized celebrity or identified as an expert (and the sole connection is that the celebrity or expert is being paid a fee).
- There must be a good reason to believe that the views expressed continue to represent the views of the endorser or expert and that the endorser continues to be a bona fide user of the product for as long as the advertisement is run.

Ordering: Prices, 900 Numbers, and Continuity Programs

- Any additional costs, such as postage and handling and excise taxes must be disclosed. All statements made regarding prices must be truthful and substantiated. For example, if the product is marketed as costing more through another outlet or at another time, there must actually be substantial sales of the product at the higher price; if a product is being offered as "two for the price of one," the second must usually be sold at additional cost. Comparative price advertising should compare only actual prices for comparable products and must not be otherwise misleading.
- Any program-length commercial advertising a continuity program must clearly inform consumers that they will automatically receive future additional shipments and disclose the minimum number of purchases required under the program, if any.
- The material terms and conditions of the continuity program, including billing and cancellation procedures, must be conveyed to consumers before their order can be accepted.
- The cost of a 900-number call advertised during a program-length commercial must be clearly and prominently disclosed during the program by at least three written announcements (at least one-half the size of the 900 number) and one oral announcement.

Warranties, Guarantees, and Refunds

- Any warranty or guarantee offered with a consumer product priced in excess of fifteen dollars must be made available to the consumer prior to purchase upon request.
- Guarantee claims made in the marketing process must identify the guarantor and clearly state the nature and manner of performance of the guarantee and any conditions, limitations, or charges in connection therewith. Such claims must also be consistent with the guarantee provided in writing with the product or service.

- If a money-back guarantee is offered with the product or service, refunds claimed must be made promptly. In order to ensure the availability of funds for refund purposes, NIMA recommends that an escrow account, based on reasonable estimates of refund requests expected, be maintained.

Monitoring/Enforcement

Subscription to this policy and these guidelines is a condition of NIMA membership. Members shall have the right to certify their compliance with these guidelines to members of the general public and the media. Willful violation of these guidelines is a basis for expulsion from NIMA.

BIBLIOGRAPHY

Bieler, Peter with Suzanne Costas, *This Business Has Legs: How I Used Infomercial Marketing to Create the $100,000,000 Thighmaster Craze.* New York: John Wiley. 1996.

Conner, Donna M. editor: *It's a Business First . . . and a Creative Outlet Second.* Irving, TX: The International Television Association. 1993.

Field, Syd. *Screenplay: The Foundations of Screenwriting.* New York: Dell Publishing Company. 1989. ISBN 0-440-57647-4.

Greensheet Direct Response Television Monitoring Report, Greensheet TV Merchandiser, Greensheet Annual Review. Tustin, CA: Jordan Whitney, Inc.

Haag, Judith H., and Hillis R. Cole, *The Complete Guide to Standard Script Formats, Part I: The Screenplay.* Los Angeles: CMC Publishing. 1980.

Haag, Judith H., and Hillis R. Cole, *The Complete Guide to Standard Script Formats, Part II: Taped Formats for TV.* Los Angeles: CMC Publishing. 1980.

Hampe, Barry, *Making Documentary Films and Reality Videos: A Practical Guide to Planning, Filming, and Editing Documentaries of Real Events.* New York: An Owl Book, Henry Holt and Company. 1997. ISBN 0-8050-4451-5.

Hampe, Barry, *Video Scriptwriting: How to Write for the $4 Billion Commercial Video Market.* New York: A Plume Book, Penguin Books, USA. 1993. ISBN 0-452-26868-0.

Handbook of Treatments. Irving, TX: International Television Association. 1993.

Hawthorne, Timothy R., *The Complete Guide to Infomercial Marketing*. Lincolnwood, IL: NTC Business Books. 1997. ISBN 0-8442-3445-1.

IMS Report. Broomall, PA: Infomercial Monitoring Service, Inc.

International Documentary Association Membership Directory and Survival Guide. Los Angeles: International Documentary Association. Published biennially.

Konigsberg, Ira, *The Complete Film Dictionary*. New York: A Meridian Book, Penguin Books, USA. 1987, 1989. ISBN 0-452-00980-4.

Reichman, Rick, *Formatting Your Screenplay*. New York: Paragon House. 1992. ISBN 1-55778-434-5.

Rosenthal, Alan, *Writing, Directing, and Producing Documentary Films and Videos*, revised edition. Carbondale & Edwardsville: Southern Illinois University Press. 1990, 1996. ISBN 0-8093-2013-4 and 0-8093-2014-2 (paperback).

Seger, Linda, *Creating Unforgettable Characters*. New York: An Owl Book, Henry Holt and Company. 1990. ISBN 0-8050-1171-4.

Seger, Linda, *Making a Good Script Great*. Second edition. Hollywood: Samuel French Trade. 1987, 1994. ISBN 0-573-69921-6.

Singleton, Ralph S., *Filmmaker's Dictionary*. Beverly Hills: Lone Eagle Publishing Company. 1986. ISBN 0-943728-08-8

Walter, Richard, *Screenwriting: The Art, Craft and Business of Film and Television Writing*. New York: A Plume Book, New American Library. 1988. ISBN 0-452-26086-8.

Zettl, Herbert, *Television Production Handbook*. Belmont, CA: Wadsworth Publishing Company. 1997.

Zettl, Herbert, *Video Basics*. Belmont, CA: Wadsworth Publishing Company. 1995.

INDEX